403(b)
Answer Book

2003 Supplement

403(b)
Answer Book

2003 Supplement

Edited by:

Donald R. Levy
Barbara N. Seymon-Hirsch
Janet M. Anderson

A Panel Publication

PUBLISHERS

1185 Avenue of the Americas, New York, NY 10036
www.aspenpublishers.com

This publication is designed to provide accurate and authoritative information in regard to the subject matter covered. It is sold with the understanding that the publisher is not engaged in rendering legal, accounting, or other professional services. If legal advice or other professional assistance is required, the services of a competent professional person should be sought.

— From a *Declaration of Principles* jointly adopted by
a Committee of the American Bar Association and
a Committee of Publishers and Associations

1 2 3 4 5 6 7 8 9 0

About Aspen Publishers

Aspen Publishers, headquartered in New York City, is a leading information provider for attorneys, business professionals, and law students. Written by preeminent authorities, our products consist of analytical and practical information covering both U.S. and international topics. We publish in the full range of formats, including updated manuals, books, periodicals, CDs, and online products.

Our proprietary content is complemented by 2,500 legal databases, containing over 11 million documents, available through our Loislaw division. Aspen Publishers also offers a wide range of topical legal and business databases linked to Loislaw's primary material. Our mission is to provide accurate, timely, and authoritative content in easily accessible formats, supported by unmatched customer care.

To order any Aspen Publishers title, go to *www.aspenpublishers.com* or call 1-800-638-8437.

To reinstate your manual update service, call 1-800-638-8437.

For more information on Loislaw products, go to *www.loislaw.com* or call 1-800-364-2512.

For Customer Care issues, e-mail *CustomerCare@aspenpublishers.com*; call 1-800-234-1660; or fax 1-800-901-9075.

Aspen Publishers
A Wolters Kluwer Company

SUBSCRIPTION NOTICE

This Aspen Publishers product is updated on a periodic basis with supplements to reflect important changes in the subject matter. If you purchased this product directly from Aspen, we have already recorded your subscription for the update service.

If, however, you purchased this product from a bookstore and wish to receive future updates and revised or related volumes billed separately with a 30-day examination review, please contact our Customer Service Department at 1-800-234-1660, or send your name, company name (if applicable), address, and the title of the product to:

Aspen Publishers
7201 McKinney Circle
Frederick, MD 21704

To the memory of Beatrice F. Seymon—
devoted mother and grandmother

Preface

403(b) Answer Book, Sixth Edition continues to be the only professional resource that systematically answers hundreds of questions on 403(b) programs, Section 457 plans, 501(c)(3) organizations, and church plans and provides insight on how to handle complicated issues not yet resolved by the IRS or the courts. *403(b) Answer Book, Sixth Edition* includes coverage of 501(c)(3) organizations, qualified domestic relations orders, nondiscrimination requirements, contribution limits, correction of plan defects, Section 403(b)(7) custodial accounts, and international tax treatment.

The 2003 Supplement to *403(b) Answer Book, Sixth Edition*, brings the practitioner up-to-date on administrative developments and changes in this ever-growing area, including:

- Treatment of participant loans as plan investments
- Duty of plan fiduciary to collect repayments on a participant loan
- Investment blackout periods, blackout notices, and duration of blackouts
- Application of securities laws when compiling plan investment information
- Participant's right to an opportunity to obtain written confirmation of investment instructions
- Department of Labor interpretive guidance relating to investment education for participants
- Gap-fillers and default provisions in beneficiary designation forms
- Survivor benefits required under ERISA for a spouse
- Common mistakes with beneficiary designations
- Three possible ways of demonstrating nondiscrimination compliance
- Special requirements applying to cross-tested 403(b) plans
- When an interest in a pooled or collective investment vehicle should be considered issued directly to eligible employee
- The SEC's position on obligation to provide eligible employees with prospectuses and other reports

- Where plan document and summary plan description conflict, term favorable to employee prevails as contract terms will be construed against the drafter
- DOL final regulations on disclosure by means of electronic media
- Curing the late filing of Form 5500
- Application of the Sarbanes-Oxley Act of 2002 to an ERISA 403(b) plan
- The fiduciary's obligation to ascertain extent to which annuity provider is covered by state guarantees
- The fiduciary's reliance on independent advice
- The scope of liability limitation or indemnification of service providers
- The three transition rules of Revenue Procedure 2003-2
- IRS clarification of "substantially equal periodic payments"
- Waiver of 60-day rollover requirement
- Commingling of 403(b) plan assets with church endowment funds and assets of 401(a) plans

Massive law amendments had been suggested quite recently by the Bush Administration, but there appears to be little prospect that any of these will be enacted any time soon; hence, these proposals are not discussed in this supplement. Similarly, the Treasury Department and the IRS have indicated that existing 403(b) regulations are being reviewed for possible consolidation and updating, but there is no anticipated date of proposal. When and if these proposals develop, they will be covered in a future supplement or edition of the book

Donald R. Levy
Barbara N. Seymon-Hirsch
Janet M. Anderson
May 2003

Editors and Contributors

Editor:

Donald R. Levy, JD, MBA, is an attorney and benefits consultant. A graduate of Harvard Law School and Harvard College, he received an MBA in accounting from New York University. Mr. Levy has over 30 years of experience as a pension administrator and tax planner. He has practiced law and has served as Vice President and Director of Employee Benefits with United States Tobacco, Vice President, Benefits, with Johnson and Higgins, and Senior Technical Consultant for Prentice Hall, where he authored the *Pension Handbook.* Mr. Levy is co-author of Aspen's *Individual Retirement Account Answer Book, Quick Reference to IRAs,* and *Employment Severance Answer Book,* and co-editor of *State by State Guide to Managed Care Law.* Mr. Levy has taught at the University of Connecticut, has been a panelist for the Practising Law Institute, and has lectured before other professional groups.

Coeditors and Contributors:

Barbara N. Seymon-Hirsch, Esq., is a Partner in Davis & Harman, LLP, a Washington, D.C. law firm specializing in federal tax and legislative matters. Ms. Seymon-Hirsch specializes in federal tax matters, concentrating particularly on issues relating to insurance product tax compliance, qualified retirement plans, Section 403(b) programs, individual retirement arrangements (including Roth IRAs), and employment tax. She received her BA from Vassar College, her JD from California Western School of Law, and her LLM in Taxation from Georgetown University Law School. Ms. Seymon-Hirsch was previously Assistant Tax Counsel with Metropolitan Life Insurance Company. She was also previously with the Internal Revenue Service in Washington, D.C. She is a member of the District of Columbia and New York bars. Ms. Seymon-Hirsch is a member of the Committee on Employee Benefits of the Tax Section of the American Bar Association and has been appointed to serve as a member of the IRS Information Reporting Program Advisory Committee (IRPAC) for 2002 and

2003. She contributes to and is coeditor of Aspen Publishers' *Annuities Answer Book.*

Janet M. Anderson, Esq., is an Associate in the Seattle, Washington, office of Mercer Investment Consulting. Her practice has covered the tax and pension laws governing Section 403(b) tax deferred annuities and Section 457 nonqualified deferred compensation plans for nearly 20 years. She has written and lectured extensively in the area of Section 403(b) tax and ERISA compliance for public and private tax-exempt organizations. She is a member of the American Bar Association, where she is a member of the Tax Section's Employee Benefits Committee and its Subcommittee on Section 403(b), Section 457, and Exempt Organization Issues. Before joining Mercer, Ms. Anderson was Senior Counsel and Assistant Secretary of The Variable Annuity Life Insurance Company (VALIC). Ms. Anderson received her BA, *cum laude,* from Georgian Court College, Lakewood, New Jersey. She received her JD from South Texas College of Law in Houston, Texas, where she received an American Jurisprudence award in Federal Procedure. She is admitted to practice before the U.S. Supreme Court, the U.S. Tax Court, the Fifth Circuit Court of Appeals, the U.S. District Court for the Southern District of Texas, and is a member of the State Bar of Texas. She is an NASD insurance investment products registered principal.

Contributors:

Karen Ackermann, JD, LLM (1949–1997), was Senior Counsel with Teachers Insurance and Annuity Association-College Retirement Equities Fund (TIAA-CREF), where she was head of the Pension Law unit. Ms. Ackermann received her JD from Rutgers University School of Law-Newark and her LLM (taxation) from New York University School of Law. She was a member of the American Bar Association Section of Taxation, Employee Benefits Committee, and the National Association of Variable Annuities (NAVA) 403(b) work/study group.

Jason Bortz, Esq., is a member of the law firm of Caplin & Drysdale, Chartered, in Washington, D.C. Mr. Bortz has broad experience in employee benefit matters, advising clients on tax, ERISA and other aspects of retirement plans, fringe benefits, and executive compensation arrangements. He serves as benefits counsel to a number of tax-exempt organizations, including private foundations, public charities, universities, international organizations, and churches. Mr. Bortz holds a BA from Hamilton College and a JD from Cornell Law School, where he was an editor of the Cornell Law Review. After law school, he served as law clerk to Chief Judge Loken of the US Court of Appeals for the Eighth Circuit.

Robert A. Browning, Esq., is a shareholder with Polsinelli Shalton & Welte PC, a law firm based in Kansas City, Missouri. He is a member of the firm's Employee Benefits and Executive Compensation Group and his practice area includes the pension and tax laws governing qualified plans, tax-sheltered annuities, and deferred compensation plans. Prior to joining Polsinelli in 1999, Mr. Browning was Senior Counsel for The Variable Annuity Life Insurance Company (VALIC). Before joining VALIC, Mr. Browning was an Associate with the law firm of Liddell, Sapp, Zivley, Hill & LaBoon in Houston, Texas, where he specialized in employee benefits and related tax law. He received his JD, with honors, from the University of Houston in 1989, and he is currently a member of the Employee Benefits Committee of the American Bar Association Section on Taxation, the Kansas City Metropolitan Bar Association, and the Heart of America Employee Benefits Conference.

Gordon M. Clay, Esq., is an Associate in the Washington, D.C. office of Steptoe & Johnson LLP, where he is a member of the firm's tax group. Mr. Clay provides corporate and tax planning advice to a variety of nonprofit organizations, including charities and private foundations. His practice includes advising clients on qualification and maintenance of tax-exempt status, restrictions on lobbying activities, IRS and FEC regulation of political campaign activities, taxation of unrelated business income, reorganizations and business ventures, Internet-based activities, reporting and disclosure requirements, charitable giving techniques, and state charitable solicitation and nonprofit corporation statutes. In addition, Mr. Clay represents corporate clients in litigation matters in various federal and state trial and appellate courts. Mr. Clay received his JD from Georgetown University Law Center, where he was executive editor of *The Georgetown Law Journal*, and is a member of the Exempt Organizations Committee of the American Bar Association Section on Taxation.

Greta E. Cowart, Esq., is a Partner with Haynes and Boone, LLP, a law firm based in Dallas, Texas. Ms. Cowart is a certified public accountant as well as a certified employee benefit specialist. She received her Bachelor of Science from Indiana University in 1982 and her JD from Indiana University School of Law in 1985. Ms. Cowart is a member of the Taxation Section and the Employee Benefits Committee of the American Bar Association and Chair of its COBRA subcommittee. A founding editor of the *Indiana State Bar Association Tax Section Newsletter,* Ms. Cowart has published extensively on many benefits issues and has practiced in the area of tax-sheltered annuities for 12 years.

John P. Curran, Esq., is Senior Counsel with Teachers Insurance and Annuity Association-College Retirement Equities Fund (TIAA-CREF), where he works in the Retirement Service Law unit of the Insurance Law Division. Mr. Curran received his JD from the Fordham University School of Law.

Michael Doran, Esq., is a former member of Caplin & Drysdale, Chartered, in Washington, D.C. His practice focuses on employee benefits, executive compensation, and related tax matters. Mr. Doran formerly served as attorney advisor in the Office of Tax Policy of the U.S. Treasury Department, where his work involved a number of regulatory and legislative projects affecting employee benefits, including regulations for Roth IRAs, COBRA, and "paperless" administration of qualified plans and Social Security reform. He is a graduate of Yale

Law School and Wesleyan University and a member of the District of Columbia bar.

Michael Footer, Esq., is a Principal of Mercer Investment Consulting in Richmond, Virginia. He has written and lectured extensively in the areas of health and welfare plans, pension and profit-sharing plans, and tax-sheltered annuities. For the past 26 years, he has been in charge of Mercer's Nonprofit 403(b) Practice in Richmond, Virginia. In his current position, Mr. Footer has had an opportunity to address design, funding, and administrative issues relating to all types of employee benefit plans with special emphasis on nonprofit organizations. Mr. Footer received his JD from George Washington University Law School in 1966 and his designation as a Chartered Life Underwriter in 1973. Mr. Footer is an active member of the American Bar Association's Employee Benefits Committee, serving on the Welfare Benefits Subcommittees and as Chairperson of the Tax Sheltered Annuity/457 Subcommittee. He is a Charter Fellow of the American College of Employee Benefits Counsel.

Evan Giller, Esq., is Senior Counsel with Teachers Insurance and Annuity Association-College Retirement Equities Fund (TIAA-CREF) where he manages the Pension Law Unit. He is responsible for ERISA, tax, and insurance law issues relating to Section 403(b) plans, qualified plans, and nonqualified defined compensation plans. He also spent five years as the Chief Compliance Officer for TIAA-CREF's pension business. Mr. Giller has served on the Employee Benefits Committee of the Association of the Bar of the City of New York. He received his JD in 1978 from the State University of New York at Buffalo Law School.

David S. Goldstein, Esq., is a Partner in the law firm of Sutherland Asbill & Brennan, LLP, in Washington, D.C. Before joining Sutherland in May 1989, he served for three and a half years on the staff of the Securities and Exchange Commission (SEC), where he was Attorney-Adviser and later Special Counsel in the Division of Investment Management. From 1981 through 1985, Mr. Goldstein was Assistant Vice President, Assistant General Counsel, and Assistant Secretary of The Variable Annuity Life Insurance Company. Mr. Goldstein is also a contributor to Aspen Publishers' *457 Answer Book.* Mr. Goldstein is a member of the District of Columbia, Texas, and Massachusetts bars; the American Bar Association, Section of Business Law (Committee on Federal Regulation of Securities and Subcommittee on Securities Activities of Insurance Companies); and the District of Columbia Bar Section on Corporation, Finance, and Securities Law. Mr. Goldstein received his BA in 1978 from Hampshire College and his JD in 1981 from Boston University.

Peter J. Gulia, Esq., is Senior Vice President of CitiStreet Retirement Services. Since 1984, Mr. Gulia has focused on the design, management, fiduciary investment procedures, and administration of retirement plans; insurance and investment product design; and lobbying on employee benefits legislation and regulations. Mr. Gulia is a contributing author of Aspen Publishers' *457 Answer Book, Governmental Plans Answer Book, Life Insurance Answer Book for Qualified Plans and Estate Planning,* and *Roth IRA Answer Book.* Mr. Gulia serves on the Board of Contributors of *Employee Benefits for Nonprofits.* He has contributed to *401(k) Advisor, CPA Administrative Report, Municipal Law Review, Planning Matters,* the journal of the International Association of Financial Planning, *Pensions & Investments* magazine, and other publications. He is frequently invited to speak to associations of employee benefits practitioners.

Gary E. Herzlich, Esq., is Senior Counsel with Teachers Insurance and Annuity Association-College Retirement Equities Fund (TIAA-CREF). He advises on Section 403(b) plans, qualified plans, nonqualified deferred compensation plans, compliance, and general pension and deferred compensation. He is currently serving as Senior Compliance Officer for TIAA-CREF. Prior to joining TIAA-CREF, Mr. Herzlich was part of an employee benefits and executive compensation group with Proskauer Rose LLP and advised clients on Section 401 qualified plans, Section 403(b) plans, nonqualified deferred compensation arrangements, and executive compensation. He also advised tax-exempt organizations on other benefit and compensation issues. Mr. Herzlich received his JD from Boston University School of Law and his LLM in Taxation from New York University Law School.

Danny Miller, Esq., is a Partner in the Washington, D.C. office of Ice Miller, an Indianapolis, Indiana-based law firm, and a member of that firm's Employee Benefits practice group. Mr. Miller received his law degree from the Vanderbilt University School of Law in 1974, at which time he began practicing in the employee benefits area. Mr. Miller has served as adjunct professor at Southern Methodist University School of Law, where for three years he taught a course on Taxation of Deferred Compensation. Mr. Miller is a member of the Employee Benefits Committee of the Tax Section of the American Bar Association and serves on the Subcommittee on Section 403(b), 457, and Exempt Organization Issues—of which he served as chair from the spring of 1989 until August 1992. Mr. Miller is also a past director and current member of the SouthWest Benefits Association based in Dallas, Texas.

Regina M. Pizzonia, Esq., is Vice President and Associate Legal Counsel of T. Rowe Price Associates, where she specializes in retirement plan matters. Ms. Pizzonia previously served as Vice President and Senior Counsel at Merrill Lynch Pierce Fenner & Smith in New York, where she focused on retail retirement products. Prior to joining Merrill Lynch, Ms. Pizzonia was with the law firm of Groom & Nordberg in Washington, D.C., where she provided ERISA advice to the firm's clients, including Fortune 100 corporations, pension plans, broker-dealers, and mutual fund companies. As Senior Associate Counsel of the United Mine Workers Health and Retirement Funds, Ms. Pizzonia provided ERISA advice to the Fund's officials regarding over $6 billion in fund assets. From 1987 to 1990, Ms. Pizzonia was a federal investigator with the U.S. Department of Labor, Pension and Welfare Benefits Administration, Office of Enforcement. Ms. Pizzonia received her BA from Fairfield University and her JD from the National Law Center at George Washington University. She also attended Oxford University, where she studied international law.

David W. Powell, Esq., is a Principal in the Washington, D.C. tax law firm of Groom Law Group, Chartered. He is a certified public accountant as well as an attorney and is a past President of the Washington Employee Benefits Forum. He received his JD from the University of Texas in 1982. Mr. Powell works with tax and ERISA issues relating to all types of employee pension and welfare benefits plans, including qualified, nonqualified, ESOP, 403(b), 457, church, governmental, health care, and flexible benefit plans. Mr. Powell frequently contributes topical articles to and is a member of the Board of Contributors of *Employee Benefits for Nonprofits* and the Editorial Advisory Board of the *Journal of Deferred Compensation*. He is a frequent speaker and writer on employee benefits topics, particularly on the topics of nonqualified deferred compensation plans and employee benefit plans for nonprofit organizations. He is also a contributor to Aspen Publishers' *457 Answer Book* and *Life Insurance Answer Book for Qualified Plans and Estate Planning*.

Douglas A. Rothermich serves as Vice President, Estate Planning and Trust Consulting for TIAA-CREF Trust Company, FSB, where he manages the delivery of estate planning and wealth transfer planning services. Prior to joining the Trust Company, Mr. Rothermich practiced law in St. Louis with the firm of Bryan Cave, LLP, a national and international law firm. He has also served as Vice President and Senior Trust counsel at Boatmen's Trust Company.

Michael S. Sirkin, Esq., is immediate past Chairman of the Tax Department of Proskauer Rose LLP, and a senior member of its Employee Benefits and Executive Compensation Group. Mr. Sirkin serves as benefits counsel to a large number of tax-exempt organizations. He advises on Section 403(b) plans, Section 401 qualified plans, nonqualified deferred compensation arrangements, fiduciary issues, and prohibited transactions. Mr. Sirkin's practice also includes advising insurance companies and benefits consultants on Section 403(b) plans and other benefit and compensation issues for tax-exempt organizations. He is a 1972 graduate of Columbia Law School. Mr. Sirkin has been an Adjunct Assistant Professor of Law at New York University School of Law, past Chairman of the Employee Benefits Committee, and a past member of the Committee on Nonprofit Organizations of the Association of the Bar of the City of New York, past Co-Chairman of the Employee Benefits Committee of New York County Lawyers' Association, and a past Chairman of the Subcommittee on Tax-Exempt and Governmental Plans of the Employee Benefits and Executive Compensation Committee of the Business Law Section of the American Bar Association. He has written and spoken extensively on Section 403(b) and other benefit and compensation issues for tax-exempt entities.

Henry A. Smith, III, Esq., is a Partner of Smith & Downey, a Baltimore, New York, and Washington, D.C. law firm that concentrates in the areas of employee benefits, executive compensation, and labor and employment law. He received a BA from Frostburg State College, an MLA from the Johns Hopkins University, and a JD from the University of Maryland School of Law. He is a member of the Maryland and District of Columbia bars, past chair of both the Maryland State Bar Association Section of Taxation and the MSBA Employee Benefits Committee, and an adjunct professor in the University of Baltimore School of Law Graduate Tax Program. Mr. Smith is coauthor of Aspen Publishers' *Nonqualified Deferred Compensation Answer Book*.

Robert J. Toth, Jr., Esq., is Senior Counsel for the Lincoln National Life Insurance Company in Fort Wayne, Indiana, one of the nation's leading issuers of 403(b) and individual nonqualified annuities. Mr. Toth is responsible for providing benefits law support to Lincoln's employer-based annuity, investment, and administrative service businesses, with a significant focus on 403(b) compliance. He has extensive experience in a wide range of ERISA-related administrative, planning, and transactional areas relating to qualified pension and welfare plans and has taught and written frequently in these areas. He has 15 years of benefit law experience, serving in both a law firm and a Fortune 100 company before joining Lincoln. He is active in the Taxation Section of the American Bar Association and is a member of the Indiana and Michigan state bar associations. Mr. Toth is a graduate of the Wayne State University Law School and the University of Michigan.

Richard A. Turner, Esq., is Associate General Counsel for The Variable Annuity Life Insurance Company, where his primary emphasis is on qualified and nonqualified retirement savings programs for tax-exempt organizations. He graduated with honors from Capital University Law School, where he served as Notes Editor on the Law Review, and holds a BA in Economics, also from Capital University. He has been in the insurance industry for over 14 years, working with 403(b) programs and other defined contribution plans, defined benefit plans, IRAs, nonqualified annuities, and variable life insurance. He is past Co-Chairman of the 403(b) subcommittee of the National Association of Variable Annuities and is a member of the Annuity Taxation Subcommittee and the Task Force on Tax Favored Savings at the American Council of Life Insurance.

Catherine W. Wilkinson, CPA, is a member of the tax practice at the law firm of Steptoe & Johnson LLP in Washington, D.C. Ms. Wilkinson provides tax planning and advice to tax-exempt organizations and represents corporations, including publicly-traded corporations, closely-held entities, and tax-exempt organizations and individuals in designing and negotiating executive compensation arrangements. This advice includes use of incentive and performance-based compensation and deferred compensation, stock options, and other forms of equity compensation, compensation paid in connection with a change in control, and the application of the intermediate sanction rules to compensation of executives of tax-exempt organizations. In addition, Ms. Wilkinson represents corporations, partnerships, tax-exempt organizations, and individuals in complex federal and state tax audits and investigations. These include routine civil audits of domestic and international organizations, and investigations relating to tax shelters and charges of tax fraud and evasion.

Acknowledgments

403(b) Answer Book, Sixth Edition is the product of the hard work and dedication of many people. Grateful acknowledgment is due Editorial Director Ellen Ros for conceiving and developing the idea of the book; Managing Editor May Wu for guiding all aspects of the book's planning and implementation; Dancy Burns, former Senior Developmental Editor, for organizing and editing the chapter contents; and Janet Mazefsky for expert indexing of the resulting work.

Special thanks are due to the authors of the chapters in both the main volume and this supplement. Don also thanks his co-editors, Barbara N. Seymon-Hirsch and Janet M. Anderson, who are also contributors, for their great expertise and tireless dedication to reviewing all the chapters, as well as raising some questions that they subsequently helped to answer. He is profoundly grateful to his wife, May, for her advice, encouragement, patience, and understanding.

Barbara thanks her daughter, Sydney Roth (who demonstrated patience beyond her two years of age), and husband, Jerry (whose extraordinary patience was sometimes tested).

Last but not least, Janet wishes to acknowledge her daughter, Christine, who has made her mother very proud.

Donald R. Levy
Barbara N. Seymon-Hirsch
Janet M. Anderson
May 2003

How to Use This Supplement

The 2003 Supplement to *403(b) Answer Book, Sixth Edition* uses straightforward language and avoids technical jargon whenever possible, yet provides professionals with the tools to become conversant in the idiom of 403(b) plans. Citations to authority are provided as research aids for those who wish to pursue particular items in greater detail.

403(b) Answer Book, 2003 Supplement provides an extensive system of cross-referencing to guide the reader toward related or more topics of interest.

Numbering System. The 2003 Supplement uses a point system of numbering questions and answers that augment material in the main volume, *403(b) Answer Book, Sixth Edition.* For example, Q 1:1 in the main volume may be followed by Qs 1:1.1, 1:1.2 in the supplement. When a question from the Sixth Edition is updated, it is repeated in its entirety in the supplement.

List of Questions. The detailed list of questions that follows the table of contents helps the reader locate areas of immediate interest. A series of sub-headings helps to organize questions by topic within each chapter.

Examples and Practice Pointers. Throughout the book are numerous examples that illustrate specific applications and situations, as well as practice pointers that highlight practical steps to take in administering 403(b) plans.

Appendices. For the reader's convenience, supplementary reference materials related to 403(b) plans are provided in the appendices that appear at the end of the book.

Cumulative Index. A detailed topical index is provided to aid in locating specific information. All entries in the index are referenced to both the Sixth Edition and the 2003 Supplement. References to questions appearing only in the supplement are identified with the prefix "S" (e.g., S 2:3.4).

Use of Abbreviations. A number of terms and statutory references are abbreviated throughout *403(b) Answer Book, Sixth Edition* and the 2003 Supplement. Among the most common of these shorthand references are:

- Code or IRC—The Internal Revenue Code of 1986, as amended

- EBSA—The Employee Benefits Security Administration (formerly the PWBA)
- ERISA—The Employee Retirement Income Security Act of 1974, as amended
- IRS—The Internal Revenue Service
- DOL—The U.S. Department of Labor
- COBRA—The Consolidated Omnibus Budget Reconciliation Act of 1985, as amended
- PBGC—The Pension Benefit Guaranty Corporation
- QDRO—Qualified domestic relations order
- SBJPA—The Small Business Job Protection Act of 1996
- TRA '86—The Tax Reform Act of 1986
- TRA '97—The Taxpayer Relief Act of 1997
- TAMRA—The Technical and Miscellaneous Revenue Act of 1988
- TVC—The Tax-Sheltered Annuity Voluntary Correction Program
- EGTRRA—The Economic Growth and Tax Relief Reconciliation Act of 2001
- JCWAA—The Job Creation and Workers Assistance Act of 2002

Contents

Contents

Contents

Contents

List of Questions

Correction of Excess Amounts

Correction of Excess Deferrals

Chapter 4 Nondiscrimination in Coverage and Benefits

Overview of Nondiscrimination Requirements

Application of Nondiscrimination Requirements for Different Types of Contributions

Chapter 5 Investments

Life Insurance Contracts

Mutual Fund Custodial Accounts

Participant Loans

Employer Responsibility for 403(b) Investments

Protection Against Liability

Making Investment Decisions

Participant-Directed Investment

Investment Communication Requirements

Communications Concerning Blackouts

Providing Investment Education and Advice

Disclosure and Reporting

Compliance with Claims Procedures

Fiduciary Matters

Chapter 10 Distributions

Requirements Governing Timing and Amount of Benefit Distributions

Chapter 11   Loans, Life Insurance, and Plan Termination

Using Trusts

Family Rights That Restrain a Beneficiary Designation

ERISA Survivor Benefits

Common-Law Marriage

Chapter 13 Qualified Domestic Relations Orders

Ineligible Plans

Chapter 16 Mergers and Acquisitions

403(b) Plan Considerations

Severance Pay and 403(b) Plans

457 Plan Considerations

Chapter 18 Tax-Sheltered Annuity Voluntary Correction Programs

Chapter 19 International Tax Treatment

U.S. Expatriate Tax

Chapter 20   Retirement and Estate Planning for 403(b) Participants

Funding Trusts with Retirement Plan Annuities

Spousal Rollovers

Retirement Equity Act of 1984

Chapter 1

Overview of Section 403(b) Arrangements

Jason Bortz, Esq.
Caplin & Drysdale, Chartered

> A Section 403(b) arrangement, also referred to as a "tax-sheltered annuity," is a form of defined contribution plan available only to employees of educational and charitable organizations. Subject to various limitations and restrictions, Section 403(b) of the Internal Revenue Code allows tax-deferred contributions to be made for such employees through an employer-funded plan or through an employee's voluntary salary reduction contributions. Section 403(b) requires that the contributions be invested in an annuity contract issued by a life insurance company (a Section 403(b)(1) annuity contract), shares of regulated investment companies held in a custodial account (a Section 403(b)(7) custodial account), a life insurance contract (subject to further limitations), or a retirement income account maintained for employees of certain church-affiliated organizations.

Introduction to Section 403(b) Programs

Q 1:6 Do Section 403(b) programs have advantages over Section 457(b) eligible deferred compensation plans?

Governmental employers are still precluded from maintaining Section 401(k) plans and, therefore, for governmental employers that are eligible to offer

Section 403(b) programs (public schools, higher education institutions, certain hospitals, and other organizations), the only other way to offer voluntary tax-deferred retirement savings is through an "eligible deferred compensation plan" under Section 457(b). In the past, Section 403(b) programs were significantly more advantageous than Section 457(b) plans because of higher limits on pre-tax salary reduction contributions, the availability of direct rollovers, and less restrictive distribution rules.

However, EGTRRA conformed many of the rules applicable to governmental Section 457(b) plans to the rules applicable to Section 403(b) programs, substantially narrowing the differences between the two types of plans. Under EGTRRA, the basic limit on pre-tax contributions during 2003 is $12,000 (increasing to $15,000 by 2006) for both a Section 403(b) plan and a Section 457(b) plan (although each type of plan still has its own particular "catch-up" limit for longer-service or older participants). Distributions from a governmental Section 457(b) plan or a Section 403(b) plan can be rolled over to another employer plan or IRA, and distributions from a governmental Section 457(b) plan are no longer subject to the restrictive "constructive-receipt" rules that formerly applied.

Additionally, EGTRRA repealed the rules requiring that contributions under a Section 403(b) program be counted against the limits under Section 457(b). Offering both types of plans allows many covered employees to double the limit on their pre-tax salary reduction contributions. (Nongovernmental tax-exempt employers are permitted to offer Section 457(b) plans only on a "top-hat" basis.)

Q 1:7 What responsibilities does an employer have under a salary reduction Section 403(b) program?

The allocation of contract rights and responsibilities depends on the terms of the annuity contract and, where applicable, the employer's plan. In the most typical case, an employee who participates in a Section 403(b) program is the direct owner of the annuity contract purchased on his or her behalf and is entitled to exercise all policyholder rights without the intervention of the employer. Where a Section 403(b) program is structured in this traditional manner, the employer's only responsibilities are to ensure that contributions are properly remitted to the issuer of the contract, and that its employees' W-2 income and tax withholding are properly adjusted. In such cases, the employer generally has no administrative responsibilities or burdens relating to distributions under the contract.

The fact that the Section 403(b) program may be funded through a group annuity contract issued to the employer as the group contract holder does not necessarily alter these relationships. In many such cases, the employer has only nominal contractual responsibilities (e.g., approval of contract amendments), and participating employees are issued individual annuity certificates that give them rights comparable to the rights of policyholders under individual contracts.

In some other cases, however, the group annuity contract is structured in a manner more like a pension trust; in those cases, the employer, as group contract holder, effectively oversees all plan terms and distributions under the contract. Although the participating employee is the beneficial owner of his or her interest in the annuity contract, the employee's rights are governed by the employer's plan document, rather than by the annuity contract.

A number of Section 403(b) programs are a hybrid of these two models. The employee's rights under the Section 403(b) contract may be subject to the terms of the employer's plan, with the employer exercising control over certain terms and the issuer of the contract taking responsibility for others.

Notwithstanding the contractual allocation of administrative responsibilities, the IRS in the recent past generally has looked to the employer for correction of any "403(b) failure" under the Employee Plans Compliance Resolution System (EPCRS). EPCRS, as applied to Section 403(b) programs, requires the employer to make necessary corrections (or, at least, to obtain the cooperation of the investment provider in making corrections) and to pay any required fee or sanction. [Rev Proc 2002-47, 2002-29 IRB 133]

However, in 2001, the IRS expanded EPCRS to permit certain "eligible organizations" other than the employer to pursue correction of operational failures for Section 403(b) programs. An eligible organization includes an insurer or other entity that issues Section 403(b) annuity contracts or provides related services (including administrative services). Correction by an eligible organization is made under Voluntary Correction of Group Failures (VCGroup), a component of EPCRS. [Rev Proc 2002-47, 2002-29 IRB 133]

Basic Requirements

Q 1:13 Has the IRS established any correction procedures for situations in which the requirements of Section 403(b) have not been satisfied?

Yes. Revenue Procedure 2002-47 [2002-29 IRB 133], which sets out EPCRS, provides comprehensive guidance for correcting a "403(b) failure." A 403(b) failure includes any "operational," "demographic," or "employer eligibility" failure under a Section 403(b) program.

EPCRS for Section 403(b) programs has three components: the Self-Correction Program (SCP), the Voluntary Correction of Tax-Sheltered Annuity Failures Program (VCT), and the Audit Closing Agreement Program (Audit CAP). Almost any tax compliance problem affecting a Section 403(b) program may be corrected under one of these three programs, often at relatively modest cost.

SCP permits self-correction of an operational failure if there are established practices and procedures for general compliance with Section 403(b) and if the failure is corrected by the end of the second year after the year in which it occurred (and prior to any IRS audit) or is insignificant, in which case there is no correction deadline. Self-correction under SCP does not require IRS review of the correction.

The VCT program provides for the issuance by the IRS of a compliance statement covering an operational, demographic, or employer eligibility failure. Under VCT, an employer submits an application to the IRS and agrees to pay a negotiated compliance correction fee that varies (in accordance with a published schedule) with the number of employees and the severity of the compliance failure. VCT is not available if there is a pending IRS audit. Correction under VCT can be initiated on an anonymous (or "John Doe") basis.

Finally, Audit CAP permits an employer undergoing an IRS audit whose Section 403(b) program has a 403(b) failure that cannot be corrected under SCP to pay a negotiated sanction to the IRS (determined as a percentage of the income tax that the IRS could collect as a result of the compliance failure) and to enter into a closing agreement for correction of the failure.

Requirements Relating to Distributions

Q 1:35 Can a participant in a Section 403(b) program take a loan from the program?

Although certain amounts held under a Section 403(b) program are subject to in-service distribution restrictions, those (and other) amounts may be borrowed by a participant under the rules of Code Section 72(p). The availability of loans provides employees with significant access to their Section 403(b) savings and, in many cases, can be an important inducement to employee participation in the program. However, many custodial accounts do not provide loans to employees (although the IRS has stated that loans from custodial accounts are permitted).

In 2001, the IRS issued final "plan loan" regulations under Section 72(p). These rules provide the first detailed guidance on loans under Section 403(b) programs (as well as other retirement savings vehicles) since the enactment of Section 72(p) in 1982. Also in 2001, the IRS proposed additional plan loan regulations that were finalized in 2002. As proposed, the regulations would have imposed a general limit on the number of loans a participant may take per year. The final regulations, however, provide that there is no general limit on the number of plan loans a participant may take per year (unless a limit is imposed by the issuer or employer). [See Treas Reg § 1.72(p)-1]

Chapter 2

Section 501(c)(3) Organizations

Catherine W. Wilkinson, CPA
Steptoe & Johnson, LLP

Gordon M. Clay, Esq.
Steptoe & Johnson, LLP

A Section 501(c)(3) organization is a type of tax-exempt organization that is eligible to maintain a Section 403(b) arrangement. This chapter discusses the formation and operation of Section 501(c)(3) organizations and the federal and state requirements for obtaining and maintaining tax-exempt status as a Section 501(c)(3) organization.

Introduction to Section 501(c)(3) Organizations

Q 2:1 What is a Section 501(c)(3) organization?

A Section 501(c)(3) organization is a nonprofit organization (i.e., corporation, community chest, fund, or foundation) that qualifies for exemption from federal income tax under Section 501(c)(3) of the Internal Revenue Code of 1986, as amended (the Code). To qualify under Section 501(c)(3), the organization must meet the following requirements:

1. It is organized and operated exclusively for religious, charitable, scientific, testing for public safety, literary, or educational purposes, or to foster national or international amateur sports competition, or for the prevention of cruelty to children or animals;

2. No part of the net earnings of the organization inures to the benefit of a private shareholder or individual;

3. No substantial part of the activities of the organization includes the carrying on of propaganda or otherwise attempting to influence legislation (except as otherwise permitted under Section 501(h)); and

4. The organization does not participate in, or intervene in, any political campaign on behalf of or in opposition to any candidate for public office.

Basic Requirements

Q 2:12 How does an organization obtain 501(c)(3) status?

Any organization formed after October 9, 1969, must file an application for tax exemption with the IRS in order to obtain 501(c)(3) status (see Q 1:16). [IRC § 508(a); Treas Reg § 1.508-1(a)(1)] The application, along with a certified copy of the organization's organizational documents, must be filed with the IRS Service Center in Cincinnati at the following address:

P. O. Box 192
Covington, KY 41012-0192

The application must be submitted with Form 8718 and the appropriate user fee. The user fee for an initial application for exemption is $500. [Rev Proc 2002-8, 2002-1 IRB 252] If the organization had gross annual receipts averaging $10,000 or less during the preceding four taxable years, or if a new organization anticipates average gross annual receipts of $10,000 or less during its first four years, the user fee is only $150. [Rev Proc 2003-8, 2003-1 IRB 236] In addition to the application for exemption, the organization is required to file an application for an employer identification number (EIN) (Form SS-4) if it has not already obtained an EIN. If the organization will be represented by an attorney, accountant, or other agent, it should file a power of attorney (Form 2848) authorizing the person or persons to represent the organization before the IRS.

Q 2:20 What are the annual filing requirements with the Internal Revenue Service?

With limited exceptions, Section 501(c)(3) organizations are required to file an annual information return with the IRS each year. [IRC § 6033(a)(1)] To meet this requirement, an organization must file Form 990—"Return of Organization Exempt From Income Tax"—along with Schedules A and B with the IRS each year. Schedule A is used to report the following:

1. Compensation of the five highest paid employees other than officers, directors and trustees;

2. Compensation of the five highest paid independent contractors for professional services;

3. Information about the organization's lobbying activities;

4. Information about the organization's transactions with insiders and certain other organizations;

5. Information about the organization's scholarship programs; and

6. Financial information showing the organization's public support.

Schedule B is used to report names, addresses, and the amount and type of contribution for each donor who contributed to the organization money or property aggregating $5,000 or more for the year.

A Section 501(c)(3) organization with annual gross receipts of less than $100,000 and total assets at year end of less than $250,000 may file a short form return—Form 990-EZ. Private foundations are required to file a more detailed information return known as Form 990-PF. If the organization has $1,000 or more in gross income from unrelated trade or business (defined in Q 2:35), the organization must file Form 990-T in addition to an annual information return (i.e., Form 990, Form 990-EZ, or Form 990-PF).

Certain Section 501(c)(3) organizations, such as churches and church-affiliated schools below college level, are exempt from the annual filing requirement. [IRC § 6033(a)(2); Treas Reg § 1.6033-2(g)(1)] Nevertheless, such organizations are required to notify the IRS of any changes to the organization's charitable purposes, operations, or activities [Treas Reg § 1.6033-2(i)(1)] The following Section 501(c)(3) organizations qualify for this exemption:

- A church, an interchurch organization of local units of a church, a convention or association of churches, or an integrated auxiliary of a church (such as a men's or women's organization, religious school (such as a seminary), mission society, or youth group)

- An exclusively religious activity of any religious order

- An organization (other than a private foundation) that normally has gross receipts in each taxable year of not more than $25,000

- A mission society sponsored by or affiliated with one or more churches or church denominations, more than one-half of the activities of which society are conducted in, or directed at persons in, foreign countries

- A state institution, whose income is excluded from gross income under Code Section 115

- An instrumentality of the United States

- A school below college level that (1) is affiliated with a church or operated by a religious order; and (2) normally maintains a regular faculty and curriculum and normally has a regularly enrolled student body in attendance at the place where educational activities are regularly carried on

- An organization that is operated, supervised, or controlled by one or more churches, integrated auxiliaries, or conventions or associations of churches

- An organization that is operated, supervised, or controlled by one or more religious orders and is engaged in financing, funding, or managing assets used for exclusively religious activities

- A governmental unit or an affiliate of a governmental unit (except that if such unit has any unrelated business income, it may need to file Form 990-T)

[Treas Reg § 1.6033-2(g)(1); Rev Proc 83-23, 1983-1 CB 687; Rev Proc 96-10, 1996-1 CB 517; Rev Proc 95-48, 1995-2 CB 418]

These filing exceptions do not, however, apply to private foundations.

Q 2:23.1   Are Forms 990 filed with the IRS confidential?

Generally, no. Code Section 6104 provides that certain information filed by tax-exempt organizations is "open for public inspection." Specifically, the statute provides for public disclosure of applications for exemption and their supporting documents and annual information returns. This means, for example, that salary information about directors, trustees, officers, and key employees of tax-exempt organizations reported on Part V of Form 990 or Part I of Schedule A for Form 990 is subject to public disclosure.

A controversy exists regarding the extent of disclosure of donor information reported on Schedule B to Form 990, "Schedule of Contributors." Schedule B is a new form introduced for tax years beginning in 2000. Prior to introduction of Schedule B, Form 990 filers were required to provide an attachment of their own design identifying large donors in connection with reporting total contributions on Line 1d of Form 990. Information provided as an attachment to Line 1d of Form 990 was not subject to public disclosure. After a number of inadvertent releases of donor information, Schedule B was introduced as a means for the IRS to capture the non-public donor information separately from the otherwise public Form 990 data, and withhold such data from public inspection. When first introduced, Schedule B bore a prominent legend "This form is generally not open to public inspection except for section 527 organizations." In November, 2001, the IRS reversed its position regarding public disclosure of information on Form 990, Schedule B. The current Schedule B provides that only the names and addresses of contributors to Section 501(c)(3) organizations (other than private foundations) are not subject to disclosure. All other information, including the amount of contributions, the description of noncash contributions and any other information provided is open to public inspection, unless it clearly identifies the donor. The tax-exempt community greeted the revised Schedule B with alarm due to a concern that, in some cases, the amount of a contribution, and particularly the description of a noncash contribution, may indirectly identify the donor and thus deter some donors. In November, 2002, in response to complaints from the tax-exempt community, the IRS advised that it will no longer include Schedule B on CD sets or other media generally made available to the public through third parties such as GuideStar (a website that posts information about tax-exempt organizations, including Forms 990). If a Schedule B is requested directly from the IRS, the requests will be handled on a case-by-case basis, and information released will be carefully reviewed to assure that it does not identify individual donors. [See IRS to Protect Privacy of Contributors to EOs, 2002 TNT 218-4 (Nov 8, 2002)]

Some donor information is also reported on Schedule A, Part IV-A. Lines 26b, 27a and b, and 28 of Schedule A, Part IV-A each call for an attachment providing the list of names of certain types of donors to the organization. Although the form provides that this information is not subject to public disclosure, the IRS apparently released a number of donor lists that were submitted with Schedule A, with only the names and addresses redacted. As with donor information reported on Schedule B, the public availability of the donor lists submitted with Schedule A raised privacy concerns. Beginning in 2001, the IRS no longer requires submission of these lists with the organizations' returns. Each filing organization should prepare the list and keep it in its records instead of submitting it to the IRS. [Cheryl Chasin, Susan L. Paul & Paul W. Jones, Form 990, Schedule A and Schedule B, IRS EO CPE Text for FY03]

Maintaining 501(c)(3) Status

Q 2:27   What is private inurement?

Private inurement occurs when any portion of the net earnings of a Section 501(c)(3) organization is paid to or used for the benefit of "any private shareholder or individual." [IRC § 501(c)(3)] This private inurement proscription generally applies to transactions that benefit persons having a personal and private interest in the activities of the organizations (sometimes referred to as "insiders" of the organization). [See Treas Reg § 1.501(a)-1(c)] If an organization violates the private inurement proscription, it is not "operated exclusively for one or more exempt purposes," as the regulations issued pursuant to Section 501(c)(3) of the Code require. [Treas Reg § 1.501(c)(3)-1(c)(2)]

Similarly, a Section 501(c)(3) organization cannot be organized or operated for the benefit of private interests. [Treas Reg § 1.501(c)(3)-1(d)(1)(ii)] This prohibition against "private benefit" is broader than the private inurement proscription, reaching transactions that benefit not only insiders but also other private individuals, such as members or beneficiaries of the organization. [See Rev Rul 77-111, 1977-1 CB 144] If an organization engages in a transaction that results in "more than incidental" private benefit, it is not "operated exclusively for one or more exempt purposes."

Although the regulations issued pursuant to Section 501(c)(3) state that an organization may engage in a transaction that results in merely "incidental" private benefit without risking loss of its tax exemption, the statutory language prohibiting private inurement is absolute. [See IRC § 501(c)(3); Rev Rul 74-146, 1974-1 CB 192; GCM 37166 (June 15 1977); GCM 35701 (Mar 4, 1974)] Some courts, however, have held that an organization may engage in a transaction that results in only incidental private inurement without risking loss of its tax exemption. [See Easter House v Comm'r, 87-1 USTC 9356 (Ct Cl 1987), *aff'd* 846 F 2d 78 (Fed Cir 1988); Founding Church of Scientology v United States, 412 F 2d 1197, 1200 (Ct Cl 1969), *cert denied,* 197 US 1009 (1970)] An organization that violates the private inurement proscription or the private benefit proscription could face loss of its tax exemption or the imposition of "intermediate sanctions" (see Q 2:28).

Q 2:29 Who is a disqualified person?

A *disqualified person* is any person who was, at any time during the five-year period preceding a transaction, in a position to exercise "substantial influence" over the affairs of the organization, a member of that person's family, or a 35 percent controll entity. [IRC § 4958(f)(1)] For example, in TAM 200244028 (Jun 21, 2002), the IRS ruled that the spouse of the president and chief executive officer of a nonprofit health care group was a disqualified person within the meaning of Section 4958.

Q 2:30 What is an excess benefit transaction?

An *excess benefit transaction* is a transaction in which the economic benefit to the disqualified person exceeds the value of the consideration received by the organization. [IRC § 4958(c)(1)(A)] The payment of excessive compensation to a disqualified person, for example, can constitute an excess benefit transaction under Section 4958. For purposes of determining whether a disqualified person's compensation package is reasonable under Section 4958, benefits provided pursuant to a qualified pension, profit-sharing, or stock bonus plan are deemed received on the date the benefit is vested. [Treas Reg § 53.4958-1(e)(2)]

Example. A family set up and ran three nonprofit, tax-exempt home health agencies (HHAs). The HHAs paid salaries to the family members working there, but rarely earned a surplus or profit. Subsequently, the family established new for-profit HHAs and transferred substantially all of the assets of the tax-exempt HHAs for less than their fair market value to the for-profit successors. The for-profit HHAs were run by the same individuals. The transfer of assets was determined to be an excess benefit transaction. [Caracci v Commissioner, 118 TC No. 25 (May 22, 2002)]

The regulations generally provide that the parties to a challenged transaction will receive the benefit of a rebuttable presumption that the transaction was reasonable if the parties satisfy the following three-part test:

1. The transaction is approved in advance by an authorized body of the organization, composed entirely of individuals who do not have a conflict of interest with respect to the arrangement;

2. Appropriate data as to comparability was obtained and relied upon by the authorized body in making the determination that the transaction was reasonable; and

3. Such determination is adequately and contemporaneously documented. [Treas Reg § 53.4958-6]

If the parties to the transaction satisfy the three-part test, the burden of proof shifts to the IRS to develop evidence that the transaction was an excess benefit transaction. [Treas Reg § 53.4958-6(b)] No adverse inference is to be drawn from an organization's failure to meet the three-part test. [Treas Reg § 53.4958-6(e)] In other words, an organization may be unable to satisfy the three-part test, but it may nevertheless escape the imposition of intermediate sanctions if consideration for the transaction is found to have been reasonable.

Example. A used car salesman created a Section 501(c)(3) organization, the purpose of which was to allow individuals to donate their used cars for a tax deduction and at the same time choose the charity to which they wanted the proceeds to go. The organization's board of directors consisted of the founder, his wife, his father-in-law, and a CPA. The founder was the president and executive director of the organization. He was in control of the organization's activities. The organization maintained no records of the number of hours the founder worked, no documentation of the services he provided, and no evidence of comparable salaries. The organization repaid several loans purportedly extended to it by the founder and his family. The loans were not documented. The founder is a disqualified person with respect to the organization because he is in a position to exercise substantial influence over the organization's affairs. The repayment of undocumented loans is an excess benefit. Moreover, the founder's salary is also presumptively an excess benefit because it was not approved by an authorized body composed entirely of disinterested individuals, appropriate data as to comparability was not obtained, and the transaction was not properly documented. [TAM 200243057 (July 2, 2002)]

Q 2:36   What is UBIT?

The unrelated business income tax (UBIT) is the tax an exempt organization must pay on income generated through unrelated trades or businesses, often referred to as an organization's unrelated business taxable income (UBTI). UBTI is computed by excluding certain types of investment and other income, enumerated in Section 512(b) of the Code, from the organization's gross income from unrelated trades or businesses and deducting those expenses and other items related to the production of the unrelated income. [IRC § 512(a)(1)] Section 501(c)(3) corporations that have UBTI will be taxed at the regular corporate rates set forth in Section 11 of the Code. [IRC § 511(a)] For this purpose, the IRS will treat an unincorporated association as a corporation. [Treas Reg §§ 301.7701-2(a), 301.7701-2(b)] Section 501(c)(3) trusts will be taxed like taxable trusts. [IRC § 511(b)]

Chapter 3

Contribution Limits

Janet M. Anderson, J.D.
Mercer Investment Consulting

In 1958, Congress enacted Section 403(b)(2), setting the first of the annual limits on the maximum amounts that could be excluded from taxable income under a Section 403(b) tax-deferred annuity. In 1974, Congress enacted the Employee Retirement Income Security Act (ERISA), imposing additional limits under Section 415(c). The Tax Reform Act of 1986 (TRA '86) added a third limit, governing salary reduction contributions. Finally, the Economic Growth and Tax Relief Reconciliation Act of 2001 (EGTRRA) repealed the Section 403(b)(2) maximum exclusion allowance, the Section 415(c)(4)(A), (B), and (C) alternative catch-up limits, and added a new catch-up limit. However, since the IRS will continue to examine maximum exclusion allowance and special alternative catch-up limit compliance through 403(b) plan audits for the next few years, this chapter includes questions and answers regarding these limits, while noting any differences brought about by EGTRRA.

Overview of Section 403(b) Contribution Limits

Q 3:8 Are salary reduction contributions ever treated as nonelective contributions?

Yes. Under Code Section 402(g) and Treasury Regulations Section 1.402(g)-1(e)(1), a 403(b) contribution is not treated as an elective deferral under a salary reduction agreement if the contribution is made pursuant to a one-time irrevocable election, at a stated percentage or dollar rate, by the employee at the time of initial eligibility to participate in the salary reduction agreement, or if the contribution is made pursuant to a similar arrangement involving a one-time irrevocable election specified in the Treasury Regulations. However, if a participant has the right or ability to terminate or modify an election, the contributions are treated as elective deferrals even if the participant never exercises this right. Irrevocability relates to the election to participate rather than to terminate participation. A viable, one-time irrevocable election salary reduction contribution would not be subject to the Section 402(g)(1) elective deferral limit of $12,000 (for 2003) or the higher expanded limit under Code Section 402(g)(7). [HR Conf Rep No 99–841, 99th Cong, 2d Sess, 405 (1986); Joint Committee on Taxation, General Explanation of the Tax Reform Act of 1986, HR 3838, 99th Cong, Pub L No 99–514, at 662 (May 4, 1987); EGTRRA, Pub L No 107-16 §§ 611(d)(1) and (3), 115 Stat 38 (2001)]

Section 403(b)(2) Contribution Limits

Includible Compensation

Q 3:17 Are salary reduction amounts included in includible compensation?

Yes. Certain salary reduction contributions are included in includible compensation. In all but a few cases, includible compensation includes tax-deferred amounts that are derived from a reduction in salary. Such items include, but are not limited to: (1) salary reduction amounts treated as elective deferrals (but not those made pursuant to a one-time irrevocable election that are not treated as elective deferrals) under a Section 403(b) program; (2) deferrals under a Section 457(b) deferred compensation plan; (3) Section 401(k) elective deferrals made by the employee; and (4) any Section 125 cafeteria plan salary reduction amounts. Section 414(h) employer "picked-up" contributions under a government pension system or Section 457(f) contributions made on a salary reduction basis are excluded from includible compensation. Non-salary reduction contributions (such as nonelective basic or matching contributions) are never included in includible compensation. [Taxpayer Relief Act of 1997, Pub L No

105-34, § 1504(a), 111 Stat 1063 (1997); IRC § 403(b)(3); Rev Rul 79–221, 1979-2 CB 188]

Years of Service

Section 402(g) Contribution Limits

Q 3:70   Who is eligible to use the 15-year cap expansion?

Employees of qualified employers that are defined as tax-exempt educational institutions, hospitals, home health service agencies, certain churches, and health and welfare organizations are eligible to use the 15-year cap expansion. In other words, those participants with at least 15 years of service with the current employer who may use the special alternative limits under Section 415(c)(4) may use the 15-year cap expansion. The years of service with the current employer do not have to be consecutive, but they must all have been with this current employer and not with multiple Section 403(b) eligible employers. [IRC § 402(g)(7)]

Q 3:71   Is there a lifetime limitation on the use of the 15-year cap expansion?

Yes. The 15-year cap expansion provision contains a $15,000 lifetime limit. In other words, no more than $15,000 of the cap expansion amount may be used by any participant (regardless of Section 403(b) employer) for 1987 or any later year. Participants who exhaust their $15,000 limit may never use the 15-year cap expansion again; their limit then will be $10,500 for 2001, $11,000 for 2002, and $12,000 for 2003 and all succeeding years. [IRC § 402(g)(7)(A)(ii)]

Section 414(v) Catch-up Limit

Q 3:75   How does an employee who is participating in both a 403(b) program and a 401(k) plan in the same calendar year meet the 402(g) limit for eligibility for using the age-50 catch-up?

An employee who is participating in both a 403(b) program and a 401(k) plan in the same calendar year can meet the 402(g) limit for eligibility for using the age-50 catch-up by contributing to both plans up to the 402(g) limit. In other words, in 2003, a participant can contribute $6,000 to the 403(b) plan and $6,000 to the 401(k) plan, for a total of $12,000, in order to become eligible for the age-50 catch-up. In such a situation, there is no guidance on whether the age-50 catch-up amount should be made to the 401(k) plan or the 403(b) plan. However, it cannot be made to both plans. [Prop Treas Reg § 1.414(v)-1(g)]

Coordination of Deferrals and Contributions

Q 3:77   Must other elective deferrals be coordinated with Section 403(b) elective deferrals?

Yes. Section 402(g) applies to elective deferrals under Sections 401(k), 403(b), and 408(k)(6) salary reduction simplified employee pension plans (SARSEPs). Additionally, deferrals to a 501(c)(18) plan or a Section 7701(j) Federal Thrift Savings Plan must be coordinated with the Section 403(b) elective deferrals. Elective deferrals to Section 401(k) plans, SARSEPs, or Section 403(b) contracts may not exceed $10,500 for 2001 ($12,000 for 2003) (or higher, under the 402(g)(7) limit).

The ability to establish Section 408(k)(6) SARSEPs was eliminated on January 1, 1997, but current plans were grandfathered. In general, savings incentive match plans for employees (SIMPLEs) have been enacted to take the place of SARSEPs. It appears that SIMPLE employee contributions made to a 401(k) plan may have to be coordinated with other elective deferrals under Section 402(g). [TRA 1986, Pub L No 99–514, Title XI, § 1147(a), at 410 (Oct 22, 1986); HR Conf Rep No 99–841, 99th Cong, 2d Sess, at 497 (1986); General Explanation of the Tax Reform Act of 1986, HR 3838, 99th Cong, Pub L No 99–514, at 776 (May 4, 1987); IRC § 7701(j)(1)(A); Small Business Job Protection Act of 1996, Pub L No 104–188, § 1422, 110 Stat 1755 (1996)]

Q 3:81   How are contributions to Section 403(b) and 457(b) plans coordinated?

A deferral to a Section 457(b) plan is not defined as an elective deferral under Section 402(g)(3). Consequently, it is not subtracted from the Section 403(b) elective deferral limit. However, for years before 2002, all Section 403(b) contributions (elective deferrals and nonelective contributions) must be coordinated with Section 457(b) deferrals pursuant to Section 457(c) and the regulations thereunder.

Section 457(c) provides that for individuals who are participants in more than one plan, the maximum amount that any one such individual may defer under Section 457(b) during a year cannot exceed $8,500 (beginning January 1, 2001), or up to the $15,000 higher limit, if applicable. Section 457(c)(2) also provides that Section 403(b) amounts are treated as amounts deferred under Section 457(b). Consequently, the maximum amount such an individual may defer under both plans equals the Section 457 maximum deferral amount. For example, if an individual is participating in a Section 403(b) contract and a Section 457(b) plan and makes an $8,500 (beginning January 1, 2001) deferral contribution (the individual's applicable Section 457 limit for that year) to the Section 457(b) plan, neither the individual nor the employer may make any contributions (elective or nonelective) to the Section 403(b) contract for that year.

Beginning January 1, 2002, elective deferrals under 401(k) plans or 403(b) programs will not have to be coordinated with deferrals under Section 457(b) plans. For example, in 2003, a participant in a 403(b) program can make full deferrals of up to $12,000 to a 403(b) program and full deferrals of up to an additional $12,000 in a 457(b) plan. Since contributions to a Section 7701(j) Federal Thrift Savings Plan are treated as 401(k) deferrals, these Section 7701(j) contributions will no longer have to be coordinated with 457(b) deferrals. [EGTRRA, Pub L No 107-16, § 615(a), 115 Stat 38 (2001)]

Q 3:81.1 How are age 50 catch-up contributions coordinated between 403(b) and 457(b) plans?

Age 50 catch-up contributions do not have to be coordinated between 403(b) and 457(b) plans. An employee who is eligible to make the age 50 catch-up contributions may contribute the full amount in each plan. In 2003, that would mean $2,000 in age 50 catch-up contributions to the 403(b) plan and another $2,000 in age 50 catch-up contributions to the 457(b) plan. [JCWAA, Pub L No 107–147, § 411(o)(9), 116 Stat 21(2002)]

Correction of Nonentitled Contributions

Q 3:88 How may amounts contributed in excess of the Code Section 403(b)(2) or 415 contribution limits be corrected?

Contributions made in excess of the applicable contribution limits may be corrected in any of three ways: (1) self-corrected as "overmax" contributions, (2) self-corrected as "excess amounts" under the Self-Correction Program (SCP), or (3) corrected as "excess amounts" under the Voluntary Correction Program with Service Approval/Voluntary Correction of Tax-Sheltered Annuity Failures (VCP/VCT) program or the Audit Closing Agreement Program (Audit CAP). The correction of excess amounts is part of the application of the Employee Plans Compliance Resolution System (EPCRS) to 403(b) plans as defined under Revenue Procedure 99-13; incorporated into Revenue Procedure 2000-16 and now superseded by Revenue Procedure 2001-17. This would include any contributions in excess of the Section 403(b)(2) limit before 2002. [Rev Proc 99-13, 1999-1 CB 409; modified and superseded by Rev Proc 2000-16, 2000-6 IRB 518; and superseded by Rev Proc 2001-17, 2001-7 IRB 1; modified and superseded by Rev Proc 2002-47, 2002-29 IRB 133; EGTRRA, Pub L No 107-16, § 632(a)(2)(B), 115 Stat 38 (2001)]

Self-corrected overmax contributions and excess amounts are virtually the same, except that the authority for self-correction for each is derived from a different source. Prior to the issuance of Revenue Procedure 99-13, there was no legal authority to correct elective deferrals in excess of the Section 403(b)(2) limit through distribution if withdrawal restrictions under Section 403(b)(7) or 403(b)(11) apply. Also, there was no information reporting mechanism for these excesses except to include them on the participant's IRS Form W-2 for the year of excess (see Q 3:95).

Correction of Excess Amounts

Q 3:97 What are excess amounts?

Excess amounts are any contributions or allocations to a 403(b) plan that are in excess of the limits under Section 415 or Section 403(b)(2) (the MEA) for the year, which are corrected pursuant to Revenue Procedure 2002-47. Excess amounts would include any contributions in excess of the Section 403(b)(2) limit made before 2002. [Rev Proc 99-13, 1999-1 CB 409, § 3(04); modified and superseded by Rev Proc 2000-16, 2000-6 IRB 518, § 5.02(3); superseded by Rev Proc 2001-17, 2001-7 IRB 1, § 5.02(3); modified and superseded by Rev Proc 2002-47, 2002-29 IRB 133, § 5.02(3); EGTRRA, Pub L No 107-16, § 632(a)(2)(B), 115 Stat 38 (2001)]

Q 3:98 How may excess amounts be corrected?

Excess amounts may be corrected in either of two ways. One way is to distribute the excess amounts and the other way is to retain the excess amounts. [Rev Proc 99-13, 1999-1 CB 409, § 4(02); modified and superseded by Rev Proc 2000-16, 2000-6 IRB 518, § 6.02(4)(b)(i) and (ii); modified and superseded by Rev Proc 2002-47, 2002-29 IRB 133, § 6.05(2)(a) and (b)]

Q 3:99 How may excess amounts be self-corrected?

Excess amounts that are self-corrected through SCP may be corrected only through distribution of excess amounts. Correction through retention of excess amounts is not permissible through self-correction. [Rev Proc 99-13, 1999-1 CB 409, § 5(02)(4); modified and superseded by Rev Proc 2000-16, 2000-6 IRB 518 § 4.02; superseded by Rev Proc 2001-17, 2001-7 IRB 1, § 6.05(2)(a) and (b); modified and superseded by Rev Proc 2002-47, 2002-29 IRB 133, § 6.05(2)(a) and (b)]

Q 3:100 May excess amounts be corrected through VCP/VCT or Audit CAP?

Yes. Under the VCP/VCT program or Audit CAP, correction may be made either by distribution or retention of excess amounts. [Rev Proc 99-13, 1999-1 CB 409, §§ 4(02)(2), 6(05); modified and superseded by Rev Proc 2000-16, 2000-6 IRB 518, § 4.02; superseded by Rev Proc 2001-17, 2001-7 IRB 1, § 6.05(2)(a) and (b); modified and superseded by Rev Proc 2002-47, 2002-29 IRB 133, § 6.05(2)(a) and (b)] (For more information on the VCP/VCT program and Audit CAP, see chapter 18.)

Q 3:101   What is correction through distribution of excess amounts?

Under this correction method, excess amounts for a year, adjusted for earnings through the date of distribution, must be distributed to affected participants and beneficiaries and included in their gross income in the year distributed. A distribution of excess amounts is generally treated in the manner described in Section 3 of Revenue Procedure 92–93 [1992-2 CB 505], relating to the corrective disbursement of elective deferrals (see Qs 3:88, 3:92). [Rev Proc 99-13, 1999-1 CB 409, § 4(02)(1); modified and superseded by Rev Proc 2000-16, 2000-6 IRB 518, § 6.02(4)(b)(i); superseded by Rev Proc 2001-17, 2001-7 IRB 1, § 6.05(2)(a); modified and superseded by Rev Proc 2002-47, 2002-29 IRB 133, § 6.05(2)(a)]

Q 3:102   Must excess amounts that are corrected under the distribution method be reported?

Yes. The distribution must be reported on IRS Form 1099-R for the year of distribution with respect to each participant or beneficiary receiving such a distribution. [Rev Proc 99-13, 1999-1 CB 409, § 4(02)(1); modified and superseded by Rev Proc 2000-16, 2000-6 IRB 518, § 6.02(4)(b)(i); superseded by Rev Proc 2001-17, 2001-7 IRB 1, § 6.05(2)(a); modified and superseded by Rev Proc 2002-47, 2002-29 IRB 133, § 6.05(2)(a)]

Q 3:103   Are excess amounts that are corrected through the distribution method eligible for rollover?

No. The distribution of excess amounts is not an eligible rollover distribution within the meaning of Code Section 403(b)(8). In addition, the employer must inform affected participants and beneficiaries that the distribution of excess amounts is not eligible for rollover. [Rev Proc 99-13, 1999-5 IRB 52, § 4(02)(1); modified and superseded by Rev Proc 2000-16, 2000-6 IRB 518, § 6.02(4)(b)(i); superseded by Rev Proc 2001-17, 2001-7 IRB 1, § 6.05(2)(a); modified and superseded by Rev Proc 2002-47, 2002-29 IRB 133, § 6.05(2)(a)]

Q 3:104   Do excess amounts corrected under the distribution method that exceed Section 415(c)(1) limits remain identified as prior years' contributions under Section 403(b)(2)(A)(ii)?

No. Excess amounts that are distributed are not treated as amounts previously excludable under Section 403(b)(2)(A)(ii) for purposes of calculating the maximum exclusion allowance for the taxable year of the distribution and for subsequent taxable years. (This is a distinct advantage over self-correcting as an overmax contribution; see Q 3:94.) [Rev Proc 99-13, 1999-5 IRB 52, § 4(02)(1); modified and superseded by Rev Proc 2000-16, 2000-6 IRB 518, § 6.02(4)(b)(i); superseded by Rev Proc 2001-17, 2001-7 IRB 1, § 6.05(2)(a); modified and superseded by Rev Proc 2002-47, 2002-29 IRB 133, § 6.05(2)(a)]

Q 3:105   How are excess amounts corrected under the retention method?

Excess amounts will be treated as corrected (even though the excess amounts are retained in the 403(b) plan), if the requirements of Section 6.05(2)(b) of Revenue Procedure 2001-17 are satisfied. [Rev Proc 99-13, 1999-5 IRB 52, § 4(02)(2); modified and superseded by Rev Proc 2000-16, 2000-6 IRB 518, § 6.02(4)(b)(ii); superseded by Rev Proc 2001-17, 2001-7 IRB 1, § 6.05(2)(b); modified and superseded by Rev Proc 2002-47, 2002-29 IRB 133, § 6.05(2)(b)]

Q 3:106   How must excess amounts that exceed the Section 415 limits be corrected under the retention method?

Excess amounts that arise from exceeding the Section 415 limits, adjusted for earnings through the date of correction, must reduce affected participants' applicable Section 415 limit for the year following the year of correction (or for the year of correction if the employer chooses), and subsequent years, until the excess is eliminated. [Rev Proc 99-13, 1999-5 IRB 52, § 4(02)(2); modified and superseded by Rev Proc 2000-16, 2000-6 IRB 518, § 6.02(4)(b)(ii); superseded by Rev Proc 2001-17, 2001-7 IRB 1, § 6.05(2)(b); modified and superseded by Rev Proc 2002-47, 2002-29 IRB 133, § 6.05(2)(b)]

Q 3:108   If excess amounts are corrected under the retention method, must it be used as the correction method for all participants who have excess amounts?

Yes. If the retention method is selected as the correction method, it must generally be used for all participants who have excess amounts. [Rev Proc 99-13, 1999-5 IRB 52, § 4(02)(2); modified and superseded by Rev Proc 2000-16, 2000-6 IRB 518, § 6.02(4)(b)(ii); superseded by Rev Proc 2001-17, 2001-7 IRB 1, § 6.05(2)(b); modified and superseded by Rev Proc 2002-47, 2002-29 IRB 133, § 6.05(2)(a)]

Q 3:109   Are excise and employment taxes waived when excess amounts are corrected?

No. Excise taxes, such as the 6 percent penalty tax under Section 4973(a)(2), FICA taxes, and FUTA taxes and corresponding withholding obligations, if applicable, that result from a failure are not waived merely because the failure has been corrected. [Rev Proc 99-13, 1999-1 CB 409; § 2(02), modified and superseded by Rev Proc 2000-16, 2000-6 IRB 518, § 6.04; modified and superseded by Rev Proc 2002-47, 2002-29 IRB 133, § 6.07]

Q 3:110 Is there an advantage to self-correction of overmax contributions as compared to self-correction of excess amounts under SCP?

Provided an employer has established practices and procedures—either individually through the employer and/or through its 403(b)-provider company —self-correction of excess amounts through SCP is more advantageous by providing an employer with firm legal reliance on Revenue Procedure 2002-47. In other words, self-correction of excess amounts provides an employer with an affirmative and reliable defense were the employer's 403(b) program to be audited by the IRS. Under Revenue Procedure 2002-47, the IRS auditor has no discretion to accept or reject the correction methods followed by the employer— provided that the correction is in compliance with Revenue Procedure 2002-47. An employer can look upon such a correction method as a safe harbor method for self-correction of amounts contributed in excess of the contribution limits. The IRS recognizes that an employer may self-correct these contributions as overmax contributions outside the purview of Revenue Procedure 2001-17 but feels that an employer is "on its own" when doing so.

Correction of Excess Deferrals

Q 3:119 May excess deferrals be corrected under the VCP/VCT program or under Audit CAP?

Yes. An operational failure to satisfy the limit on elective deferrals under Section 403(b)(1)(E) may be corrected under the VCP/VCT program or under Audit CAP (see chapter 18 for more information). [Rev Proc 2001-17, 2001-7 IRB 1; modified and superseded by Rev Proc 2002-47, 2002-29 IRB 133]

Chapter 4

Nondiscrimination in Coverage and Benefits

Robert A. Browning, JD
Polsinelli Shalton & Welte

Section 403(b) provides that eligible employers may make current contributions toward the purchase of an annuity contract, but employees will not be taxed on such contributions or earnings until the amounts are distributed to them. However, in order to receive this tax-favored treatment, the contract must be purchased under a plan that meets certain coverage and nondiscrimination requirements. These rules generally require that the salary reduction feature of the plan, if any, must be made available to any employee of the organization willing to contribute more than $200 per year, and that employer contributions under the plan satisfy coverage and nondiscrimination requirements similar to those that apply to qualified 401(a) plans. Compliance with the rules is important, since the effect of violating the nondiscrimination requirements of Section 403(b)(12) is loss of 403(b) status for the employer's entire 403(b) program. This chapter gives an overview of the coverage and nondiscrimination requirements applicable to 403(b) programs.

Overview of Nondiscrimination Requirements

Q 4:1   What coverage and nondiscrimination rules apply to 403(b) programs?

There are separate rules with respect to contributions made pursuant to a salary reduction agreement (i.e., employee pre-tax contributions) and all other types of contributions. [IRC 403(b)(12)(A)] With respect to salary reduction contributions, a plan meets the nondiscrimination requirements of Section 403(b)(12) so long as all employees of the employer (other than certain excludable employees) may elect to make salary reduction contributions of more than $200 per year. This is sometimes referred to as the *universal availability* requirement of Section 403(b)(12), and it is unique to 403(b) programs. [IRC 403(b)(12)(A)(ii)]

With respect to contributions other than salary reduction contributions, 403(b) programs are generally subject to the same nondiscrimination rules as qualified plans. These rules apply to plan coverage, contributions, and other benefits, and are contained in Sections 401(a)(4), 401(a)(5), 401(a)(17), 401(a)(26), 401(m), and 410(b). [IRC 403(b)(12)(A)(i)]

Notice 89-23 [1989-1 CB 654] provides that, until further guidance is published, the nondiscrimination requirements of Section 403(b)(12) are satisfied if the employer operates its 403(b) plan in accordance with a reasonable, good-faith interpretation of Section 403(b)(12). The Notice also sets forth certain transitional safe harbors to facilitate compliance with Section 403(b)(12). When IRS Notice 89-23 was issued in 1989, it was intended to apply for a limited period to alleviate compliance problems for tax-exempt employers. It has since been extended several times, and, as of the publication date of this book, it continues to apply for an indefinite period (see SQ 4:33).

Therefore, not only are there two separate sets of discrimination rules for 403(b) arrangements—one set of rules for salary-reduction contributions and another set for all other employee and employer contributions—but for each set of rules there are three possible ways of demonstrating compliance:

1. Adherence to the statutory rules referenced under Section 403(b)(12);
2. Application of a "reasonable good-faith interpretation" of Section 403(b)(12) (as permitted under Notice 89-23); or
3. Application of one of the safe harbors set forth in Notice 89-23.

Q 4:3   When must 403(b) programs comply with the nondiscrimination rules?

The coverage and nondiscrimination requirements of Section 403(b)(12), including the universal availability requirement for salary reduction contributions, generally apply to plan years beginning on or after January 1, 1989. However, as a result of delays in finalizing the IRS regulations governing the nondiscrimination requirements applicable to qualified plans, the compliance date for many of the nondiscrimination rules applicable to non-salary reduction 403(b) contributions was deferred until the first day of the first plan year commencing after October 1, 1997 (for tax-exempt employers), or the first day of the first plan year commencing after December 31, 1998 (for governmental employers and nonelecting 414(e) church plans). [Ann 95-48, IRB 1995-23 (May 11, 1995); Notice 96-47, 1996-2 CB 213] Until those dates, governmental plans were deemed to satisfy and tax-exempt employers (including nonelecting 414(e) church plan sponsors) could rely on a reasonable, good-faith interpretation of many of the nondiscrimination requirements.

The Taxpayer Relief Act of 1997 (TRA '97) permanently exempted governmental plans (including Section 403(b) arrangements) from many of the nondiscrimination requirements. [IRC 401(a)(5)(G)] As a result, the only nondiscrimination requirements applicable to governmental 403(b) programs (such as those sponsored by public schools) are the universal availability requirement for salary reduction contributions and the requirement that non-salary reduction contributions satisfy the limit on considered compensation under Section 401(a)(17). [IRC § 403(b)(12)(C)]

There are special effective dates for the application of certain nondiscrimination rules for "nonelecting" church plans (church plans that have not elected, pursuant to Section 410(d), to be subject to the participation, vesting, and funding requirements of the Employee Retirement Income Security Act of 1974 (ERISA)). As indicated in Q 4:2, certain church plans, as defined in Section 414(e), may not qualify as churches or church-controlled organizations under Section 3121(w)(3), and therefore are generally subject to the nondiscrimination rules under Section 403(b)(12). As noted above, the coverage and nondiscrimination regulations are generally applicable to tax-exempt employers on the first day of the first plan year commencing after October 1, 1997. However, Notice 2001-46 [2001-32 IRB 122] provides that the effective date of regulations under Sections 401(a)(4), 401(a)(5), 401(l), and 414(s) for nonelecting church plans have been extended until further notice, but not earlier than the first plan year beginning on or after January 1, 2003.

Application of Nondiscrimination Requirements for Different Types of Contributions

Q 4:4   What types of contributions may be made to a 403(b) program?

A 403(b) program may include the following types of contributions:

1. Salary reduction contributions (i.e., employee pre-tax deferrals);

2. After-tax employee contributions;

3. Non-matching (discretionary or nonelective) employer contributions (sometimes referred to as "employer basic" contributions); and

4. Employer matching contributions.

The nondiscrimination rules vary for each type of contribution. The rules that apply to salary reduction contributions (see SQ 4:5) are designed to provide "universal" coverage, regardless of the employee's income. The rules that apply to non-salary reduction contributions (see SQs 4:6 through 4:8) are designed to provide broad coverage and to prevent discrimination in favor of highly compensated employees (HCEs), as that term is defined in Section 414(q).

Q 4:4.1   Who is a highly compensated employee?

For plan years beginning after December 31, 1996, an HCE is any employee who

1. Was a 5 percent owner at any time during the plan year or the preceding year; or

2. Received compensation from the employer during the preceding plan year in excess of $90,000 (indexed for inflation, 2003 figure) and, *if elected by the employer*, was among the top 20 percent of the most highly compensated employees during the preceding plan year when ranked on the basis of compensation during that year. [IRC § 414(q)(1)]

Notice 97-45 [1997-2 CB 296] describes how the employer may make this "top paid group" election and also describes a method for determining HCEs on a calendar-year basis rather than a plan-year basis.

All members of a controlled group or affiliated service group associated with an employer are taken into account in determining HCEs. However, the IRS has indicated that tax-exempt and governmental employers may rely on a reasonable, good-faith interpretation of the controlled group and affiliated service group rules under Code Sections 414(b), 414(c), 414(m), and 414(o) until further guidance is issued. [IRS Notice 96-64, 1996-2 CB 229]

Notice 89-23 [1989-1 CB 654] includes a special definition of an HCE that may be used for purposes of the rules in the notice. This alternative definition, which basically limits HCEs to 5 percent owners or individuals who receive compensation in excess of $50,000, as adjusted in the manner described in Code Section 45(d), was only useful before 1997, when the Section 414(q) definition described above became more liberal than the special definition provided in Notice 89-23.

Q 4:5   What nondiscrimination rules apply to salary reduction contributions?

Generally, the right to make salary reduction contributions must be universally available. This means that if an eligible employer (other than a Section 3121(w)(3) church or church-controlled organization) allows any employee to make salary reduction contributions under a 403(b) plan, the employer may not exclude any statutorily eligible employee from participating in the salary reduction arrangement except to require that annual contributions be greater than $200. [IRC 403(b)(12)(A)(ii)] However, the following categories of employees may be statutorily excluded:

1. Nonresident aliens with no U.S.-source income;

2. Employees who normally work fewer than 20 hours per week;

3. Students providing services described in Section 3121(b)(10); and

4. Employees eligible to make salary reduction contributions to other employer plans maintained under Sections 401(k), 457, or 403(b).

[IRC § 403(b)(12)]

With regard to categories 2 and 3, such employees may be excluded for discrimination testing purposes only if the plan or program excludes *all* employees in that category. Therefore, in order to exclude employees who normally work fewer than 20 hours per week, the plan cannot cover any employee who works less than that amount.

It is important to note that salary reduction contributions under a 403(b) plan that are the result of a one-time irrevocable election made at the time of initial eligibility to participate in the salary reduction arrangement are deemed to be employer contributions, not salary reduction contributions. [IRC § 403(b)(12)] Therefore, mandatory employee contributions are not treated as salary reduction contributions for purposes of the nondiscrimination requirements of Section 403(b).

Notice 89-23, however, provides that employers may apply a reasonable, good-faith interpretation of the nondiscrimination requirements of Section 403(b)(12) and also provides a safe harbor for satisfying the universal availability requirement with respect to salary reduction contributions to a 403(b) arrangement. See SQs 4:33 and 4:36 and Qs 4:34, 4:35, and 4:37 for more details on the relief provided by Notice 89-23, including additional categories of employees that may be excluded from a 403(b) arrangement without violating the discrimination requirements.

The average deferral percentage (ADP) test applicable to salary reduction contributions under Section 401(k) plans does not apply to salary-reduction contributions under Section 403(b) arrangements. For HCEs, this can be a significant advantage. Conversely, the universal availability requirement of Section 403(b)(12)(A)(ii) does not apply to salary reduction contributions under a Section 401(k) plan.

Q 4:6   What nondiscrimination rules apply to employee after-tax contributions?

Since no rules (other than the universal availability requirement described in SQ 4:5) prohibit discrimination in salary reduction (i.e., pre-tax) contributions, one might expect a similar treatment for after-tax contributions to 403(b) plans, but that is not the case. Employee after-tax contributions are considered non-salary reduction contributions for purposes of Section 403(b)(12) and are therefore subject to the same rules that apply to after-tax contributions to qualified plans. For nongovernmental 403(b) arrangements, employee after-tax contributions and employer matching contributions are subject to the actual contribution percentage (ACP) test under Section 401(m). [IRC § 401(m)(1)] Governmental 403(b) arrangements are deemed to satisfy the ACP test for employee after-tax and employer matching contributions. However, for nongovernmental employers, the right to make such after-tax contributions is a "benefit, right, or feature" that must be tested under the regulations of Section 401(a)(4). Therefore, not only must after-tax contributions to a nongovernmental 403(b) plan satisfy the numerical ACP test, but the right to make such contributions must be available to a nondiscriminatory group of employees.

Q 4:7 What rules apply to matching contributions?

For nongovernmental employers, employer matching contributions (as well as employee after-tax contributions) are subject to the ACP test under Section 401(m).

In addition, the right to receive matching contributions at a specific rate or percentage is itself a "benefit, right, or feature" that must be tested under Section 401(a)(4).

In order to satisfy the ACP test, the average contribution rate (expressed as a percentage of compensation) of the HCEs for the testing year cannot exceed the *greater of*

1. 125 percent of the average contribution rate for all eligible non-highly compensated employees (NHCEs) for the prior year; or
2. The lesser of
   (a) 200 percent of the average contribution rate for all eligible NHCEs for the prior year, or
   (b) the average contribution rate for all eligible NHCEs for the prior year, plus 2 percent.

[IRC § 401(m)(2)]

The following table illustrates which of the three contribution limit rules applies, depending on the range of average matching and after-tax contributions for NHCEs:

Average NHCE (%)	Applicable Rule
Less than 2	200%
2 to 8	+2%
Over 8	125%

For example, if the average matching and after-tax contributions rate for NHCEs for the prior year was 1 percent of compensation, then the maximum average for HCEs is 2 percent (200% × 1%). If the average rate for NHCEs for the prior year was 3 percent, then the maximum average for HCEs is 5 percent (3% + 2%). If the average rate for NHCEs for the prior year was 9 percent, then the maximum average for HCEs is 11.25 percent (9% × 125%).

All HCEs who are *eligible for* after-tax or matching contributions during the testing year, and all NHCEs who were eligible during the prior year, are counted, including those who make no after-tax contributions and those who receive no matching contributions. The employer may elect to perform the Section 401(m) ACP test by using current year NHCE contributions instead of prior year NHCE contributions. However, once the employer elects to use current year contribution data, the employer cannot revert to "prior year" testing unless certain requirements are met. [Notice 98-1, 1998-3 IRB 42]

If the average Section 401(m) contribution rate for HCEs exceeds the limit, the excess contributions must be returned or forfeited. Specific timing requirements must be met to avoid excise taxes. [IRC § 401(m)(6)]

Governmental 403(b) arrangements are deemed to satisfy the nondiscrimination requirements with respect to matching contributions. Therefore, they are not subject to the 401(m) ACP test.

Q 4:7.1   What is a safe-harbor 403(b) plan?

Nongovernmental Section 403(b) plans may also satisfy the requirements of Section 401(m) through the use of a "design-based" safe harbor. Just as 401(k) plans can be structured as safe-harbor plans to avoid the ADP and ACP tests, 403(b) arrangements may be structured as safe-harbor arrangements that are "deemed" to satisfy the ACP tests. However, the safe harbor only applies with respect to matching contributions (i.e., it does not apply to employee after-tax contributions). Section 401(m)(11) provides that a plan shall be treated as satisfying the requirements of Section 401(m) with respect to matching contributions (i.e., it is treated as satisfying the ACP test for matching contributions) if the plan meets certain minimum contribution requirements, certain notice requirements, and certain additional limitations. The IRS has provided guidance on the application of this design-based safe harbor in Notice 98-52 and Notice 2000-3.

The contribution requirement may be satisfied by (1) a basic matching formula, (2) an enhanced matching formula, or (3) a nonelective contribution formula. Regardless of the formula, all "safe harbor" contributions must be 100 percent vested, and they must be subject to withdrawal restrictions that are similar to those that otherwise apply to elective deferrals.

Under the basic matching formula, the plan will be deemed to satisfy the ACP test if, under the terms of the plan, the employer is required to make matching contributions on behalf of each eligible NHCE equal to 100 percent of the elective contributions that do not exceed 3 percent of the employee's compensation, and 50 percent of the elective contributions that exceed 3 percent of compensation but do not exceed 5 percent of compensation. The enhanced matching formula requires that the employer make matching contributions on behalf of each eligible NHCE that, for any rate of elective contributions, provides an aggregate amount of matching contributions at least equal to the aggregate matching contributions that would have been provided under the basic matching formula. Under either formula, the rate of matching contributions may not increase as the employee's rate of elective contributions increases, and the rate of matching contributions that applies to any HCE must not be greater than the rate of matching contributions that would apply to any NHCE who has the same rate of elective contributions. The employee's right to matching contributions cannot be subject to an allocation condition, such as a requirement that the participant be employed on the last day of the plan year or a rquirement to work at least 1,000 hours during the plan year.

Under the nonelective contribution formula, the plan will be deemed to satisfy the ACP test if, under the terms of the plan, the employer is required to make a safe harbor nonelective contribution on behalf of each eligible NHCE equal to at least 3 percent of the employee's compensation. This contribution must be based on a nondiscriminatory definition of compensation, and the employee's right to the contribution must not be subject to any "last day" or "1,000 hours of service" requirement.

The notice requirement is satisfied if each eligible employee for the plan year is given written notice of his or her rights and obligations under the plan, and the notice satisfies both a content requirement and a timing requirement.

The content requirement is satisfied if the notice is sufficiently accurate and comprehensive to inform the employee of his or her rights and obligations under the plan and is written in a manner calculated to be understood by the average employee eligible to participate in the plan. The timing requirement is satisfied if the notice is provided within a reasonable period before the beginning of the plan year (or, in the year an employee first becomes eligible, within a reasonable period before the employee becomes eligible). (The timing requirement is deemed to be satisfied if the notice is provided at least 30 days (and no more than 90 days) before the beginning of each plan year.) In the case of a newly established plan or a newly eligible employee, the notice may be provided within the 90-day period ending on the date the employee becomes eligible for the plan.

In addition to the contribution requirement and the notice requirement, the plan must satisfy certain other limitations and restrictions on matching contributions. These include the following:

1. If the plan uses the basic matching formula, there may not be any other matching contributions under the plan;

2. If the plan uses an enhanced matching formula or the nonelective contribution formula, matching contributions may not be made with respect to employee contributions or elective deferrals in excess of 6 percent of compensation; and

3. If the plan uses an enhanced matching formula or the nonelective contribution formula, and the plan provides for matching contributions at the employer's discretion, the plan must limit such discretionary matching contributions to an amount which, in the aggregate, will not exceed 4 percent of the employee's compensation.

Notice 98-52 also provides that safe harbor contributions may be made to another defined contribution plan. Therefore, the nondiscrimination requirement for matching contributions under a Section 403(b) arrangement could be satisfied, for example, by "safe harbor" nonelective contributions to another Section 401(a) plan of the employer (such as a profit-sharing or money purchase plan).

Q 4:8 What rules apply to employer nonmatching contributions?

With respect to 403(b) arrangements of nongovernmental employers, contributions that are not made pursuant to a salary reduction agreement (i.e., employer discretionary or nonelective contributions) must meet the requirements of Sections 401(a)(4), 401(a)(5), 401(a)(17), 401(a)(26), and 410(b) in the same manner as if the plan were a qualified plan under Section 401(a). For purposes of these tests, students performing services described in Section 3121(b)(10) and employees who normally work fewer than 20 hours per week may be statutorily excluded (provided that all such employees are excluded from participation in the 403(b) program). In addition, the statute allows nonresident aliens with no U.S.-source income to be excluded. Notice 89-23 [1989-1 CB 654] allows additional employees to be excluded for purposes of the safe-harbors set forth in that notice. Governmental 403(b) arrangements are deemed to satisfy the nondiscrimination requirements under Sections 401(a)(4), 401(a)(5), and 410(b), but they must satisfy the requirements of Section 401(a)(17), which limits the amount of compensation that can be taken into account for purposes of contributions or benefits. This limit, which is $200,000 for 2003, is indexed for inflation. Under a special transition rule, certain grandfathered employees of certain governmental employers may be permitted to take into account more than $200,000 of compensation. [Treas Reg § 1.401(a)(17)-l]

Notice 89-23, however, provides that employers may apply a reasonable, good-faith interpretation of the nondiscrimination requirements of Section 403(b)(12). The Notice also provides three safe harbor formulas (and many special definitions) for satisfying the requirements of Section 403(b)(12) that apply to non-salary reduction contributions (see SQ 4:33).

Minimum Participation Rules

Q 4:9　Which employees must be allowed to participate in the plan?

Section 401(a)(26) generally provides that a plan must benefit at least the lesser of 50 employees or 40 percent of the employees. However, effective for plan years beginning on or after January 1, 1997, the requirements of Section 401(a)(26) apply solely to defined benefit plans. Because the vast majority of 403(b) arrangements are defined contribution plans, the requirements of Section 401(a)(26) rarely affect the determination of which employees must be allowed to participate in a 403(b) arrangement. Therefore, there is generally no requirement that employer contributions under a 403(b) defined contribution arrangement be made for at least 50 employees or 40 percent of the employees.

Section 410(a) of the Code, which sets forth the minimum age and service requirements that can be imposed by plans that are intended to be "qualified" under Section 401(a), does not apply to 403(b) plans. However, if an employer-sponsored 403(b) arrangement is subject to ERISA, similar provisions apply. Section 202(a) of ERISA provides that, in general, employees may not be excluded from a plan on account of age or service if they have attained age 21 and have completed at least one year of service. Employees must generally be allowed to participate within six months after they have met those requirements. Normally, a year of service means a plan or employment year in which an employee has completed at least 1,000 hours of service, although other methods of determining a year of service may be used. Regulations issued by the IRS and the Department of Labor (DOL) set forth myriad requirements and alternatives for measuring years and hours of service. [See, e.g., DOL Reg §§ 2530.200b-3(c), 2530.200b3(d), and 2530.200b-3(e)]

It should be noted that the age and service rules described in Section 202(a) of ERISA do not preempt the universal availability requirement that applies to salary reduction contributions to Section 403(b) arrangements. Therefore, for 403(b) plans that are subject to ERISA, regardless of any age or service requirements applicable to employer contributions under the plan, employees who are under age 21 or have less than one year of service must be permitted to make salary reduction contributions. Also, the rule under Section 403(b)(12) that permits the exclusion for nondiscrimination testing of employees who "normally work less than 20 hours per week" does not preempt the rule under Section 202(a) of ERISA that prohibits the exclusion of "part-time" employees who may otherwise complete at least 1,000 hours of service in a year and become eligible to participate in the plan. Therefore, for an ERISA-covered 403(b) arrangement, the exclusion of employees who normally work less than 20 hours per week may violate Section 202(a) of ERISA, even though it does not violate the nondiscrimination requirements of Section 403(b)(12).

Coverage Rules

Q 4:14   How does the Section 410(b) ratio percentage test work?

Under the ratio percentage test defined in Section 410(b)(1), a plan satisfies coverage requirements if the percentage of nonexcludable NHCEs covered by the plan is at least 70 percent of the percentage of nonexcludable HCEs covered. Nonexcludable employees are all employees other than the "excludable" employees. Excludable employees include those who have not satisfied the minimum age and service requirements of the plan (applied as if Section 410(a) applied to the 403(b) plan), union employees, students, employees who normally work fewer than 20 hours per week, and nonresident aliens. If a plan covers employees who do not meet the statutory age or service requirements of Section 410(a), then, for purposes of meeting the Section 410(b) rules, it can be tested as two separate plans: one covering employees who meet the statutory requirements and a second covering employees who do not. To be deemed covered under a plan for a year for purposes of Section 410(b), a participant must actually be receiving a contribution (or be eligible to receive a matching contribution) or accruing a benefit. Inactive or terminated participants are not counted. [Treas Reg § 1.410(b)-6]

The following table illustrates the application of the ratio percentage test to an employer's 403(b) plan:

Plan	Nonexcludable Employees		
Status	NHCEs	HCEs	Total
Covered	180 (67%)	27 (90%)	207 (69%)
Not covered	90 (33%)	3 (10%)	93 (31%)
Total	270 (100%)	30 (100%)	300 (100%)

Here 300 nonunion employees are nonexcludable due to age, service, or other factors. Of those, 270 are NHCEs and 30 are HCEs. The plan covers 67 percent of the NHCEs and 90 percent of the HCEs. Because 67 percent divided by 90 percent equals 74 percent, which exceeds 70 percent, the plan passes the ratio percentage test. In fact, if 28 of the 30 HCEs (or 93 percent) were covered, the plan would still pass (67% ÷ 93% = 72%). However, if 29 HCEs (or 97 percent) were covered, the plan would not pass (67% ÷ 97% = 69%).

Q 4:20   How is the average benefits percentage calculated?

An average benefits percentage can be calculated for each employee on either a defined contribution or a defined benefit basis. If the average benefits percentage is being determined on a contributions basis, then the rate of contribution as a percentage of compensation applicable to each nonexcludable employee is calculated. For a defined contribution plan, this rate would be equal to the amount of contributions and forfeitures allocated to the employee for the year, divided by his or her compensation (limited for the year as provided in

Section 401(a)(17)—$200,000 for 2003). If a defined benefit plan is maintained by the employer, the amount of benefit accruing under that plan is converted to an equivalent rate of contribution using actuarial assumptions. [Treas Reg § 1.401(a)(4)-8] Nonexcludable employees not receiving allocations or accruing benefits are credited with zero. However, for purposes of the average benefits percentage test, the only employees who can be excluded on the basis of age or service requirements are those who do not meet the lowest age and service eligibility requirements of any plan of the employer. [Treas Reg § 1.410(b)-6(b)(2)]

Nondiscrimination Rules

Q 4:25   How is it determined whether employer contributions to nongovernmental 403(b) arrangements are discriminatory under Section 401(a)(4)?

A plan can meet the coverage rules of Code Section 410(b) and still be discriminatory. As a simple example, a plan could cover 100 percent of all statutorily eligible employees but provide substantial contributions for HCEs and de minimis contributions for NHCEs. To prohibit this, Section 401(a)(4) provides that a plan cannot discriminate in favor of HCEs with respect to the benefits or contributions provided. Compliance can be demonstrated by testing an individual plan or aggregating that plan with any other eligible plans of the employer. If an aggregated group of plans is demonstrated to be nondiscriminatory with respect to benefits or contributions, then each of the plans contained in the group is deemed to be nondiscriminatory. [Treas Reg § 1.410(b)-7(d)]

The regulations under Section 401(a)(4) are extremely voluminous and complex, extending to over 300 pages. They deal not only with the quantitative value of the benefits or contributions provided under a plan, but also the qualitative provisions that cover the eligibility for, and distribution of, benefits from a plan. This latter category is generally referred to as the *benefits, rights, and features* of a plan (see SQ 4:32).

Virtually all 403(b) plans are of the defined contribution type. Therefore, this section of the chapter will deal with the rules governing compliance of defined contribution plans. However, because employers sponsoring 403(b) plans may also sponsor defined benefit plans, this section will also cover the rules applicable to defined benefit plans with which it is necessary to comply in order to aggregate such plans with a 403(b) plan to demonstrate compliance of the 403(b) plan.

Q 4:25.1   What definition of compensation must be used under Section 403(b)(12)(A)(1)?

For purpose of the average benefits test under Section 410(b) and the nondiscrimination requirements of Section 401(a)(4), the plan must use a definition of compensation that satisfies Section 414(s). Section 414(s) provides that *compensation* may be defined as either (1) Section 415(c)(3) compensation or (2) an alternative definition permissible under applicable Treasury regulations, so long as such alternative definition does not discriminate in favor of HCEs. Treasury Regulations Sections 1.414(s)-1 and 1.415-2 set forth several definitions of compensation that are deemed to satisfy Section 414(s), and Treasury Regulations Section 1.414(s)-1 sets forth the requirements for determining whether an altenative definition of compensation will be considered nondiscriminatory under Section 414(s).

It should be noted that under any of the definitions of compensation that are deemed to satisfy Section 414(s), the employer may elect to exclude certain "elective" amounts (i.e., amounts contributed by the employer pursuant to a salary reduction agreement, and which are not includible in the employee's gross income under Code Section 125, 132(f)(4), 402(e)(3), 402(h), or 403(b)). In addition, any of the definitions of compensation that are deemed to satisfy Section 414(s) may be modified to exclude the following items (even if they are includible in gross income):

- Reimbursements or other expense allowances
- Fringe benefits (cash and noncash)
- Moving expenses
- Deferred compensation
- Welfare benefits

The following definitions of compensation are deemed to satisfy Section 414(s):

Section 415 "long form" compensation—includes all remuneration described in Treasury Regulations Section 1.415-1(d)(2) and excludes all other compensation, including the items specifically listed as excludable in Treasury Regulation Section 1.415-2(d)(3).

Section 415 "short form" or "safe-harbor" compensation—includes *only* the remuneration described in Treasury Regulations Section 1.415-1(d)(2)(i) and excludes all other compensation, including items listed as excludable in Treasury Regulations Section 1.415-1(d)(3).

W-2 compensation—includes wages (as defined in Code Section 3401(a)) and all other payments for which the employer is required to furnish the employee a written statement under Code Sections 6041(d), 6051(a)(3), and 6052.

Section 3401(a) wages—includes wages, as defined in Section 3401(a), but determined without regard to rules limiting the remuneration to be included on the basis of the nature or location of the employment or the services performed.

Section 414(s) safe-harbor compensation—technically, this is Section 415 "long form" compensation reduced by reimbursements or expense allowances, fringe benefits, moving expenses, deferred compensation, and welfare benefits. As previously indicated, however, any of the definitions of compensation listed above (including Section 415 safe-harbor compensation, W-2 compensation, or Section 3401(a) wages) may also be modified to exclude these items, and such modified definition will be considered a Section 414(s) safe-harbor definition of compensation.

Q 4:26 What safe harbors are provided under Section 401(a)(4)?

There are several design-based safe harbors provided under the Section 401(a)(4) regulations that will allow a 403(b) plan to comply without any complicated testing. Furthermore, Notice 89-23 [1989-1 CB 654] allows employers to apply a "reasonable good-faith interpretation" of Section 401(a)(4) and alternatively provides two additional design-based safe harbors that will allow a 403(b) plan to comply with the nondiscrimination requirements applicable to non-salary reduction contributions under Section 403(b)(12). It is possible that the availability of the Notice 89-23 "good-faith" interpretation and the safe harbors will ultimately be discontinued, and the regulations under Section 401(a)(4) will be applied. Therefore, the safe harbor rules of both Section 401(a)(4) and Notice 89-23 are explained, even though the rules under Notice 89-23 are usually more liberal.

The Section 401(a)(4) rules limit discrimination in contributions or benefits in favor of HCEs. There are no restrictions on disparities in contributions or benefits among NHCEs. For example, a contribution formula providing 15 percent of compensation for NHCEs earning over $50,000 and 1 percent of compensation for NHCEs earning under $50,000 is not prohibited by the rules. However, a formula that provides a greater percent of compensation for HCEs than for NHCEs will be subject to the limitations of Section 401(a)(4).

The following types of contribution formulas meet a 401(a)(4) safe harbor and require no testing:

1. A formula that provides the same contribution percentage or a flat dollar amount for all employees, or one that provides higher contributions for employees earning over a dollar breakpoint that complies with the permitted disparity rules of Section 401(1); and

2. A formula that provides contributions based on a uniform points formula taking into account the age, service, and/or compensation of the employee, provided that the average contribution (as a percentage of compensation) for all NHCEs is at least as great as the average contribution for all HCEs. Permitted disparity under Section 401(1) cannot be taken into account for this purpose.

[Treas Reg § 1.401(a)(4)-2]

Under the permitted disparity rules, employees earning above the Social Security Wage Base are allowed to receive an additional percentage contribution on compensation above the wage base equal to the lesser of (1) the percentage of total compensation contributed to the plan or (2) 5.7 percent. [IRC § 401(1)] For example, a contribution formula of 4 percent of compensation plus 4 percent of compensation in excess of the wage base would meet the safe harbor. However, formulas of (1) 4 percent of compensation plus 5 percent above the wage base or (2) 7 percent of compensation plus 6 percent above the wage base would not meet the safe harbor. The "5.7 percent" in (1) will be adjusted to conform with any increase in the contribution rate for the retirement insurance portion of an employer's Social Security contributions.

In designing a contribution formula with permitted disparity, it is permissible to reduce the breakpoint where the change in contribution rate takes place relative to an amount as low as 20 percent of the current wage base. If the breakpoint is 80 percent of the wage base or less, the maximum percentage is reduced from 5.7 percent to 4.3 percent; if it is above 80 percent of the wage base, the maximum is reduced to 5.4 percent.

To use these safe harbors, certain other applicable plan provisions must be uniform for all eligible employees. These include the provisions for determining eligibility, crediting service, vesting, and defining compensation.

Q 4:30   How is cross-testing used?

The general test can be applied to any plan on a defined contribution or defined benefit basis (see Q 4:28). It may be advantageous to test defined contribution plans on a benefits basis. This is generally called cross-testing of the plans.

The general test is used only in situations where all other methods for demonstrating that a plan does not discriminate in favor of HCEs have failed. These situations will always involve plans with contribution or accrual rates that are higher for HCEs than for NHCEs. Generally, if the HCEs with the highest rates tend to be older than the NHCEs, testing based on benefits will produce the best results. If some very young HCEs have high rates, testing based on contributions may be more favorable.

A common approach to 403(b) plan contribution design is to have higher rates of contribution for older or longer service employees. For example, the following schedule of contribution rates might apply:

Age	*Contribution Rate (%)*
Below 35	1
35–44	4
45–54	6
55–59	8
60 and over	10

In a typical employee group, the HCEs are likely to be older than the NHCEs. Therefore, based on the contribution rates, the schedule above might produce discrimination in favor of HCEs. However, it requires a significantly higher contribution rate for older employees to provide a given amount of retirement benefits at age 65 than it does for younger employees. Therefore, if the contribution rates in the above schedule are converted to equivalent annual benefit amounts payable at age 65, it is very likely that there would be no resulting discrimination in favor of HCEs.

To demonstrate that the above schedule of contributions is not discriminatory, it is necessary to convert, for each individual participant, the amount of contribution to an equivalent annual pension benefit payable at age 65 using actuarial assumptions in accordance with Treasury Regulations Section 1.401(a)(4)-8. The allowable permitted disparity is added to the benefit rate. Each employee is then assigned to a rate group based on his or her specific annual accrual rate as a percentage of compensation. The rate groups must be set up so that all employees within a range of no more than 5 percent (not five percentage points) above and below the midpoint are included in the same rate group. [Treas Reg § 1.401(a)(4)-2(c)(2)(v)] For example, if the midpoint of a rate group were 2 percent, then the range of the rate group would be 1.9 percent to 2.1 percent. All employees for whom the annual contribution rate plus permitted disparity converts to an equivalent benefit accrual rate of 1.9 percent to 2.1 percent would be included in that rate group. A plan with a contribution formula similar to that illustrated above could easily have 25 to 50 independent rate groups that must be evaluated.

Once the rate groups are established and each individual is assigned to a group based on an equivalent rate of benefit accrual, then the general test can be applied to the entire array of rate groups. For this purpose, each rate group is assumed to include all employees in that group and all higher groups. [Treas Reg § 1.401(a)(4)-2(c)(1)]

Example 4-4. The table below illustrates a simplified rate group analysis based on a plan in which the equivalent accrual rates range from 1 percent to 1.5 percent. All statutorily eligible employees of the employer are included in the plan.

	Covered Employees		
Rate Group (%)	NHCEs (%)	HCEs (%)	Ratio Percentage
0.95–1.05	300 (100)	50 (100)	100
1.06–1.16	250 (83)	50 (100)	83
1.17–1.28	200 (67)	40 (80)	84
1.29–1.41	150 (50)	35 (70)	71
1.42–1.56	100 (33)	30 (60)	55

Note that 100 of the 300 NHCEs (33 percent) and 30 of the 50 HCEs (60 percent) received the highest rate of benefit accrual. The ratio percentage for this rate group is 55 percent (33% ÷ 60%), which is below the 70 percent required to pass the ratio percentage test. Thus, the plan fails that test. However, if the plan can pass the average benefits percentage leg of the average benefits test by demonstrating that the average benefit (including permitted disparity) for NHCEs is at least 70 percent of that for HCEs, then it could still pass the general test. In fact, because 86 percent (300 ÷ 350) of the employees are NHCEs, the ratio percentage to pass the average benefits test is reduced to 25 percent (for this purpose, the average of the safe and unsafe harbors described in Qs 4:17 and 4:18 can be used). An individual rate group is exempt from the reasonable classification requirement of the average benefits test. The lowest ratio percentage of any rate group is 55 percent— well in excess of the 25 percent ratio percentage required if the average benefits test is to be used.

Even if the plan did not pass the general test, either because there was a rate group below 25 percent or because the plan could not pass the average benefits percentage leg of the average benefits test, alternative methods might be tried before significant revisions to the plan are made. For instance, there is some flexibility in the rate groups identified, provided that the rates for HCEs are not consistently higher than those for NHCEs within all rate groups. [Treas Reg § 1.401(a)(4)-2(c)(2)(v)(A)] Because the range of accrual rates was between 1 percent and 1.5 percent, the first rate group could be 0.9 percent to 1 percent, or could be 1 percent to 1.1 percent. Revising the starting point in this manner would revise all subsequent rate groups. A small change of this type could move some NHCEs and HCEs into different rate groups, which could permit the plan to pass, particularly if it had failed by a small amount.

If changing rate groups does not work, a small change in contribution rates for some HCEs could be made. In Example 4-4, only the highest rate group fails the ratio percentage test. If the number of HCEs in that group were reduced from 30 to 23, then the rate group would pass. It might not be too disruptive to reduce the contribution percentage slightly for seven of the HCEs. Of course, any revision in contribution rates should be designed so that the plan will continue to pass the general test in the future. Ad hoc adjustments designed merely to get through the current year may be undesirable.

Q 4:30.1 What special requirements apply to cross-tested 403(b) plans?

The general test works in the same way when annual benefit accruals are converted to equivalent contribution rates, and when plans of different types are aggregated. This can be a very complex process if multiple plans of different types are included in the test.

The IRS has recently issued final regulations that restrict the types of defined contribution plans that can be cross-tested on a benefits basis. [Treas Reg §§ 1.401(a)(4)-8 and 1.401(a)(4)-9] Under the new cross-testing regulations, which are effective for plan years beginning on or after January 1, 2002, in order for a defined contribution plan to use cross-testing, it must first satisfy a threshold requirement. Except for certain plans that are aggregated with defined benefit plans, a defined contribution plan must do one of the following:

1. Provide broadly available allocation rates, as defined in the regulations;

2. Provide certain age-based allocation rates that are based on either a gradual age and service schedule or a uniform target benefit allocation; or

3. Satisfy a minimum allocation gateway.

A plan provides "broadly available" allocation rates for a plan year if each allocation rate under the plan is currently available during the plan year to a group of employees that satisfies the ratio percentage test under Section 410(b). A plan has age-based allocation rates that are based on either a gradual age or service schedule if the schedule of allocation rates under the plan's formula is available to all employees in the plan and provides for allocation rates that increase "smoothly" and at "regular intervals." These terms have specific meanings, as defined in the regulations.

Finally, a plan will satisfy the minimum allocation gateway if either (1) each NHCE receives a minimum allocation that is at least one-third of the allocation rate of the HCE with the highest allocation rate, or (2) each NHCE receives a minimum allocation of at least 5 percent of his or her Section 415(c)(3) compensation, measured over a period of time permitted under the definition of plan year compensation.

Therefore, unless a plan satisfies the "broadly available" test or the "age-based" or "service-based" allocation test, then in order to apply cross-testing, the plan must provide a minimum allocation for NHCEs equal to at least the lesser of 5 percent of Section 415(c) compensation or one-third of the allocation rate of the HCE with the highest allocation rate. There are special rules for defined contribution plans that are aggregated with defined benefit plans.

Q 4:32 What are nondiscriminatory benefits, rights, and features?

Non-salary reduction contributions under a nongovernmental 403(b) arrangement must be provided under a plan that does not discriminate in favor of HCEs with respect to certain "benefits, rights, and features." [Treas Reg §1.401(a)(4)-4] These include all optional forms of benefit (such as the right to an annuity form of payment) and all rights and features made available to employees under the plan (such as the right to make after-tax contributions, the right to receive a specific rate or percentage of matching contributions, or the right to take a hardship withdrawal).

Benefits, rights, and features (or BRFs, as they are often called) will be considered to be provided in a nondiscriminatory manner only if they satisfy both the current availability test and the effective availability test. The *current availability* test is satisfied if the group of employees to whom a particular BRF is available satisfies the Section 410(b) ratio percentage test. The *effective availability* test is satisfied if, based on all the relevant facts and circumstances, the group of employees to whom a BRF is effectively available does not substantially favor HCEs.

Therefore, if a 403(b) program provides for a 50 percent match for some employees and a 100 percent match for other employees, both matching percentages must be a available to a group of employees that will satisfy the Section 410(b) ratio percentage test. In other words, each matching rate must be available to a percentage of nonexcludable NHCEs that is at least 70 percent of the percentage of nonexcludable HCEs who are eligible for that rate of matching contributions.

Q 4:33   How is Notice 89-23 applied?

Notice 89-23 [1989-1 CB 654] provides that employers may rely on a reasonable, good-faith interpretation of Section 403(b)(12). This means that, with respect to non-salary reduction amounts (i.e., employer contributions), sponsors of nongovernmental 403(b) plans may rely on a reasonable, good-faith interpretation of Sections 401(a)(4), 401(a)(5), 401(a)(17), and 401(a)(26), as well as Sections 401(m) and 410(b). Alternatively, 403(b) plans that satisfy one of the three safe harbors described below (and that satisfy the requirements of Section 401(m), if applicable) are deemed to satisfy the underlying requirements of Section 403(b)(12). In addition, for plan years after December 31, 1995, 403(b) plans must independently satisfy Section 401(a)(17). [Ann 95-48, IRB 1995-23 (May 11, 1995)] Therefore, beginning with the 1996 plan year, 403(b) plans (including governmental plans) with employer contributions must comply with the compensation limit under Section 401(a)(17) and the regulations thereunder. (Section 401(a)(17) does not apply to 403(b) salary reduction contributions.)

With respect to salary reduction amounts, Notice 89-23 provides that an employer may rely on a reasonable, good-faith interpretation of Section 403(b)(12). Alternatively, Notice 89-23 provides a safe harbor for salary reduction contributions. Under the safe harbor, salary reduction contributions will be deemed to satisfy Section 403(b)(12) so long as (1) each employee of the common-law employer sponsoring the plan is eligible to defer annually more than $200 pursuant to a salary reduction agreement and (2) the opportunity to make such contributions is available to all employees on the same basis. (See Q 4:34 for the definition of common-law employee.)

Three special safe harbors are permitted solely for non-salary reduction contributions to 403(b) plans under Notice 89-23. Under these safe harbors, the IRS will deem all *nonmatching* employer contributions under any of the 403(b) plans included in the employer's "aggregated 403(b) annuity program" to satisfy the coverage requirements of Section 410(b) and the nondiscrimination requirements of Section 401(a)(4) if the "aggregated 403(b) program" (see Q 4:34) satisfies one of the following three safe harbors:

1. *Maximum disparity safe harbor.* If at least 50 percent of all statutorily eligible NHCEs of the employer are receiving contribution allocations under the 403(b) plan, and at least 70 percent of all participants receiving allocations are NHCEs, then a safe harbor is satisfied if the highest

contribution rate (as a percentage of compensation) for any HCE is no greater than 180 percent of the lowest contribution rate for any NHCE.

2. *Lesser disparity safe harbor.* If at least 30 percent of all statutorily eligible NHCEs of the employer are receiving contribution allocations under the 403(b) plan, and at least 50 percent of all participants receiving allocations are NHCEs, then a safe harbor is satisfied if the highest contribution rate (as a percentage of compensation) for any HCE is no greater than 140 percent of the lowest contribution rate for any NHCE.

3. *No disparity safe harbor.* If at least 20 percent of all statutorily eligible NHCEs of the employer are receiving contribution allocations under the 403(b) plan, and at least 70 percent of all participants receiving allocations are NHCEs, then a safe harbor is satisfied if the contribution rate for all NHCEs is at least as great as that for any HCE. Alternatively, 80 percent can be substituted for 20 percent, and 30 percent for 70 percent, and the safe harbor will be satisfied.

Example 4-5. Assume that a not-for-profit employer has 1,000 statutorily eligible employees of which 960 are NHCEs and 40 are HCEs. A plan of the employer that covers 480 NHCEs and all 40 HCEs and provides a contribution rate of 9 percent for HCEs and 5 percent for NHCEs would satisfy the first safe harbor. In fact, any variation in contribution rates among the covered group would be permitted, as long as the highest HCE contribution did not exceed 9 percent and the lowest NHCE contribution was not less than 5 percent. If the plan covered fewer than 480 NHCEs, but at least 288, and provided a 5 percent contribution for NHCEs, then HCEs could receive a contribution as high as 7 percent (140% ×5%) under the second safe harbor. The provisions of the third safe harbor do not allow disparate contribution rates.

For purposes of Notice 89-23, HCEs are generally identified by reference to the definition of HCE under Section 414(q) and the regulations thereunder. However, Notice 89-23 provides that the employer may elect to include in its class of HCEs only those employees who, during the plan year, are 5 percent owners of any entity within the same controlled group as the employer or who receive compensation in excess of $50,000 (indexed for inflation). (It is unclear whether this alternative definition of HCEs is still available, because the most recent Section 414(q) definition of HCE, which became effective in 1997, is now more liberal than this "alternative definition.") The requirements of Notice 89-23 are applied as of the last day of the plan year, but any HCE participating in the 403(b) plan who terminates in the final quarter of the year must be included.

Compensation, for purposes of Notice 89-23, has the same meaning as in Section 414(s), and as limited by Section 401(a)(17), *except* that it includes only compensation paid by a 403(b) eligible employer.

If the vesting schedules applicable to employee accounts are not uniform for all employees in the testing group, then an adjustment in contribution rates must be made in accordance with the principles of Revenue Ruling 74-166. [1974-1 CB 97]

If a contribution by an employee is made as a result of a one-time irrevocable election when first eligible for the plan, it is considered an employer contribution for purposes of Section 401(a)(4) and Notice 89-23. Also, contributions "picked up" for employees by government entities (as permitted under Section 414(h)) are treated as employer contributions.

Q 4:36 Which categories of employees may be excluded under Notice 89-23?

Notice 89-23 provides that, for purposes of applying any of the safe harbors under the Notice, the following employees may be excluded (but only if all similarly situated employees are not eligible to participate):

- Nonresident aliens, as described in Section 410(b)(3)(C)
- Students performing services described in Section 3121(b)(10)
- Employees who normally work less than 20 hours per week
- Employees who made a one-time irrevocable election to participate in a 414(d) governmental plan instead of the 403(b) plan
- Employees covered by a collective bargaining agreement (if retirement benefits were the subject of good-faith bargaining)
- Certain professors providing services on a temporary basis to another institution (if certain conditions apply)
- Certain individuals who have taken a vow of poverty, if their religious order provides for their retirement
- Certain other employees of governmental entities

In addition to the employees listed above, the following employees may be excluded for purposes of the safe harbor regarding salary reduction contribution (but only if all similarly situated employees are not eligible to participate):

- Employees who are participants in a Section 457(b) deferred compensation plan
- Employees who are eligible to participate in a 401(k) plan or another 403(b) program of the employer that provides for salary reduction contributions
- Employees whose contributions to the plan under its maximum deferral percentage would be $200 or less

For purposes of the safe harbors applicable to non-salary reduction contributions, a 403(b) plan may also exclude employees who have not satisfied the minimum age and service requirements set forth in the plan (so long as such requirements are permissible under Section 410(a), applied as if Section 410(a) were applicable to 403(b) plans), but only if all employees not meeting those requirement are excluded from participation in such non-salary reduction contributions. Notice 89-23 also allows for separate testing of "otherwise excludable employees" (i.e., employees who would be excludable under the previous sentence but for the fact that they, or other employees of the same or lower age, or with the same or fewer years of service, are not excluded from coverage under the plan).

Chapter 5

Investments

Peter J. Gulia, Esq.
CitiStreet Retirement Services

Section 403(b) of the Internal Revenue (Code) permits participants' retirement savings to be invested in fixed and variable annuity contracts, life insurance contracts, and mutual fund shares. This chapter explains the different 403(b) investment options and an employer's responsibility for any selection of those options.

Because almost all 403(b) plans and programs provide for participant-directed investment, this chapter includes an explanation of Section 404(c) of the Employee Retirement Income Security Act of 1974 (ERISA)—a rule that allows plan fiduciaries to avoid liability for participants' investment directions. Also, this chapter explains the Department of Labor interpretive guidance relating to investment education for participants.

403(b) Investment Options

Q 5:2   Can a Section 403(b) contribution be invested in a stable value fund?

Section 403(b) contributions can be invested in a stable value fund only under limited circumstances.

What most pension consultants mean when they refer to a *stable value fund* is a portfolio of investments that may include insurance company guaranteed interest contracts (GICs), bonds or bond funds, bank investment contracts (BICs), and other kinds of investments. Sometimes a stable value fund will include a bank or insurance company guarantee so that the fund can credit a guaranteed return even when the portfolio's actual return (without the guarantee) is lower.

Section 403(b) contributions can be invested only in an annuity contract or a custodial account that holds mutual fund shares (see Q 5:1). Therefore, Section 403(b) contributions can be invested in a stable value fund only if the "fund" is an annuity contract or the portfolio is a mutual fund that is registered with the Securities and Exchange Commission (SEC) and managed as a regulated investment company for federal income tax purposes. These Section 403(b) rules may limit certain techniques that otherwise might be used in making up a stable value fund.

A Section 403(b) stable value fund may be feasible when it is a Section 403(b)(9) retirement income account for church employees (see Qs 5:16–5:19).

Q 5:3   Can 403(b) amounts be invested in brokerage accounts?

No. Section 403(b) amounts can be invested only in an annuity contract or a custodial account that holds mutual fund shares (see Q 5:1). While a custodial account can hold mutual fund shares (see SQ 5:13), it cannot hold other securities. Therefore, if an account can include securities other than mutual fund shares, it is not a Section 403(b)(7) custodial account. [IRC § 403(b)(7)(A)(i)]

Fixed Annuity Contracts

Q 5:5   What is a fixed annuity contract?

A *fixed annuity contract* is a form of annuity contract that has guaranteed minimum interest and typically credits a current interest rate that is declared from time to time (often each month) at the sole discretion of the insurer. The fixed annuity holder hopes that the insurer will continue to declare reasonably market-sensitive interest rates; the insurer, however, has no obligation to do so. A fixed annuity is regulated by insurance law but not by securities law. [Securities Act of 1933 § 3(a)(8), 15 USC § 77c(a)(8); Securities Act Rule 151]

Life Insurance Contracts

Q 5:12   How are life insurance premiums paid under a 403(b) arrangement?

Life insurance premiums may be paid under a 403(b) arrangement either by employer matching or nonelective contributions or by salary reduction contributions, as long as the incidental benefit limit is met. [Ltr Rul 9215055] For Section 403(b) purposes, the determination of whether a participant has no more than incidental life insurance is a simple calculation of the ratio of life insurance premiums to all 403(b) contributions. The permitted ratio varies depending on whether the contract is an ordinary or nonordinary life insurance contract.

Under the incidental benefit rule, an ordinary life insurance contract is a contract that provides both a nondecreasing death benefit and a nonincreasing premium, while a nonordinary life insurance contract is any other kind of life insurance. A contract of the type that insurance practitioners call whole life usually will meet the definition of ordinary life insurance; the type of contract that insurance practitioners call term or universal life insurance usually will be treated as nonordinary.

For an ordinary life insurance contract, the amount used to pay the premiums under the contract must be less than 50 percent of all Section 403(b) contributions. For a nonordinary life insurance contract, up to 25 percent of the amount of all Section 403(b) contributions may be used to pay the premiums under the contract. Also, if a participant has both kinds of life insurance contracts, the sum of 50 percent of the ordinary life insurance premiums and all nonordinary premiums cannot be more than 25 percent of all Section 403(b) contributions. An insurance contract may include provisions for disability waiver of premiums or disability income if the total premiums still meet the 25 percent rule. [Treas Regs §§ 1.401-1(b)(1)(i) and (ii), 1.403(a)-1(d), 1.403(b)-1(c)(3); Rev Ruls 76-353, 1976-2 CB 112; 74-307, 1974-2 CB 126; 73-501, 1973-2 CB 128; 70-611, 1970-2 CB 89; 69-408, 1969-2 CB 58; 68-453, 1968-2 CB 163; 68-31, 1968-1 CB 151; 66-143, 1966-1 CB 79; 65-25, 1965-1 CB 173; 61-164, 1961-2 CB 99; 61-121, 1961-2 CB 65; 60-84, 1960-1 CB 159; 60-83, 1960-1 CB 157; 60-59, 1960-1 CB 154; 57-213, 1957-1 CB 157; 56-633, 1956-2 CB 279; 55-748, 1955-2 CB 234; 54-67, 1954-1 CB 149; 54-51, 1954-1 CB 147; Ltr Ruls 8725088, 8029100, 1966 unnumbered rulings (Mar 14–15, 1966)]

Further, to meet the incidental benefit rule, the 403(b) arrangement must require that each life insurance contract be distributed to the participant or converted to a payout option upon retirement or commencement of benefits. That rule is in addition to the requirement that premiums must be no more than 25 percent or 49 percent of all Section 403(b) contributions.

An insurance contract that insures the life of the participant's spouse or child is not a permitted investment under a 403(b) arrangement. [Rev Rul 69-146, 1969-1 CB 132]

The premiums or mortality expense charges of a 403(b) life insurance contract must be based on gender-neutral rates. [Arizona Governing Comm for Tax Deferred Annuity and Deferred Compensation Plans v Norris, 463 US 1073 (1983)]

Even when a 403(b) life insurance contract meets all of the above requirements, the cost of life insurance protection (sometimes called the yearly renewable term (YRT) or PS–58 cost) for a death benefit of the amount that is the difference between the face amount of the contract and the current cash value (sometimes called the net amount at risk) is taxable income each year. [Treas Reg §§ 1.72-16(b)(2), 1.72-16(b)(4), 1.72-16(b)(5), 1.403(b)-1(c)(3)]

Mutual Fund Custodial Accounts

Q 5:13 What is a mutual fund custodial account?

A *mutual fund* is a corporation, partnership, or business trust that invests commonly for investors who have selected that fund. Pooling is the key aspect of mutual fund investing; by banding together, the shareholders may get diversification and management that they could not get as individuals.

"Mutual fund" is the popular name for what the securities laws call a "registered investment company." The formal name comes from the Investment Company Act of 1940, a federal law that regulates how a mutual fund is operated. (The Code calls a mutual fund a "regulated investment company.") [IRC §§ 403(b)(7)(C), 851(a)]

For Section 403(b) purposes, a participant may not hold mutual fund shares directly. [IRC § 403(b)(7)(A)(i)] Instead, they must be held in a *custodial account*, and the custodian must be a bank (including an insured federal credit union or a corporation subject to state banking laws). [IRC §§ 401(f), 403(b)(7)(B), 408(n), 581] A nonbank trustee, such as a securities broker-dealer, may serve as custodian upon IRS approval. [IRC §§ 401(f)(2), 403(b)(7)(B); Treas Reg § 1.401-12(n)] The custodian must apply the distribution restrictions of Section 403(b)(7)(A)(ii), as well as other Section 403(b) requirements and restrictions. Either "open-end" or "closed-end" mutual fund shares may be held in a Section 403(b)(7) custodial account.

A typical Section 403(b)(7) custodial account provides for investment in mutual funds of a single mutual fund "complex" or "family." A participant who wants to redirect a portion of his or her 403(b) investment to a mutual fund sponsored by a different complex must redeem the investment in the fund that is no longer desired, wait to receive cash proceeds, and then effect a direct transfer according to Revenue Ruling 90-24 [1990-1 CB 97] (see SQ 5:64, Q 5:65).

Depending on the diligence of the participant, both custodians' record keepers, and any intermediaries, the transaction may take a few business days.

Some providers offer a Section 403(b)(7) custodial account that permits investment in mutual funds of many different mutual fund families. Such an account provides that both the redemption and purchase aspects of an account investment direction are credited on the same New York Stock Exchange day so that the participant's amounts are not "out of the market" for even one day.

An account that permits investment in bonds or stocks other than mutual fund shares is not a proper 403(b) investment (except for a church retirement income account) because Section 403(b)(7) permits a custodial account to hold only mutual fund shares.

For more information about mutual fund custodial accounts, see chapter 7.

Participant Loans

Q 5:19.1 Is a participant loan a plan investment?

Yes and no. Under a typical annuity contract, a participant loan involves a use of the contract rights and an adjustment in the contract's value. Under a typical custodial account, a participant loan is, in form, an investment of the account. In either case, a typical participant loan affects only the account of the participant, who in effect is both borrower and lender. [DOL Reg § 2550.408(b)-1(f)]

For information about the many ERISA and Code rules concerning participant loans, see chapter 11.

Q 5:19.2 Must a plan fiduciary collect repayments on a participant loan?

A typical participant loan affects only the account of the participant, who is in effect both borrower and lender (see SQ 5:19.1). If a plan fiduciary has a duty to manage plan assets, a plan administrator may use discretion, usually restricted only by an arbitrary and capricious review standard, in collecting on a defaulted loan. [See, e.g., Colaluca v Climaco, Climaco, Seminatore, Lefkowitz & Garofolo LPA, 1997 US App LEXIS 2108 (6th Cir 1997)] A prudent plan fiduciary might ask a borrowing participant to direct that none of the plan fiduciaries collect loan repayments. A plan fiduciary will not be liable for a loss that results from following such a direction. [ERISA § 404(c)(1)(B)]

Employer Responsibility for 403(b) Investments

Q 5:26   How should an employer select investments for a 403(b) plan or program?

If an employer makes available a voluntary 403(b) program that is not covered by ERISA (see chapter 9), the employer need not be responsible for selection of any 403(b) investment options. Thus, an employer might prefer to allow a broad range of investment options, while deliberately avoiding any selection decisions other than those assuring minimum contractor responsibility and efficiency to serve the employer's administrative convenience.

If an employer maintains an employer-sponsored 403(b) plan that is not subject to ERISA (e.g., a church plan or governmental plan), the employer must make any investment selection as a fiduciary under applicable state law (see SQ 5:28).

If an employer maintains a 403(b) plan subject to ERISA (see chapter 9), the employer must make any investment selection as an expert fiduciary under ERISA (see Q 5:31).

Q 5:28   What is an employer's investment responsibility for an ERISA plan?

If a 403(b) plan is subject to ERISA (see chapter 9), the plan fiduciaries have a legal duty to act solely in the best interest of the plan's participants for the exclusive purpose of providing retirement benefits to participants and their beneficiaries.

ERISA requires that a fiduciary act with the care, skill, prudence, and diligence under the circumstances then prevailing that a prudent person acting as a fiduciary and familiar with retirement plan matters would use in the conduct of managing a retirement plan. [ERISA § 404(a)(1)(B); DOL Reg § 2550.404a-1(b)] Simply put, the plan fiduciary must act as an expert would. [Marshall v Snyder, 1 EBC (BNA) 1878, 1866 (EDNY 1979)] Or, as the Joint Committee on Taxation noted, "The [ERISA fiduciary] standard measures the decisions of plan fiduciaries against the decisions that would be made by experienced investment advisers." [Joint Comm on Taxation, Overview of the Enforcement and Administration of the Employee Retirement Income Security Act of 1974, JCX-16-90 at 12 (June 6, 1990)]

Under ERISA's "prudent expert" rule, a fiduciary must make a reasonably careful inquiry into the merits of a particular investment decision. A fiduciary's lack of familiarity with a particular form of investment is not an excuse for making an imprudent investment. If a fiduciary does not have sufficient knowledge to evaluate the merits or soundness of a proposed investment, the fiduciary then has a duty to obtain expert advice in making the decision. [See, e.g., Katsaros v Cody, 744 F 2d 270, 279 (2d Cir), *cert denied sub nom* Cody v Donovan, 469 US 1072 (1984); Marshall v Glass/Metal Assn and Glaziers and

Glassworkers Pension Plan, 507 F Supp 378, 384 (D Hawaii 1980)] However, the fiduciary must make its own decision using that advice. [Whitfield v Cohen, 682 F Supp 188, 194–195 (SDNY 1988); Donovan v Tricario, 5 EBC (BNA) 2057 (SD Fla 1984) (unpublished)]

A fiduciary does not have to make the "right" decision; rather, the fiduciary must consider sufficient information. The legal standard is whether the fiduciary's procedure made a well-informed decision possible. If a fiduciary has diligently investigated the relevant information, a court will not interfere with and will uphold the fiduciary's judgment. Following this, any review of a fiduciary's decision is based on the circumstances and the review conducted at the time the fiduciary made the decision, and not from the vantage point of "20/20 hindsight." [See, e.g., Katsaros v Cody, 744 F 2d 270, 279 (2d Cir), *cert denied sub nom* Cody v Donovan, 469 US 1072 (1984); Lanka v O'Higgins, 810 F Supp 379 (NDNY 1992); Whitfield v Cohen, 682 F Supp 188 (SDNY 1988)]

It may be wise to ensure that participants have a choice of insurers, unless plan administration convenience is an important concern. Few cases, however, have challenged a decision to operate a retirement plan through one insurance company (as many plan sponsors do).

Likewise, a 403(b) plan should include variable investment options (mutual fund custodial accounts and variable annuity contracts), both for investment opportunity and diversification and because such funds are not subject to the risk of an insurer's insolvency. [See, e.g., State of Connecticut Insurance Commissioner Declaratory Ruling No IC-91-51 (Dec 17, 1991)]

A plan sponsor should consider making a written investment policy statement. If the plan provides for participant-directed investment (see SQs 5:44–5:49), the statement should specify that the plan sponsor's policy is to make available a broad range of no fewer than three different diversified investment options that have varying degrees of risk and return and that the selection is intended to enable the participant to achieve a balanced portfolio consistent with modern portfolio theory (see SQ 5:48). Consistent with the plan sponsor's continuing fiduciary duty, the plan sponsor should revise or reapprove the investment policy statement each year.

Q 5:29 May a plan fiduciary consider guaranty coverage when selecting an insurance company?

Yes, a plan fiduciary may consider guaranty coverage when selecting an insurance company. When making fiduciary decisions, a plan fiduciary should consider all available information that can be relevant to the decision. [See ERISA § 404(a)(1)] In the Labor Department's view, a plan fiduciary selecting an insurer "should consider . . . the availability of additional protection through state guaranty associations and the extent of their [sic] guarantees." [DOL Interpretive Bulletin 95-1, reprinted in 29 CFR § 2509.95-1(c)(6); DOL Adv Op 2002-14A (Dec 18, 2002)] However, because an expert fiduciary considers all relevant information, a plan fiduciary also should consider the disruption or inconvenience to the plan that might arise from the rehabilitation or liquidation of an insolvent or impaired insurer.

Q 5:30   How should an ERISA plan fiduciary evaluate a provider's fees?

An ERISA plan fiduciary must discharge its duties with expert prudence solely in the interest of the plan's participants and their beneficiaries. [ERISA § 404(a)(1)] This means that a plan fiduciary that selects investment options or service providers must

1. Establish a careful procedure for selecting investment options or service providers;
2. Select investment options that are appropriate for the plan;
3. Select service providers that are capable of meeting the plan administrator's needs;
4. Decide that fees paid to each investment or service provider are reasonable in light of the scope and quality of services provided; and
5. Monitor investment options and service providers once selected to evaluate whether they continue to be sound choices.

According to the DOL, a plan fiduciary should "consider fees as one of several factors in [its] decision making; compare all services received with the total cost; and realize that cheaper is not necessarily better." [DOL PWBA, "A Look At 401(k) Plan Fees" (1998)] Also, because a plan fiduciary must make its decisions for the benefit of a large group rather than any individual, the DOL recognizes that "[an] employer may not be able to accommodate each employee's preferences[.]"

A plan fiduciary is relieved from liability to the extent that a fee applies to a participant's or beneficiary's account because of his or her investment direction. "For example, individual service fees may be charged to a participant for taking a loan from the plan[,] or for executing participant investment directions." [DOL PWBA, "A Look At 401(k) Plan Fees" (1998)] Likewise, although some plan investment options may have benefits and charges different from other plan investment options, a plan fiduciary is not responsible for a participant's choice among plan investment options. [ERISA § 404(c); DOL Reg § 2550.404c-1(b)(2)(ii)]

Q 5:32   What should a fiduciary do when a decision involves an investment or service provider with whom he or she has a relationship?

ERISA imposes the highest duty of loyalty, including especially a fiduciary duty to avoid self-dealing. If a fiduciary is faced with the possibility of self-dealing because of his or her relationship with an investment or service provider, ERISA permits that fiduciary to remove himself or herself from that particular decision. Such removal is called a *recusal.*

A fiduciary does not participate in a prohibited transaction if the fiduciary absents himself or herself from all consideration of the proposed decision and does not exercise any authority, control, or responsibility concerning the proposed decision. [DOL Reg § 2550.408b-2(f), Ex 7] In addition to not voting on the proposed decision, the fiduciary should physically absent himself or herself from the meeting (or that portion of the meeting) that considers the proposed decision. [DOL Adv Op 84-09A, n2] To rely on a recusal, it is important that the nonvoting and absenting fiduciary avoid any attempt to influence others who retain decision-making authority. [See DOL Adv Op 86-11A]

> **Example 5-1.** The Read-to-Your-Children Foundation sponsors a 403(b) plan that is governed by ERISA. Patti is one of five members of the foundation's pension committee. Her sister, Diane, is a partner of Cheswyck Investment Counsel LLP, which, along with other competitors, has proposed certain investment advisory services for the foundation's 403(b) plan. When the pension committee turns to the investment advisor selection, Patti formally recuses herself, announces to the committee members her potential conflict of interest (without saying what it is), instructs the committee's secretary to record her recusal in the minutes of the meeting, and then leaves the room. Patti does not talk about Cheswyck or any of the competitor investment advisors with any of the committee members. By doing all that, Patti has made a successful recusal. If Cheswyck gets the contract, Patti must also avoid involvement in reviewing Cheswyck's performance.

Recusal can be a better choice than resignation when the fiduciary has a conflict of interest only for one or a few matters and the fiduciary's consideration of other matters is valuable for the benefit of the plan.

Q 5:33 What should a plan fiduciary do if the other fiduciaries make a decision that is imprudent?

Under the common law of trusts, any action by fewer than all the trustees, even though a majority, is void unless the trust document states that the trustees may act by a majority. [American Law Institute, Restatement (Second) of Trusts § 194] However, in modern retirement plan practice, many plan fiduciary committees act by majority vote.

When a plan fiduciary is outvoted, resignation, without further action to protect the interests of participants and beneficiaries, generally is not enough to protect the outvoted fiduciary from personal liability.

According to the Department of Labor,

> where a majority of [fiduciaries] appear ready to take action [that] would clearly be contrary to the prudence requirement of [ERISA §] 404(a)(1)(B) . . . , it is incumbent on the minority [fiduciaries] to take all reasonable and legal steps to prevent the action. Such steps might

include preparations to obtain an injunction from a Federal District court . . . , to notify the Labor Department, or to publicize the vote if the decision is to proceed as proposed. If, having taken all reasonable and legal steps to prevent the imprudent action, the minority [fiduciaries] have not succeeded, they will not incur liability for the action of the majority. Mere resignation, however, without taking steps to prevent the imprudent action, will not suffice to avoid liability for the minority [fiduciaries] once they have knowledge that the imprudent action is under consideration.

Likewise, a fiduciary's insistence that his or her "objections and the responses to such objections [if any] be included in the record of the meeting" will not be sufficient to protect the outvoted fiduciary. "[R]esignation by the [fiduciary] as a protest against [a fiduciary] breach will not generally be considered sufficient to discharge the [fiduciary's] positive duty under [ERISA Section] 405(a)(3) to make reasonable efforts under the circumstances to remedy the breach." [DOL Interpretive Bulletin 75-5, 40 Fed Reg 31599 (July 28, 1975), redesignated at 41 Fed Reg 1906 (Jan 13, 1976), reprinted in 29 CFR § 2509.75-5] Arguably, an ERISA plan fiduciary might be protected from liability if the other fiduciaries' breach was not *clearly* a breach. However, when considering whether any decision might be *clearly* a fiduciary breach, the outvoted fiduciary still must act as an expert fiduciary. [ERISA § 404(a)(1)]

For a non-ERISA plan, the common law of trusts provides a similar or greater duty. An outvoted trustee remains liable for a cotrustee's breach unless the outvoted trustee takes prudent steps to prevent the other trustees' breach or to compel the other trustees to correct the breach. [American Law Institute, Restatement (Second) of Trusts §§ 184, 224; National Conference of Commissioners on Uniform States Laws, Uniform Trust Act § 703(b)(2) (1998 draft)] The outvoted trustee has a right to engage independent legal counsel and (if he or she acts or acted in good faith) a right to have the trust advance or reimburse his or her expenses (including attorneys' fees). [F.M. English, Right of Coexecutor or Trustee to Retain Independent Legal Counsel, 66 ALR 2d 1169 (1959); Lee R. Russ, Award of Attorneys' Fees Out of Trust Estate in Action by Trustee Against Cotrustee, 24 ALR 4th 624 (1983)]

For a church plan, an outvoted fiduciary who fails to take protective action might nevertheless avoid liability to the extent that the breach would not have been prevented or corrected but for requiring the fiduciary to take an action that would have interfered with his or her free exercise of religion. [US Const amend I]

For a governmental plan, an outvoted fiduciary who fails to take protective action might be protected by sovereign immunity, governmental immunity, or public officer immunity.

Protection Against Liability

Q 5:34   Can an ERISA plan exempt a plan fiduciary from liability?

No. ERISA provides that "any provision in an agreement or instrument which purports to relieve a fiduciary from responsibility or liability for any responsibility, obligation, or duty under [the fiduciary responsibility provisions of ERISA] shall be void as against public policy." [ERISA § 410(a)]

Q 5:35   Can a non-ERISA plan exempt a plan fiduciary from liability?

A provision in a non-ERISA plan or trust document may provide that a plan fiduciary does not have a duty that otherwise would be a fiduciary duty. [American Law Institute, Restatement (Second) of Trusts § 174] Likewise, a non-ERISA plan or trust document may vary a fiduciary's duties. [See, e.g., Hayim v Citibank, AC 730 (1987)] Finally, a provision in a non-ERISA plan or trust document may relieve a plan fiduciary from liability for a breach of fiduciary responsibility. [American Law Institute, Restatement (Second) of Trusts § 222]

An exemption clause cannot protect a fiduciary who acts in bad faith or with reckless indifference to the participants' or beneficiaries' interests. [American Law Institute, Restatement (Second) of Trusts § 222(2)]

A provision that might exempt a fiduciary from liability is strictly construed to limit the potential exemptions from fiduciary responsibility. [American Law Institute, Restatement (Second) of Trusts § 222(1) and comment a]

Q 5:36   Can an employer indemnify an ERISA plan fiduciary?

Yes. Although an ERISA plan cannot indemnify a fiduciary against his or her fiduciary breach, nothing precludes an employer from indemnifying a plan fiduciary, as long as the employer uses its own money rather than plan assets.

ERISA Section 410(a) provides that "any provision in an agreement or instrument which purports to relieve a fiduciary from responsibility or liability for any responsibility, obligation, or duty under [the fiduciary responsibility provisions of ERISA] shall be void as against public policy." "The Department of Labor interprets [ERISA Section 410(a)] to permit [i]ndemnification by a plan fiduciary [usually the employer] of the fiduciary's employees who actually perform the fiduciary services." However, "[t]he Department of Labor interprets [ERISA Section] 410(a) as rendering void any arrangement for indemnification of a fiduciary of an employee benefit plan *by the plan*. Such an arrangement would have the same result as an exculpatory clause in that it would, in effect, relieve the fiduciary of responsibility and liability to the plan by abrogating the plan's right to recovery from the fiduciary for breaches of fiduciary obligations." Further, "[w]hile indemnification arrangements do not [necessarily] contravene the provisions of [ERISA Section] 410(a), parties entering into an indemnification agreement should consider whether the agreement complies with the other [fiduciary responsibility] provisions of [ERISA] and with other applicable laws." [DOL ERISA Interpretive Bulletin 75-4, 40 Fed Reg 31599 (July 28, 1975), redesignated at 41 Fed Reg 1906 (Jan 13, 1976), reprinted in 29 CFR § 2509.75-4]

Q 5:37   Can an employer indemnify a non-ERISA plan fiduciary?

Yes. Nothing in the common law of trusts precludes a third person from providing indemnification to a fiduciary, unless receiving that indemnification is a breach of the fiduciary's duty to avoid self-dealing with those whose interests might be contrary to the purposes of the trust or the interests of the participants and beneficiaries.

Whether a church will indemnify a retirement plan fiduciary may be further provided by the church's organizing documents.

Making Investment Decisions

Q 5:40   What information should a plan sponsor consider when making a fiduciary investment selection?

When making a fiduciary investment selection, a plan sponsor should obtain and carefully consider at least the following information concerning each proposed investment:

- The insurance or investment contract
- The prospectus and statement of additional information (for any mutual fund, variable annuity contract, or variable life insurance contract)
- A "plain language" description of the charges, fees, penalties, or other adjustments that may be imposed under any proposed investment
- A complete explanation of the ownership of the insurance agent, securities dealer, or investment advisor
- A disclosure of any business relationship that the insurance agent or securities dealer that proposes an investment has with the investment issuer, or a written confirmation that there is no relationship
- The sales commission (expressed as a percentage of the contribution for the first year and for later years)
- A written confirmation that the insurance agent, securities dealer, or investment advisor has disclosed any other conflict of interest or related-party transaction that relates to each proposed investment
- A written confirmation that no recommendation is restricted by any agreement or business relationship with any investment issuer
- For an investment advisory service, the disclosure statement (including SEC Form ADV) and the investment advisory agreement

- The amount (if any) that a mutual fund distributor or transfer agent pays as compensation to the custodian or plan record keeper
- A written confirmation that there can be no fees other than those already disclosed

[See Glaziers and Glassworkers Local 252 Annuity Fund v Newbridge Securities Inc, 20 EBC (BNA) 1697 (3d Cir 1996); In Re Unisys Savings Plan Litigation, 74 F 3d 420 (3d Cir 1996); Morgan v Independent Drivers Assn, 15 EBC (BNA) 2515 (10th Cir 1992); Brock v Robbins, 830 F 2d 640 (7th Cir 1987); Donovan v Mazola, 716 F 2d 1226 (9th Cir 1983); McLaughlin v Bendersky, 705 F Supp 417 (ED IL 1989); Benvenuto v Schneider, 678 F Supp 51 (EDNY 1988); Donovan v Tricario, 5 EBC (BNA) 2057 (SD Fla 1984) (unpublished)]

The plan sponsor should retain all these records (see Q 5:68), and require updated information when it conducts regular reviews (see Q 5:31) of the plan's investment selection.

Q 5:41   May an employer provide different investment options for different classes of employees?

Generally, it may be difficult to provide different investment options for different classes of employees.

For instance, if a 403(b) plan includes contributions other than elective salary reduction contributions, the plan is subject to coverage and nondiscrimination requirements that are almost the same as those that apply to a Section 401(a) qualified retirement plan. [IRC § 403(b)(12)(A)(i)] (That is not the case for a 403(b) plan that is a governmental plan.) [IRC § 401(a)(5)(G), as amended by the Tax Reform Act of 1997, § 1505(a)(1)] Under those rules, a right to a particular form of investment is an "other right or feature" [Treas Reg § 1.401(a)(4)-4(e)] that is subject to specific nondiscrimination testing. Therefore, unless the employer is confident that each class or group of employees will meet the nondiscrimination requirement, it might be unwise to limit investment options by class or group. An exception permits separate testing of those employees who belong to a collective bargaining unit. [Treas Reg § 1.410(b)-7(c)(5)]

This nondiscrimination rule for investment options probably does not apply to an elective 403(b) program. Nevertheless, some practitioners believe that the rule should be applied to such a program to give meaning to the requirement that every employee be permitted to enter into a salary reduction agreement. [IRC § 403(b)(12)(A)(ii)]

If an employer limits employees' Section 403(b) investment choices for reasons other than neutral concerns about the administrative burden on the employer, that involvement [DOL Reg § 2510.3-2(f)] might cause a voluntary 403(b) program that otherwise would have avoided ERISA coverage (see chapter 9) to become subject to ERISA's design, disclosure, reporting, and fiduciary requirements. Inasmuch as most employers prefer to steer clear of

ERISA, it may be better to avoid unnecessarily restricting employees' Section 403(b) investment choices.

Q 5:42   May an employer limit a 403(b) program to socially responsible investments?

An employer may impose any limitation it chooses in providing a 403(b) program. Nonetheless, before limiting Section 403(b) investment choices, an employer should carefully consider the consequences of that choice.

First, limiting a 403(b) program to less than a "reasonable choice" of investments may make the program a plan subject to ERISA. Consequently, it may be better to permit (but not mandate) socially responsible investment.

More broadly, if the employer makes any 403(b) investment selection, it does so as a fiduciary, whether under ERISA or state-law fiduciary standards. Whichever the fiduciary standard, "social investing" is contrary to the fiduciary duty of prudence if the particular investment or investment program involves subordinating the interests of participants and beneficiaries to any objective other than seeking the maximum feasible investment return. [American Law Institute, Restatement (Third) of Trusts §§ 170, 227; Uniform Law Commission, Uniform Prudent Investor Act (1994), official comment to § 5; DOL Interpretive Bulletin 94-1, 59 Fed Reg 32606 (June 22, 1994), reprinted in 29 CFR § 2509.94-1] Furthermore, even if an investment is prudent, the fiduciary duty of loyalty bars the fiduciary from acting in the interest of itself or a third person rather than according to the exclusive interest of participants and beneficiaries. [American Law Institute, Restatement (Third) of Trusts, §§ 170, 227; ERISA § 404(a)(1)(A)]

Even if social investing results in no breach of fiduciary duty, an employer should also consider the likelihood (and expense) of lawsuits by participants and beneficiaries. The Evangelical Lutheran Church in America and its Board of Pensions have defended lawsuits, for example, concerning certain investment decisions for the Board's Section 403(b)(9) defined contribution retirement income accounts that may have at least considered the church's social investment policy. Although the Board of Pensions avoided a public trial of its fiduciary decision making, the parties incurred the unpleasantness and expense of litigation. [Basich v Board of Pensions, Evangelical Lutheran Church in Am & Basich Evangelical Lutheran Church in Am, No C8-95-882 and No CX-95-883, 540 NW 2d 82, 19 EBC (BNA) 2231 (Minn App 1995), *cert denied*, 117 S Ct 55, 136 L Ed 2d 18 (1996) (The Board's decisions concerning social investment policy are at least related to religious doctrine or church management, and therefore "[t]he Establishment Clause of the First Amendment and the Freedom of Conscience Clause of the Minnesota Constitution deprive [a civil] court of subject matter jurisdiction . . . ," notwithstanding that the plan specified that "[a]ll controversies, disputes, and claims arising [under the plan] shall be submitted to the Minnesota Fourth Judicial District Court, Hennepin County."), reversing No CT 93-16711 District Court for County of Hennepin, Fourth Judicial District; Basich v Board of Pensions, Evangelical Lutheran Church in Am, 493

NW 2d 293, 296 (Minn App 1992) (Retirement plan participants do not have standing to bring a derivative suit)]

A better course may be for an employer to seek out socially responsible investment funds as Section 403(b) investment options, in addition to other prudently selected investment options, and then allow participants to choose socially responsible investing.

Participant-Directed Investment

Q 5:44   What rules apply to a participant-directed plan?

The rules that apply to a participant-directed plan turn on whether the plan is (or is not) subject to ERISA.

If a plan that provides for participant-directed investment is subject to ERISA, the plan sponsor and other plan fiduciaries may avoid liability for participants' investment decisions by meeting the requirements of ERISA Section 404(c) (see SQ 5:47).

If a plan that provides for participant-directed investment is not subject to ERISA (a church plan or governmental plan), state law will govern whether and how the plan sponsor may avoid liability for participants' investment decisions. Since the regulations under ERISA Section 404(c) are based on the common law of trusts, which is likely to be relevant in almost all states, voluntary compliance with most or all of the ERISA Section 404(c) requirements may be wise to help a church plan sponsor avoid liability. A governmental plan sponsor may be completely shielded from any monetary liability by state law.

Q 5:45   What does ERISA Section 404(c) provide?

If a retirement plan allows participants to choose their own investments, the employer may worry about potential complaints from participants whose investments perform poorly. Following ERISA Section 404(c) gives the employer a way to avoid liability for the consequences of a participant's unwise decisions. ERISA Section 404(c) provides that if participants have control over the investment of their plan accounts, plan fiduciaries will not be responsible for participants' investment decisions.

DOL regulations interpret ERISA Section 404(c) by offering formal guidance on what requirements a plan must meet to ensure that participants have sufficient control over the investment of their retirement plan accounts to justify shifting legal responsibility to them. [DOL Reg § 2550.404c-1] Nevertheless, some employee benefits lawyers have suggested that compliance with the regulations might not protect the plan sponsor fiduciary. [Sacher, Miller, and Schoenecker, "Win, Lose, or Draw: Analysis of the Proposed 404(c) Regulation," 17 *J Pension Planning & Compliance*, 3 (Fall 1991) at 15]

Q 5:46 Must an employer comply with ERISA Section 404(c)?

No. Complying with ERISA Section 404(c) is entirely optional. If, however, an ERISA 403(b) plan meets all the requirements of ERISA Section 404(c), the employer and other plan fiduciaries should be shielded from liability for participants' investment decisions.

If a plan meets the ERISA Section 404(c) regulations for the most part but does not fully comply, plan fiduciaries might still be relieved from responsibility if they can show the court that their management of the plan was consistent with ERISA Section 404(c). [See Daniele and Hennessy, "Participant-Directed Retirement Plans under the Final Section 404(c) Regulations," 19 *Pension Rep* 1992 (Oct 19, 1992) at 1825; but see Brennan, "Relief at Last?: DOL Final Regulations on Participant-Directed Individual Account Plans," 19 *J Pension Planning & Compliance* 1 (Spring 1993) at 50–52] Further, some employee benefits lawyers believe that even if a plan plainly does not comply with ERISA Section 404(c), a plan fiduciary may avoid liability if it can show that it properly followed the participant's or beneficiary's direction. [Eccles and Gordon, "Now That the § 404(c) Regulations Are Final, Who Cares?" 1 *ERISA Litig Rptr* 11 (Dec 1992) at 15–23]

A fiduciary that overrules a participant's investment direction because it believes that the direction no longer is prudent cannot rely on the protection of ERISA Section 404(c) with respect to the overruled participant. [DOL Adv Op 96-02A]

Q 5:47 Does complying with ERISA Section 404(c) mean an employer is absolved of liability?

Not completely. If a plan complies with ERISA Section 404(c), the plan fiduciary is relieved from liability for participants' investment directions (within the choices available). However, the plan sponsor is still responsible for the selection (and periodic monitoring) of an appropriate menu of plan investment choices available to participants. [DOL Reg § 2550.404c-1(a)(1)] If the plan sponsor makes any selection of the menu of plan investment options, it must act prudently in selecting and reviewing the investment options available for the plan (see SQ 5:28). Also, the plan fiduciary is responsible for providing necessary information to participants and promptly implementing their investment instructions.

A plan sponsor that chooses to provide participant investment education may be responsible for the quality of information given. If the plan sponsor itself provides information, it is responsible for the accuracy, completeness, and appropriateness of that information. [29 CFR § 2509.96-1(e); American Law Institute, Restatement (Second) of Torts § 552] If, instead, a plan sponsor selects a service provider for participant investment education, the plan sponsor may be responsible if it did not make a prudent selection.

Further, according to the DOL's unofficial view, a plan sponsor's designation (or continuation) of a provider for participant investment education is itself a fiduciary act. [DOL Interpretive Bulletin 96-1, 61 Fed Reg 29586 (June 11, 1996), reprinted in 29 CFR § 2509.96-1(e)] This view seems incorrect, however, if the provider does not perform services for the plan and is not paid from plan assets, and the employer specifically warns that it does not express any view concerning the capability of the provider. [ERISA § 3(21)(A); but see Reich v McManus, 883 F Supp 1144 (ND Ill 1995); DOL Adv Op 83-60A] Further, the DOL states that

> in the context of an ERISA Section 404(c) plan, neither the designation of a person to provide education nor the designation of a fiduciary to provide investment advice to participants and beneficiaries would, in itself, give rise to fiduciary liability for loss, or with respect to any breach of [fiduciary duties], that is the direct and necessary result of a participant's or beneficiary's exercise of independent control.

[DOL Interpretive Bulletin 96-1, 61 Fed Reg 29586 (June 11, 1996), reprinted in 29 CFR § 2509.96-1(e)]

Q 5:48   What is required to comply with ERISA Section 404(c)?

If a plan provides for participant-directed investment for all or some portion of plan investments and chooses to comply with the ERISA Section 404(c) regulations, the plan (or the participant-directed portion of the plan) must meet these basic requirements:

1. *Broad range of investments.* A participant must have the right to choose from a "broad range" of at least three diversified investments with varying degrees of risk and return (see SQ 5:49).
2. *Investment information.* A participant must receive sufficient information to enable him or her to make informed investment decisions (see SQs 5:50–5:52). If the plan passes through voting rights of securities, the participant must receive all proxy voting materials (see Q 5:76).
3. *Investment changes.* A participant must have the right to change investments at least once each quarter or more frequently, and to receive written confirmation of account transactions (see SQs 5:60, 5:61).

Q 5:49   What constitutes a broad range of investments?

Under ERISA Section 404(c), participants must have the right to choose from a broad range of at least three "core" diversified investments with varying degrees of risk and return. The requirement can be met by the investment options of a single variable annuity contract or the funds of a single mutual fund complex.

Participant-directed investment selection must allow the participant to achieve a balanced portfolio or "a portfolio with aggregate risk and return characteristics . . . appropriate for the participant." [DOL Reg

§ 2550.404c-1(b)(3)] Likewise, each of the core investments must be such that "when combined with investments in the other alternatives [it] tends to minimize through diversification the overall risk of a participant's . . . portfolio." [DOL Reg § 2550.404c-1(b)(3)(i)] The regulation is based on modern portfolio theory. [For a summary of the use of modern portfolio theory in trust law, see American Law Institute, Restatement (Third) of Trusts (Prudent Investor Rule) § 227(a) (1992)]

Many employee benefits lawyers suggest that as a bare minimum an ERISA Section 404(c) plan should have a stock fund, a bond fund, and a money market fund. In selecting the options to be made available under a participant-directed investment plan, however, plan fiduciaries might ask themselves whether they could accept full legal responsibility for managing plan assets if that plan's investment universe were limited to the investments proposed to be made available to participants. ERISA Section 404(c) is based on the premise that under a participant-directed plan, a participant is, in effect, his or her own investment trustee.

At least three of the core investment options must be "look-through" investments, such as variable annuity separate accounts or mutual funds or a fixed annuity contract. [DOL Reg § 2550.404c-1(b)(3)(i)(C)] A "look-through" investment must be sufficiently diversified. [DOL Reg § 2550.404c-1(b)(3)(ii)]

Investment Communication Requirements

Q 5:50 What investment information must be furnished to a participant in a participant-directed plan?

The ERISA Section 404(c) regulations require that a participant be furnished with and have the opportunity to obtain sufficient information to become able to make informed investment decisions. [DOL Reg § 2440.404c-1(b)(2)(i)(B)] The regulations under ERISA Section 404(c) divide that information into two categories:

1. That which must routinely be furnished to every participant and
2. That which must be furnished upon a participant's request.

If a plan fiduciary wants ERISA Section 404(c) relief from responsibility for participants' investment directions, participants must receive written information, at least for the materials required to be routinely furnished. (The regulations do not say whether foreign language materials must be furnished to a participant who cannot read English, and it is not clear what information, if any, must be provided to a participant who cannot read any language.) Furnishing the required information does not constitute giving investment advice for ERISA purposes. [ERISA § 3(21)(A); DOL Interpretive Bulletin 96-1, 61 Fed Reg 29586 (June 11, 1996), reprinted in 29 CFR § 2509.96-1(d)(1)]

Q 5:51 What investment materials must be furnished to every participant in a participant-directed plan?

To obtain ERISA Section 404(c) relief, the following materials must be furnished to every participant in a participant-directed plan:

1. A description of every investment option available under the plan, including a general description of
   a. The identity of the investment manager,
   b. Investment objectives,
   c. Risk and return characteristics,
   d. Diversification of assets included in the portfolio, and
   e. Transaction fees and expenses that affect the participant's account balance (including management and investment advisors' fees, initial or deferred sales charges, and redemption or exchange fees).

   A document that meets the requirements of a profile prospectus under the federal securities laws meets the requirements of the ERISA Section 404(c) regulations. [See 17 CFR § 230.498]

2. If the investment option is subject to the Securities Act of 1933, upon the participant's initial investment in that option, a copy of the most recent prospectus provided to the plan.

3. The name, address, and telephone number of the plan fiduciary (and, if applicable, the other person(s) designated by the plan fiduciary) responsible for providing information upon request (see SQ 5:52).

4. An explanation of when and how participants may give investment instructions, including an explanation of any limitations on plan investment instructions and of any restrictions on transfers to or from an investment option.

5. An explanation that the plan is intended to have participant-directed investment under ERISA Section 404(c), thereby relieving fiduciaries of liability for losses that are the result of the participant's investment directions.

Q 5:52 What investment materials must be furnished to a participant in a participant-directed plan upon request?

The following materials must be furnished to a participant upon request; they may be requested for a particular investment option or for all investment options:

- A copy of the prospectus (including any statement of additional information) for any or all investment options
- A description of annual operating expenses (such as investment management fees or administration fees) that reduce the rate of return to the

participant's account, and the aggregate amount of such expenses expressed as a percentage of average net assets of the investment option

- A copy of the financial statements and reports for any or all investment options
- Information on the value of shares or units in any or all investment options
- Information on the historical investment performance of any or all investment options, determined net of expenses, on a reasonable and consistent basis

[DOL Reg § 2550.404c-1(b)(2)(i)(B)(2)]

In fulfilling requests for the foregoing information, the plan fiduciary (or other person) may use whatever information was most recently furnished to it and need not furnish any information that it does not have. However, a plan fiduciary might have a duty to obtain the information available to it. [ERISA § 404(a)]

Q 5:53 What may a plan administrator's general fiduciary duty to provide accurate information require?

Although not expressly stated by ERISA Section 404(c), a plan administrator's general fiduciary duty to provide accurate and not misleading information may require that any communication to participants include

1. A statement that past performance is not an indication of future performance;
2. A calculation or estimate of investment performance according to SEC-prescribed formulas;
3. A display of historical investment performance according to certain one-, five-, and ten-year periods ending as of the most recent available quarter-end date; and
4. Several other disclosures customary for securities law purposes.

If a plan sponsor relies on materials provided by an investment company or securities broker-dealer, the plan administrator can help protect itself by requiring the company or broker-dealer to furnish a copy of its letter obtaining approval of the material from the National Association of Securities Dealers (NASD).

Q 5:54 Is it advisable for an employer to provide foreign-language investment materials for its non-English-speaking employees?

If an employer makes available a non-ERISA program, it should not provide any materials because doing so may establish a plan subject to ERISA (see Q 9:2). Although an employer is permitted to summarize information furnished by the providers, the difficult choices inherent in providing a translation or even summarizing information may cause the employer to exceed the "hands-off" role required by the safe-harbor regulation. [DOL Reg § 2510.3-2(f)]

The plan administrator should provide foreign-language investment materials for a plan only if it has determined, upon expert fiduciary prudence, that the expense is necessary to the administration of the plan. [ERISA § 404(a)(1)] In making such a determination, the plan fiduciary should consider whether some of those who cannot read English also cannot read any language.

It is difficult for a provider to offer foreign-language materials, because federal securities law prohibits the use of foreign-language materials unless the issuer also furnishes the complete prospectus in the same foreign language. [Investment Company Act Release No 6082 (June 23, 1970); SEC No-Action Letter, American Funds Distributors Inc (publicly available Oct 16, 1989)] Unless a fund's governing board is presented with responsible evidence that sales to individuals who read the foreign-language prospectuses would sufficiently benefit the fund in relation to the expense, the fund's directors or trustees may have a duty to disapprove the translation expense. [See generally Investment Company Act § 36, 15 USC § 80a-35; American Law Institute, Principles of Corporate Governance]

Communications Concerning Blackouts

Q 5:54.1   What is a blackout?

A plan has a blackout if participants, beneficiaries, or alternate payees are restricted for at least three consecutive business days from giving an investment direction or taking a plan loan or distribution, when such transactions ordinarily would be permitted. [DOL Reg § 2520.101-3(d)(i)] If the restriction is imposed for fewer than three days, it is not a blackout.

> **Note.** Although DOL Regulations Section 2520.101-3(d)(i) does not define the term "business days," it excludes Saturdays, Sundays, and holidays—days on which plan transactions usually would not be processed. Thus, if a plan's customary procedure is to process an instruction received on a holiday on the next business day, the holiday does not count for purposes of the blackout period.

During a blackout, DOL Regulations Section 2520.101-3(d)(i) does not impose restrictions on transactions resulting from the following:

- Application of securities law
- A regularly scheduled restriction explained in the summary plan description
- A qualified domestic relations order (QDRO)
- The plan's procedure for determining whether a court order is a QDRO
- An act (or failure to act) on the part of a participant, a beneficiary, or alternate payee

- A third person's claim or action "involving the account of an individual participant"

Example 5-2. Plan X's procedure provides that a distribution does not become payable until 15 days after a participant initiates an address change. This procedure gives the participant and the plan administrator the opportunity to detect, by reading a confirmation, whether someone has impersonated the participant. The procedure imposes a restriction on the distribution, but it does not constitute a blackout.

Q 5:54.2   What is the rule regarding blackout notices?

If an individual-account retirement plan governed by ERISA will have a blackout, the plan administrator must send affected participants, beneficiaries, and alternate payees a notice explaining the blackout. [ERISA § 101(i), as added by the Sarbanes-Oxley Act of 2002]

The most common reason for a blackout is a change in record keepers. Another reason is a change in the record keeper's computer system.

Practice Pointer. Although ERISA does not require the trustee or administrator of a church plan or governmental plan to send a blackout notice, a cautious fiduciary might want its lawyer's advice on whether sending such a notice would be prudent under other law.

Q 5:54.3   What must a blackout notice include?

A blackout notice must include the following information:
1. The reason for the blackout
2. An explanation of each investment and other plan right affected
3. The expected beginning of the blackout
4. The expected ending of the blackout
5. An investment warning (see below)
6. The name of an individual in the plan administrator's office to contact for further information

[ERISA §101(i); DOL Reg § 2520.101-3(b)(1)(iv)–(v)]

A blackout notice may describe the beginning or end (or both) of the blackout period by referring to a calendar week rather than a particular day.

If the ability of participants, beneficiaries, or alternate payees to give investment directions is restricted during the blackout, the blackout notice must warn recipients that they should evaluate the appropriateness of their current investment decisions, because they will not be able to direct investments or diversify assets credited to their accounts during the blackout.

The notice must be written in language that can be understood by the average participant.

The blackout regulation includes a model notice. A plan that uses paragraphs 4 and 5A of the model notice in its blackout notice satisfies the requirement to inform plan participants, beneficiaries, and alternate payees that they should evaluate the appropriateness of their current investment decisions in light of their inability to direct their investments or diversify assets credited to their plan account during the blackout.

Using the model notice does not provide any assurance concerning the regulation's other requirements (see SQ 5:54.5). [DOL Reg § 2520.101-3(e)(1)]

The above requirements meet only the plan administrator's duty under ERISA Section 101(i). A plan fiduciary may have additional duties to communicate information about a blackout that participants, beneficiaries, and alternate payees need to know.

Q 5:55.4   To whom must a plan administrator send a blackout notice?

A plan administrator must send a blackout notice to each participant, beneficiary, or alternate payee who could be affected by an inability to give an investment direction or take a loan or distribution. [DOL Reg § 2520.101-3(a)]

Q 5:54.5   When must a plan administrator send a blackout notice?

A plan administrator must furnish the notice at least 30 days (but no more than 60 days) before the blackout begins. [DOL Reg § 2520.101-3] An exception may be available if the blackout period is the result of a corporate merger, an acquisition, a divestiture, or similar business transaction. In such a case, the plan administrator must furnish the notice as soon as is "reasonably practicable" [DOL Reg § 2520.101-3(b)(2)(ii)(c)]

Another exception might apply if a plan administrator "documents" its decision that there are unforeseeable or extraordinary circumstances beyond its control or if delaying an action would constitute a breach of its fiduciary duties. Even then, a plan administrator must furnish the blackout notice "as soon as [is] reasonably possible under the circumstances." [DOL Reg § 2520.101-3(b)(2)(ii)(B)]

Q 5:54.6   What must a plan administrator do if a blackout does not end as scheduled?

If there is a change in either the beginning or ending of a blackout, the plan administrator must send another notice to affected participants, beneficiaries, and alternate payees as soon as is "reasonably practicable." This notice must explain any "material" change in the information furnished in the original (or most recent) blackout notice. [DOL Reg § 2520.101-3(b)(4)]

Q 5:54.7   What are the consequences of failing to furnish a blackout notice?

The potential consequences of failing to furnish a blackout notice include fiduciary liability for investment losses in participants' accounts, civil penalties, and criminal punishment.

Fiduciary liability. Failing to furnish a required blackout notice is a clear breach of the plan administrator's fiduciary duties. [ERISA § 404(a)(1)] ERISA provides that a fiduciary is liable to make good losses that result from the fiduciary's breach. [ERISA §§ 502, 509] Although it might be difficult to prove causation, some lawyers believe a participant, beneficiary, or alternate payee could allege that he or she would have made different investment directions had he or she received the proper notice.

Civil penalty. If a plan administrator fails to furnish a required blackout notice, the DOL may impose a penalty. The maximum penalty is $100 per affected participant, beneficiary, or alternate payee multiplied by the number of days that the plan administrator failed to furnish the notice. [DOL Reg § 2560.502e-5, -7]

> **Example 5-3.** Wellness Healthcare Network maintains a Section 403(b) retirement plan that has 30,000 participants. Wellness, as plan administrator, changes the plan's record keeper. Accordingly, it imposes a blackout period starting at 4:00 p.m. on Friday, January 31, 2003. The "conversion" and reconciliation are completed in three business days, and the blackout ends at the close of business on Wednesday, February 5, 2003. Although Wellness should have sent a blackout notice no later than January 1, 2003 (30 days before the start of the blackout period), it did not send a blackout notice. In this case, the penalty is $108 million ($100 × 30,000 [$3 million] × 36 days).

Criminal punishment. A willful failure to furnish a blackout notice may be punished by a fine up to $500,000 and up to ten years' imprisonment, in addition to punishment for related crimes. [ERISA § 501]

Providing Investment Education and Advice

Q 5:55   Does a plan sponsor have to give advice to participants?

No. The ERISA Section 404(c) regulations explicitly state that the plan sponsor or other plan fiduciary has no duty to provide advice to participants concerning their investment choices. [DOL Reg § 2550.404c-1(c)(4); DOL Interpretive Bulletin 96-1, reprinted in 29 CFR § 2509.96-1(b)]

Nonetheless, some plan sponsors may wish to provide a means by which participants can have guidance with investment choices. If so, it may be advisable to have such services performed by professionals who are appropriately regulated in that conduct, such as registered investment advisors.

If a plan sponsor chooses to provide any information beyond the required information, it should do so carefully. Although not expressly stated in the ERISA Section 404(c) regulations, a plan administrator's general fiduciary duty to provide accurate and not misleading information may require that any communication to participants

1. Be based on generally accepted investment theories that take into account the historic returns of standard market indices of different asset classes (such as stocks, bonds, and money market instruments) over a defined period of time.

2. Expressly state all relevant facts and assumptions.

3. Expressly state that the participant or beneficiary should consider his or her assets, income, and investments other than those under the plan.

4. Refer to all available plan investment options (or refer to none of the plan investment options).

5. Include a statement that past performance is not an indication of future performance.

6. Include a calculation or estimate of investment performance according to SEC-prescribed formulas.

7. Include a display of historical investment performance according to certain one-, five-, and ten-year periods ended as of the most recent available quarter-end date.

8. Include several other disclosures customary for securities law purposes.

[DOL Interpretive Bulletin 96-1, 61 Fed Reg 29586, (June 11, 1996), reprinted in 29 CFR § 2509.96-1]

In the DOL's view, if a plan sponsor chooses to engage a service provider for participant investment education, it must use fiduciary diligence and expertise in making or reviewing a selection. [29 CFR § 2509.96-1(e)] A plan sponsor is not responsible, however, to the extent that the participant selects the education provider. [29 CFR § 2509.96-1(e)]

Q 5:55.1 Should a plan administrator follow securities laws when it compiles plan investment information?

Yes. ERISA requires that a plan fiduciary communicating participant-directed investment choices use the same expertise that someone in the business of communicating consumer investment choices would use. [ERISA § 404(a)(1)] Although an ERISA plan fiduciary that is not a securities broker-dealer or investment advisor might not be regulated by securities laws, those laws may be used as evidence of what an expert would do in presenting investment information.

Practice Pointer. If a plan fiduciary who is not an expert in securities law prepares any communication concerning plan investment options, it might consider asking the plan's regular employee benefits lawyer to consult with a securities lawyer about the form, content, and accompanying disclosures for such a communication.

Q 5:59   May an investment advisor give advice about its own funds?

Yes. Notwithstanding ERISA's prohibited transaction rule that precludes many self-dealing or other conflict-of-interest transactions, an investment advisor may give a participant, beneficiary, alternate payee, or plan advice about investing in the advisor's (or an affiliate's) funds if

1. The advisor adjusts its investment advisory fee to subtract the amount of the fee received by each mutual fund manager [PTCE 77-4, 42 Fed Reg 18732 (Apr 8, 1977)]; or

2. The advisor's investment advisory method reflects the work of an independent consultant, and there are significant restraints on the opportunity for the advisor to influence the work of that independent consultant. [DOL Adv Op 2001-09A (Dec 14, 2001)]

Of course, a participant, beneficiary, or alternate payee who considers whether to engage an investment advisor on such a basis should read carefully all disclosure information (see Q 5:58) and evaluate whether the investment advisor's methods make sense. Further, a plan fiduciary that considers whether to approve the availability of an investment advisor's services should carefully evaluate whether the advisor's disclosure information is such that a participant, beneficiary, or alternate payee may independently decide to engage the investment advisor. [See DOL Interpretive Bulletin 96-1, 61 Fed Reg 29586 (June 11, 1996), reprinted in 29 CFR § 2509.96-1(e)]

Procedures for Investment Instructions

Q 5:60   How often must a 403(b) plan allow investment changes?

A 403(b) plan may impose reasonable restrictions on the frequency of investment changes. At a minimum, however, participants must have the right to make investment changes at least once within any three-month period; for example, a calendar quarter. [DOL Reg § 2550.404c-1(b)(2)(ii)(C)(1)]

Further, a restriction on investment changes is "reasonable" only if "it permits participants . . . to give investment instructions with a frequency which is appropriate in light of the market volatility to which the investment alternative may reasonably be expected to be subject." [DOL Reg § 2550.404c-1(b)(2)(ii)(C)] Thus, for especially volatile mutual funds and variable annuity separate accounts, a right to daily instructions may be required. [DOL Reg § 2550.404c-1(b)(2)(ii)(C)]

Q 5:61   Must a participant-directed plan have procedures for accepting or conveying investment instructions?

An ERISA Section 404(c) plan must ensure that a participant has a reasonable opportunity to give investment instructions (in writing or otherwise) to an identified plan fiduciary (or other person designated by the plan fiduciary) that is obligated to comply with those instructions, except when the regulations permit refusal of the instruction (see SQ 5:63). Also, a participant must have an opportunity to obtain written confirmation of his or her investment instructions.

Practice Pointer. The plan sponsor should make sure that the plan has a procedure for participants, beneficiaries, and alternate payees to request account corrections.

Under the ERISA Section 404(c) regulations, the plan fiduciary is relieved of fiduciary responsibility for a particular investment direction only if the participant affirmatively gives that investment direction. [ERISA § 404(c)(1)(i), 57 Fed Reg 46923 (Oct 13, 1992)] According to the DOL, if a participant neglects or refuses to give investment instructions for his or her plan account, the plan fiduciary (employer) must invest that participant's account as a fiduciary. [Preamble to DOL Reg § 2550.404(c)-1] The employer must decide which investments are appropriate to meet that participant's retirement needs and must periodically monitor that participant's account.

Q 5:62   May a plan administrator direct investment for a "lost" participant?

According to the DOL, a plan administrator may follow a uniform procedure of "overriding" a participant's last investment direction when the participant is missing and his or her investment direction no longer seems prudent to the plan administrator. (It is unclear how a plan administrator determines that an investment direction is no longer prudent for the best interests of an individual it cannot locate.) Following such a procedure will not cause a plan to lose protection as an ERISA Section 404(c) plan for participants other than those whose investment directions are "overridden." [DOL Adv Op 96-02A] However, when the plan administrator changes the investment of a missing participant's account, it does so under a full fiduciary duty to act as an expert investor in managing that participant's account according to the participant's best interests.

Alternatively, there should be no liability for following the participant's last investment direction, even if the participant cannot be located and even if that investment direction seems unwise. As long as the plan administrator has met all ERISA Section 404(c) requirements, the plan administrator may rely on the participant's last investment direction.

Q 5:63   When may a plan refuse a participant's investment instruction?

A plan may refuse to implement a participant's investment instruction

1. If the responsible plan fiduciary (or other person receiving the instruction) knows the participant to be legally incompetent [DOL Reg § 2550.404c-1(c)(2)(iii)];

2. If the instruction could result in a loss greater than the participant's account balance [DOL Reg § 2550.404c-1(d)(2)(ii)(D)]; or

3. In certain situations (such as prohibited transactions) that pose danger to the plan's compliance with the Code or ERISA. [DOL Reg § 2550.404c-1(d)(2)(i)]

Q 5:64   How does a participant change Section 403(b) investments?

When a participant has not yet been severed from employment and has not reached age $59\frac{1}{2}$ (and therefore is not yet entitled to a distribution), he or she can change investments within a 403(b) arrangement by instructing an insurer or custodian to make a direct transfer (see Q 5:65) payable to another insurer or custodian. [Rev Rul 90-24, 1990-1 CB 97, revoking Rev Rul 73-124, 1973-1 CB 200 (for transactions occurring after 1991); Ltr Rul 9104021] However, an employer's plan might preclude a transfer to an investment not authorized by the plan administrator.

After severance from employment or attainment of age $59\frac{1}{2}$, a participant (or beneficiary) may make an investment change either by a direct transfer or by a rollover (see chapter 10). [IRC §§ 402, 403(b)(8); Temp Treas Reg § 1.403(b)-2T]

Financial Services Modernization

Q 5:71   How does the Gramm-Leach-Bliley Act affect 403(b) investment options?

Enacted just before the turn of the century, the Gramm-Leach-Bliley Act [113 Stat 1338, Pub L 106-102 (Nov 12, 1999)] may be the broadest change in American regulation of "financial services" since the 1930s. The Act amends 26 previous acts of Congress, beginning with the Banking Act of 1933. The Act does not preempt state laws regulating banking, insurance, and securities.

The Act permits a new form of financial holding company that can offer a wide range of banking, insurance, securities, and investment advice services. Likewise, a financial subsidiary of a national bank may provide any of these financial activity services. [Act §§ 101–161]

Rather than establish one regulator for all financial services, the Act continues regulatory regimes based on a principle of "functional" regulation. Because of this, banks will no longer be generally exempt from registration requirements under the Securities Exchange Act or the Investment Advisers Act. [Act §§ 201–241] Insurance continues to be regulated by the states. [Act § 104(a); 15 USC § 1011 et seq (McCarran-Ferguson Act of 1945)] But a state regulator cannot discriminate against banks that engage in insurance businesses. [Act §§ 301–308] To make sure that consumers are not confused by differences between banking and insurance or securities "products," the Act includes several new provisions for consumer protection by disclosure and prohibitions against inappropriate sales practices. [Act § 305]

Chapter 8

Application of Federal Securities Laws to Section 403(b) Arrangements

David S. Goldstein, Esq.
Sutherland Asbill & Brennan LLP

> Of the several federal laws that pertain to securities, three have particular relevance for Section 403(b) arrangements: the Securities Act of 1933, the Securities Exchange Act of 1934, and the Investment Company Act of 1940. This chapter briefly discusses the general relevance of these laws to Section 403(b) arrangements.

Q 8:6 How does traditional SEC staff analysis of investment contracts in connection with employee benefit plans apply to Section 403(b) programs?

Section 403(b) programs differ from qualified plans in that there usually is not a separate trust or other plan asset in which employees can have an interest that could be considered a security. Nevertheless, the investment contract theory can be applied to an eligible employee's interest in an insurance company separate account supporting a Section 403(b) variable annuity contract or a Section 403(b)(7) bank custody account holding mutual fund shares to find a security. Therefore, even though a Section 403(b) program does not generally take the form of a separate legal entity and cannot easily be deemed to hold a security in the form of an interest in a separate account or bank custody account, interests in such pooled or collective investment vehicles can be considered to be issued directly to the eligible employee in connection with a Section 403(b) program. Likewise, interests in certain types of fixed 403(b) annuity contracts can be deemed to be securities of an insurance company issued directly to the eligible employee.

Whether, in fact, an interest in a pooled or collective investment vehicle should be considered issued directly to the eligible employee depends on the facts and circumstances. In most cases, such as where individual variable annuity contracts are issued to each eligible employee in a pure salary reduction program, an interest in a separate account (in the form of a variable annuity) is being issued directly to the employee. In such a case, the interest usually must be registered as a security with the SEC under the 1933 Act and the separate account as an investment company under the 1940 Act. Such registrations, in turn, trigger other federal securities law requirements, such as the issuing insurance company's obligation to deliver prospectuses to eligible employees and the selling broker-dealer's responsibility to provide eligible employees with confirmation statements. In other cases (such as group variable annuity contracts issued in circumstances where the employer or other program fiduciary plays a significant intermediary role in making investment options available), the interest may be treated as being issued to the employer or other group contract owner. [Aetna Life Insurance and Annuity Company (Jan 6, 1997)]

Q 8:14   What is the status of bank custody accounts holding mutual fund shares pursuant to Section 403(b)(7)?

In response to a no-action letter request from the Investment Company Institute, the SEC staff took a position many years ago that it would not recommend enforcement action to the Commission if bank custody accounts holding mutual fund shares did not register as investment companies under the 1940 Act and if interests in such accounts were not registered under the 1933 Act. [Investment Company Institute (Oct 21, 1974)] The SEC staff position was predicated on several conditions including (1) that the custodian or trustee has no investment discretion with regard to the account and does not otherwise manage the account in any way, (2) that the prospectus and various reports from the mutual fund be provided to the eligible employee, and (3) that the prospectus contain appropriate disclosure about 403(b) programs and custody accounts. A similar position was taken by the SEC staff several years later in response to a no-action letter request from an employer sponsoring a 403(b) program that included 403(b)(7) custody accounts. [Cleveland Clinic Foundation (Aug 12, 1979)]

A recent request to reduce the obligation to provide eligible employees with prospectuses and other reports was denied by the SEC staff. [Lincoln National Life Insurance Company (Jan 30, 2003)]

Chapter 9

ERISA Requirements

Michael S. Sirkin, Esq.
Proskauer Rose LLP

Gary E. Herzlich, Esq.
Teachers Insurance and Annuity Association-
College Retirement Equities Fund

The Employee Retirement Income Security Act of 1974, commonly referred to as ERISA, affects a broad range of plans, funds, and programs. It applies to any such arrangement established or maintained by an employer to provide retirement income or deferral of income to employees. ERISA provides participants—and their spouses and beneficiaries—with extensive rights and imposes stringent duties on fiduciaries. Depending upon its structure, a 403(b) arrangement may be subject to the reach of ERISA. Great care must be taken to structure and administer the arrangement properly and, where applicable, ensure compliance with the requirements of ERISA. This chapter explains the circumstances under which a 403(b) arrangement is subject to ERISA and discusses the relevant requirements and issues with regard to vesting schedules, joint and survivor annuities, beneficiary designations, amendments to the plan, disclosures and reporting, and fiduciary matters.

Circumstances Under Which a 403(b) Arrangement Is Subject to ERISA

Q 9:10 Does an employer's vote in an insurance company demutualization cause the arrangement to become subject to ERISA?

No. In PWBA Opinion Letter 2001-03A [Feb 15, 2001], the DOL dealt with the issue of whether the exemption from ERISA is effected if an employer, as contract holder, votes on the approval of the demutualization and selects an allocation method for distributing the proceeds among employees covered by the group contract. The Opinion Letter was specifically addressed to the demutualization of the Prudential Insurance Company of America.

In reaching the conclusion that such action does not result in the arrangement becoming subject to ERISA, the DOL recognized that:

1. The actions of Prudential independent of the employer gave rise to the employer's need, as the titled group contract holder, to take action on behalf of the covered employees with regard to the demutualization;

2. The employer would be acting in accordance with specific provisions in New Jersey law governing the demutualization and pursuant to the requirements of Prudential's Plan of Reorganization that is being approved and supervised by the New Jersey Commissioner of Insurance; and

3. The vote on the demutualization and the decision on the method of allocation of proceeds thereunder are unique, one-time acts that do not involve the employer retaining any discretion regarding the ongoing administration or operation of the 403(b) arrangements.

Note. The Pension and Welfare Benefits Administration (PWBA) has been renamed the Employee Benefits Security Administration (EBSA). The name change became effective February 3, 2003.

Joint and Survivor Annuity Requirements

Q 9:18 What spousal rights are afforded by ERISA Section 205?

A Section 403(b) plan that is subject to ERISA is required to provide (1) accrued benefits payable to a vested, married participant who does not die before the annuity starting date in the form of a qualified joint and survivor annuity (in the case of a single participant, these benefits must be payable in the form of a single-life annuity), and (2) accrued benefits payable to a vested, married participant who dies before the annuity starting date in the form of a qualified preretirement survivor annuity to the surviving spouse.

Generally, spousal consent is required for a married participant to receive benefits in any form other than a joint and survivor annuity. Spousal consent is not required in the case of an automatic cash-out of an account whose value is equal to or less than $5,000. Final regulations effective in 2000 eliminated the look-back rule for most distributions and allow a mandatory distribution of an account value of $5,000 or less, even though that participant's account value may have exceeded $5,000 at an earlier distribution date. However, the look-back rule is not eliminated if the participant is receiving a distribution of an optional form of benefit under which at least one scheduled payment is still payable. Spousal consent is also not required if it is established to the satisfaction of a plan representative that there is no spouse, the spouse cannot be located, or the plan participant is legally separated or the participant has been abandoned (within the meaning of local law) and the participant has a court order to such effect.

A plan may also provide that a qualified joint and survivor annuity and a qualified preretirement survivor annuity will not be provided if the participant and the spouse have not been married throughout the one-year period ending on the earlier of (1) the participant's annuity starting date or (2) the date of the participant's death. [ERISA § 205(g); Treas Reg § 1.401(a)-20]

Amendments

Q 9:26 Must a prospective cutback of benefits under a 403(b) plan be preceded by an ERISA Section 204(h) notice?

ERISA Section 204(h) requires a plan administrator to provide advance written notice, commonly referred to as a 204(h) notice, in the event of an amendment to an applicable pension plan that provides for a significant reduction in the rate of future benefit accrual. The Economic Growth and Tax Relief Reconciliation Act of 2001 (EGTRRA) revised ERISA Section 204(h) and added Section 4980F to the Internal Revenue Code. Code Section 4980F imposes a tax on the failure of an applicable pension plan to provide advance written notice in the event of an amendment to the plan that provides for a significant reduction in the rate of future benefit accrual. It appears that these rules do not apply to a Section 403(b) plan because the revised rules, including those under the proposed regulation, apply only to a defined benefit plan and to an individual account plan that is subject to the minimum funding standards of Code Section 412. Final regulations issued by the DOL in April 2003 clarify that ERISA Section 204(h), as revised, no longer applies to an individual account plan that is subject to the minimum funding standards of ERISA Section 302 but is not subject to the minimum funding standards of Code Section 412. This is the case with Section 403(b) plans. Indeed, the final regulations specify that the requirement does not apply to Section 403(b) plans.

Q 9:27   What is the significance of the ERISA Section 204(g) anticutback rule?

ERISA Section 204(g) prohibits an ERISA 403(b) plan from eliminating an optional form of benefit with regard to those benefits attributable to service performed prior to adoption of the amendment. A plan may be amended, however, to eliminate an optional form of benefit on a prospective basis.

While the language of ERISA Section 204(g) appears to be clear, in two scenarios its impact may not be readily apparent. First, in the case of a plan that in the past has changed funding vehicles or in the future intends to do so, ERISA Section 204(g) requires the plan to preserve the optional forms of benefits offered by the prior funding vehicle or funding vehicles with regard to those benefits that accrued during the time those forms of benefit had been offered. The second, and perhaps less apparent, scenario involves the case where a 403(b) plan permits participants to move assets into the plan from a prior plan. In such a case, the receiving 403(b) plan may permit the participant's assets to move into the plan either by means of a transfer pursuant to Revenue Ruling 90-24 [1990-1 CB 97], commonly referred to as a 90-24 transfer, or by means of a rollover. Where the plan permits 90-24 transfers into the plan, ERISA Section 204(g) would apply, and the receiving plan would have to preserve the optional forms of benefits with regard to transferred assets. Where the plan permits movements of assets into the plan by means of rollover, however, ERISA Section 204(g) would not apply. Thus, from an administrative standpoint of dealing with ERISA Section 204(g), frequently it has been more desirable to limit asset movement to rollovers and to bar the availability of 90-24 transfers between plans.

Congress, the Department of the Treasury, and the IRS recognized the practical problems employers faced complying with ERISA Section 204(g). After concluding that payment forms could be replicated through alternative means, they determined that the burdens placed on employers outweighed the benefits individuals gained from the preservation of optional forms of benefit.

The Economic Growth and Tax Relief Reconciliation Act of 2001 (EGTRRA) reflects recent regulatory relaxation of the anticutback rule. Pursuant to recent modifications, a defined contribution plan to which benefits are transferred will not be treated as violating the anticutback rule of Code Section 411(d)(6), or the parallel Section 204(g) of ERISA, merely because the transferee plan does not provide some or all of the forms of distribution previously available under the transferor plan if:

1. The plan receives a direct transfer of the participant's or beneficiary's accrued benefits, or the plan results from a merger or other transaction that has the effect of a direct transfer (including consolidations of benefits attributable to different employers within a multiple employer plan);

2. The terms of both the transferor plan and the transferee plan authorize the transfer;

3. The transfer occurs pursuant to a voluntary election by the participant or beneficiary that is made after the participant or beneficiary received a notice describing the consequences of making the election; and

4. The transferee plan allows the participant or beneficiary to receive any distribution to which the participant or beneficiary is entitled under the transferee plan in the form of a single sum distribution.

Except to the extent provided by regulations promulgated by the Secretary of the Treasury, a defined contribution plan similarly will not be treated as violating Code Section 411(d)(6), or the parallel Section 204(g) of ERISA, merely because the plan is amended to eliminate a form of distribution previously available under the plan if:

1. A single sum distribution is available to the participant at the same time or times as the form of distribution being eliminated; and

2. The single sum distribution is based on the same or greater portion of the participant's accrued benefit as the form of distribution being eliminated by the amendment.

EGTRRA directs the Secretary of the Treasury to issue regulations under both Code Section 411(d)(6) and Section 204(g) of ERISA. The regulations are to be issued no later than December 31, 2003, and are to apply to plan years beginning on or after January 1, 2004, unless an earlier date is specified by the Secretary of the Treasury. In September 2002, the IRS issued Notice 2002-46 [2002-28 IRB 96] requesting comments for proposed rulemaking.

Disclosure and Reporting

Q 9:33 What is a summary plan description?

A summary plan description (SPD) is an understandable and detailed summary description of an employee benefit plan's provisions that must be provided to plan participants and beneficiaries. The importance of SPDs cannot be overstated. As a practical matter, the SPD is often the only document provided to participants summarizing the salient features of a plan. For this reason, SPDs are usually at the center of benefit and plan communication disputes.

ERISA and the various DOL regulations impose numerous requirements as to the information that must be included in an SPD. [ERISA § 102(a)(1), 102(b); DOL Reg §§ 2520.102-2, 2520.102-3]

The regulations contain a laundry list of items and information that must be included in the SPD:

- The plan's eligibility requirements for participation and benefits
- A description of provisions regarding nonforfeitable benefits

- A statement identifying the circumstances that may result in disqualification or ineligibility for benefits, or in denial, loss, forfeiture, or suspension of benefits that a participant or beneficiary might otherwise reasonably expect the plan to provide

- A foreign-language notice offering foreign-language assistance and explaining the procedures for obtaining such assistance if (1) the plan has fewer than 100 participants and 25 percent or more of such participants are literate only in the same foreign language, or (2) the plan has more than 100 participants and the lesser of 500 (or more) or 10 percent of the participants are literate only in the same foreign language [DOL Reg § 2520.102-2(c)]

- The name of the plan and, if different, the name by which the plan is commonly known by its participants and beneficiaries

- The type of plan and the type of plan administration

- The name and address of the entity that maintains the plan

- The name and address of the plan's agent for service of legal process, as well as a statement that service may be made upon the plan administrator

- The name, business address, and telephone number of the plan administrator

- The names, titles, and addresses of the principal place of business of each funding agent

- The plan's vesting provisions, age and service requirements, and normal retirement age [DOL Adv Op No 85-05A (Feb 5, 1985)]

- A description of procedures governing qualified domestic relations orders or, alternatively, a statement regarding how to obtain a copy of such procedures

- If applicable, a statement that the plan is maintained pursuant to one or more collective bargaining agreements and that the agreements may be obtained by participants and beneficiaries upon written request or are available for inspection

- The source of contributions to the plan

- The identity of any funding medium or organization through which benefits are provided

- The date of the end of the plan year

- The basis on which plan records are maintained (e.g., calendar or fiscal year)

- The employer identification number assigned to the plan by the IRS and the plan number

- The plan's claims review and appeals procedures

- The plan's requirements concerning eligibility for participation and benefits

- A statement of ERISA rights (the DOL has provided a model statement)

- A statement concerning termination insurance coverage
- A description of how and when the plan may be terminated and of benefits, rights, and obligations of participants and beneficiaries on termination (including a summary of the disposition of plan assets on termination) [DOL ERISA Tech Rel 84-1 (May 4, 1984)]
- A description of any joint and survivor benefits and requirements concerning election

[DOL Reg § 2520.102-3]

In general, SPDs must contain information that is "sufficiently accurate and comprehensive to reasonably apprise such participants and beneficiaries of their rights and obligations under the plan." [ERISA § 102(a)(1)]

The law does not require that SPDs contain information specifically tailored to each participant's individual situation. Rather, an SPD should focus on describing general rules in a comprehensible and understandable manner. [Maxa v John Alden Life Ins Co, 972 F 2d 980, 985 (8th Cir 1992), *cert denied*, 113 S Ct 1048 (1993); see also Bowerman v Wal-Mart Stores, Inc, 226 F 3d 574, 590 (7th Cir 2000), and Watson v Deaconess Waltham Hosp, 298 F 3d 102, 115 (1st Cir 2002)]

Q 9:36 Does a disclaimer in an SPD, stating that the plan documents govern, negate inaccuracies in the SPD?

Considering the comprehensive nature of the information that is required to be provided in SPDs, there should not be, in theory, any inconsistencies between the SPD and the plan document. However, SPDs often contain disclaimer provisions to the effect that, in the event of any inconsistency between the plan and the SPD, the plan will govern.

Even though this type of disclaimer is frequently found in SPDs and the law is not fully settled, a significant line of case law holds that "[w]here . . . the terms of a plan and those of a plan summary conflict, it is the plan summary that controls." [Heidgerd v Olin Corp, 906 F 2d 903, 908 (2d Cir 1990) (severance pay plan document referred to restriction not described in SPD); see also Feifer v Prudential Ins Co, 306 F 3d 1202 (2d Cir 2002) (plan summary providing for long-term disability payments without offsets, controlled for duration plan summary was in circulation); Bergt v Retirement Plan for Pilots Employed by Mark Air, Inc, 293 F 3d 1139 (9th Cir 2002) (where plan document and SPD conflict, term favorable to employee will prevail; contract term construed against the drafter)]

Although a limited number of cases have upheld the power of disclaimers, the trend appears to be toward their invalidation. [Helwig v Kelsey-Hayes Company, 93 F 3d 243, 249 (6th Cir 1996) (disclaimer ineffective against SPD's promise of lifetime health coverage); Manginaro v The Welfare Fund of Local 771, 21 F Supp 2d 284, 296 (SD NY 1998) (plan shortened limitation on actions omitted from SPD held not enforceable despite disclaimer)] Therefore, it is important that all plan communications, including SPDs, be reviewed periodically for consistency with plan documents.

As an added measure, a plan fiduciary may wish to distribute plan documents to plan participants. In reviewing inaccurate SPD language, several courts have found that the plan document controlled where it was distributed to the plan participants, because the participants seeking relief could not be said to have "relied upon" the SPD. [Chiles v Ceridian Corp, 95 F 3d 1505 (10th Cir 1996); Aiken v Policy Management Systems Corp, 13 F 3d 138, 141–42 (4th Cir 1993)]

Q 9:39   What methods of distribution does ERISA require to satisfy its reporting and disclosure requirements?

Where certain material is required to be furnished by operation of law, or upon request, the plan administrator must "use measures reasonably calculated to ensure actual receipt of the material by participants and beneficiaries." [DOL Reg § 2520.104b-1] The plan administrator, as defined in ERISA Section 3(16)(A), is responsible for providing the required communications. [ERISA §§ 101(a), 104(b)]

Material that is required to be furnished upon written request to the administrator should be mailed to the address provided by the requesting individual or personally delivered. [DOL Reg § 2520.104b-1(b)(2)]

Material that is required to be furnished to all participants (and all beneficiaries receiving benefits under a plan) "must be sent by a method or methods of delivery likely to result in full distribution." In-hand delivery to employees at their worksites is an acceptable method of distribution. It is also acceptable to insert the information in a periodical or publication (for example, a union newsletter or employer publication), provided that the plan's distribution list is comprehensive and up to date and that there is a prominent notice on the front of the publication as to the inclusion of the information. However, "stacking" the material at a specified location (such as a plan office, union hall or office, or worksite) is not an acceptable method of distribution.

Material may be mailed by first-, second-, or third-class mail. However, distribution by third-class mail is acceptable only if return and forwarding postage is guaranteed and address correction is requested. Moreover, any letter that is returned with an address correction must be re-sent by first-class mail or personally delivered. [DOL Reg § 2520.104b-1(b)(1)]

The DOL issued final regulations in April 2002 addressing standards for the disclosure of employee benefit information, including SPDs and summaries of material modifications (SMMs), by means of electronic media. This information may be distributed to participants who have effective access to electronic documents at their workplace. The regulations also require that a plan participant affirmatively consent to receive the specified documents in this manner.

Q 9:43 Can a failure to timely file a Form 5500 be cured?

Yes, with limitations. The PWBA (now called the EBSA) established the Delinquent Filer Voluntary Compliance Program (DFVC) to encourage, through the assessment of reduced civil penalties, delinquent plan administrators to comply with their annual reporting obligations under Title I of ERISA.

Under Section 502(c) of ERISA, the Secretary of Labor has the authority to assess civil penalties of up to $1,100 per day against plan administrators who fail or refuse to file complete and timely annual reports (Form 5500 Series Annual Return/Reports) as required under ERISA Section 101(b)(4). The program established by the PWBA provided that civil penalties for noncompliance with the annual reporting requirements may be asessed at $50 for each day that an annual report is filed after the date that it was required to be filed, without regard to any extensions. Plan administrators who fail to file an annual report may be assessed a penalty of $300 per day, up to $30,000 per year, until a complete annual report is filed. The DOL may waive all or part of a civil penalty assessed on an administrator's showing that there was reasonable cause for the failure to file a complete and timely annual report.

Plan administrators who fail to file timely annual reports for plan years beginning after 1987 may take advantage of the DFVC program by complying with filing requirements and paying the specified civil penalties. However, the DFVC program is not available to plan administrators who either: (1) have been notified in writing of the DOL's intention to assess a civil penalty under Section 502(c) of ERISA for failure to file a timely annual report or (2) otherwise have been notified in writing by the DOL of a failure to file a timely annual report under Title I of ERISA.

Prior to receiving the notice described above, a plan administrator must file with the appropriate IRS office a complete Form 5500 or Form 5500-C Series Annual Report (the DFVC program does not apply to Form 5500-R filers), with all required schedules and attachments. A copy of the first page of the Form 5500 must also be sent to the DOL, along with the applicable penalty. Guidance issued in March 2002 eliminated the prior requirement to mark in red ink on the submission "DFVC Program."

In an effort to further encourage participation in the DFVC Program, the March 2002 guidance also reduced the penalty fees. The per day late fee penalty is reduced from $50 per day to $10 per day, with a cap of $750 for small plans and $2,000 for large plans. In addition, for plans that are delinquent in annual filings for multiple plan years, there is a per-plan penalty fee cap of $1,500 for small plans and $4,000 for large plans, provided the plan administrator submits all of the annual reports due in a single DFVC Program submission. In the case of a small plan sponsored by a Code Section 501(c)(3) organization, however, the applicable penalty amount is not to exceed $750, regardless of the number of delinquent annual reports submitted as part of the same DFVC submission. The plan administrator is personally liable for payment of these civil penalties, which may not be paid from the assets of an employee benefit plan. The payment of penalties assessed under the DFVC program does not preclude assessment of nonfiling or late-filing penalties by other federal agencies, including the IRS and PBGC. Under the Internal Revenue Code, these penalties apply unless it is shown that the failure to timely file is due to reasonable cause. If there is reasonable cause, a cover letter should be attached to the completed Form 5500 explaining the failure to timely file under Treasury Regulations. This statement of reasonable cause must be made under penalty of perjury.

The guidance explains that the DFVC program has two components. Under the first component, eligible plan administrators are required to file the delinquent annual report. For administrators of apprenticeship and training plans and "top hat" plans, this requirement is satisfied by filing the notice described in Labor Regulations § 2520.104-22 and the statement described in Labor Regulations § 2520.104-23. Under the second component of the DFVC program, filers must send the applicable penalty amount along with the required portions of the delinquent Form 5500 to:

> DFVC Program
> EBSA
> P.O. Box 530292
> Atlanta, GA 30353-0292

For Form 5500s for 1998 and earlier, the filer needs to include only the first page of the delinquent Form 5500 return. Filers who are using the 1999 Form 5500 or a subsequent version of the form must include a copy of all pages of the Form 5500, dated and signed, but without any schedules or attachments. *If the submission is for a small plan sponsored by a Code Section 501(c)(3) organization, the notation "501(c)(3) Plan" must appear in the upper-right-hand corner of the first page of the Form 5500.* Administrators of apprenticeship and training plans and top-hat plans filing under Section 4 of the DFVC program who are making filings for 1999 or later years must sign and date the Form 5500 and complete lines 1a–1c, 2a–2c, 3a–3c, and 8a or 8b as applicable.

Q 9:43.1   Does the Sarbanes-Oxley Act of 2002 apply to an ERISA 403(b) plan?

The Sarbanes-Oxley Act of 2002 [Pub L No 107–204] amended ERISA to require plan administrators of individual account plans to provide written notice to affected participants and beneficiaries of any blackout period during which their rights to direct or diversify investments or obtain a loan or a distribution under a plan may be temporarily suspended, limited, or modified. The DOL has provided a model notice under Section 101(i) of ERISA as part of a final rule issued on January 24, 2003. The final rule also implements a civil penalty under Section 502 of ERISA, establishing a civil penalty applicable to a plan administrator's failure or refusal to provide notice of a blackout period. These provisions could apply to an ERISA 403(b) plan in a scenario whereby a change in the plan's funding vehicles or a change in the plan's record keeper results in the imposition of a temporary investment allocation limitation, or a loan or distribution restriction, on participants and beneficiaries.

The Sarbanes-Oxley Act also prohibits a director or officer from purchasing or selling during any blackout period any equity security of the company acquired in connection with his or her employment. Although these insider trading restrictions of the Sarbanes-Oxley Act appear to apply to an ERISA 403(b) plan, application of these restrictions seems to have no practical meaning in the context of a 403(b) plan because an employer maintaining a 403(b) plan does not issue public stock.

Compliance with Claims Procedures

Q 9:44   What is a benefits claim?

A benefits claim is a request made by or on behalf of a participant or beneficiary for plan benefits. [DOL Reg § 2560.503-1(e)]

Q 9:45   When is a benefits claim deemed filed?

Under regulations effective for claims filed beginning in 2002, every employee benefit plan is required to establish and follow reasonable procedures governing the filing of benefit claims, notification of benefit determinations, and appeal of adverse benefit determinations. [DOL Reg § 2560.503-1(b)] If a plan fails to establish or follow claims procedures consistent with the requirements of DOL Regulations Section 2560.503-1, a claimant shall be deemed to have exhausted the administrative remedies available under the plan and shall be entitled to pursue any remedy under ERISA Section 502(a) on the basis that the plan failed to provide a reasonable claims procedure that would yield a decision on the merits of the claim. [DOL Reg § 2560.503-1*(1)*] The time period for a determination begins when a claim is filed in accordance with the plan's reasonable procedures, without regard to whether all the necessary information accompanies the filing.

Q 9:47   When must a claimant be informed that a benefits claim has been denied?

A claimant whose claim is denied in whole or in part must be notified in writing within a reasonable time after the plan receives the claim, not to exceed 90 days. If an extension is required, the claimant must receive written notice of the extension before the end of the initial 90-day period. The notice must specify the circumstances requiring the extension and the date by which the plan expects to render the final decision. The extension cannot exceed 90 days from the end of the initial 90-day period.

If a plan fails to establish or follow claims procedures consistent with the requirements of DOL Regulations Section 2560.503-1, a claimant shall be deemed to have exhausted the administrative remedies available under the plan and shall be entitled to pursue any remedy under ERISA Section 502(a) on the basis that the plan failed to provide a reasonable claims procedure that would yield a decision on the merits of the claim.

Q 9:48   What information must a claim denial contain?

A written notice of claim denial issued by the plan administrator or insurer must give the following information in a manner calculated to be understood by the claimant:

1. The specific reason(s) the claim was denied;
2. Specific reference to the pertinent plan provisions on which the denial was based;
3. An explanation of what additional material or information is necessary, and why, for the claimant to perfect the claim; and
4. An explanation of the appeals procedure by which the claimant can submit the claim for review and the time limits applicable to such procedures, including a statement of the claimant's right to bring a civil action under Section 502(a).

[DOL Reg § 2560.503-1(g)]

Q 9:49   What are a claimant's procedural rights on an appeal of a claim denial?

The claimant must have at least 60 days after receipt of written notice of a claim denial to file a request for review of the denied claim. The claimant or an authorized representative must be permitted to make a written application to the plan requesting a review of the claim and must be permitted to review pertinent documents and submit issues and comments in writing. Plan procedures need not allow the claimant or a representative to appear in person; review of denied claims can be required to be made solely upon written submissions. Plan procedures must provide for a review that takes into account all comments, documents, and records submitted by the claimant relating to the claim, without regard to whether the information was submitted or considered in the initial review. [DOL Reg § 2560.503-1(h)]

Q 9:50   When must an appeal be decided?

Generally, a decision on appeal must be made within 60 days after the plan receives the request for review. If an extension is required, the claimant must receive written notice of the extension before the end of the initial 60-day period. The notice must specify the circumstances requiring the extension and the date by which the plan expects to render the final decision. The extension cannot exceed 60 days from the end of the initial 60-day period.

If the named fiduciary that has responsibility for reviewing claims is a committee or board that holds meetings at least quarterly and a claim is received at least 30 days in advance of the next meeting, the claim must be heard at the next meeting. If an extension is required, the decision must be made by the third meeting after initial receipt of the request for appeal. [DOL Reg § 2560.503-1(i)]

Q 9:51   What information must a decision on appeal contain?

A written notice of appeal denial issued by the named fiduciary for hearing appeals must give the following information in a manner calculated to be understood by the claimant:

1. The specific reason(s) the appeal was denied;

2. Specific reference to the pertinent plan provisions on which the denial was based;

3. A statement that the claimant is entitled to receive upon request and free of charge access to copies of information relevant to claimant's claim for benefits; and

4. A statement of the claimant's right to bring an action under ERISA Section 502(a).

[DOL Reg § 2560.503-1(j)]

Q 9:53   Are any plans exempt from the requirement of providing a reasonable claims procedure?

To the extent benefits are provided or administered by an insurance company or similar, state-regulated organization, the claims procedure for those benefits might provide for filing benefit claims with, and notice of decision by, the insurance company or similar, state-regulated organization.

The person or committee designated as named fiduciary for hearing appeals (appeals committee) must have the power to reverse the denial of a claim and order payment of the benefit when the appeals committee determines it is appropriate. The appeals committee may be (though in many cases it would be preferable if it were not) the same individual or committee that decided the original claim. The appointment of an appeals committee should be expressly provided for in the plan documents and should be carefully documented so as to clearly define the appeals committee's powers and responsibilities.

If plan benefits are provided through insurance, the insurer will often require that the appeals committee (and the person determining initial claims) be the insurer or a committee designated by the insurer. This can ensure uniform interpretations consistent with the insurer's practices.

Fiduciary Matters

Q 9:63.1   How broad is the scope of the fiduciary's duty in selecting an annuity provider?

DOL Advisory Opinion 2002-14A expands on DOL Regulations Section 2509.95-1(c) and DOL Internal Bulletin 95-1. The Advisory Opinion clarifies that the fiduciary should ascertain, among other factors, the amount and extent to which the annuity provider is covered by state guarantees. It stresses that the fiduciary has a duty to engage a qualified independent expert to evaluate such factors if the fiduciary did not have the necessary level of expertise to evaluate the creditworthiness of an annuity provider.

Q 9:74   Does a fiduciary have an obligation to seek the assistance of an expert to satisfy the prudence requirement?

Fiduciaries have an affirmative duty to seek the advice and counsel of independent experts when their own ability is insufficient under the circumstances. Not all plan fiduciaries can be expert in all phases of employee benefit plan investments and administration, nor can they have knowledge of the entire range of activities integral to the operation of a plan. A fiduciary who lacks the expertise needed to address an issue prudently should promptly seek and retain a professional who has the expertise to assist the fiduciary in the decision. For example, plan trustees breached the prudence standard in connection with a $2 million loan to a bank when they considered only the information presented by the interested parties who sought the loan and failed to conduct an independent investigation. [Katsaros v Cody, 744 F 2d 270, 279 (2d Cir), *cert denied*, 469 US 1072 (1984)] Merely seeking independent advice is not enough. A fiduciary who consults and relies on an independent expert is required to provide the expert with complete and accurate information, investigate the expert's qualifications, and justify reliance on the expert. [Chao v Hall Holding Co, 285 F 3d 415 (6th Cir 2002)]

Q 9:81   Can a prohibited transaction be corrected?

Yes. A prohibited transaction can be corrected by undoing the transaction to the extent possible, but in any case placing the plan in a financial position no worse than the position it would have been in had the party in interest acted under the highest fiduciary standards. [ERISA § 502(i)] This requirement may be even more severe than the imposition of the penalty, as the "undoing" of a transaction may be far costlier than the amount of penalty involved. The party in interest, however, cannot choose between paying the penalty and "undoing" the transaction, as the penalty is continuously imposed for each year the prohibited transaction occurs, until it is corrected.

Effective April 14, 2000, the DOL established a Voluntary Fiduciary Correction (VFC) program, which is designed to encourage the voluntary and timely correction of certain transactions and the restoration of losses to employee benefit plans resulting from fiduciary breaches. Transactions may be corrected without a determination that there is an actual breach; there need only be a possible breach.

If an applicant is in full compliance with all of the terms and procedures set forth under the VFC program, the EBSA will issue a "no-action letter" with respect to the transaction identified. Pursuant to the no-action letter, the EBSA will not initiate a civil investigation under Title I of ERISA regarding the applicant's responsibility for any transaction described, or assess a civil penalty under ERISA Section 502(l) on the correction amount paid to the plan or its participants. Relief is limited to the transactions identified in the application and the persons who are correcting those transactions. Correction under the VFC program does not preclude any other governmental agency, including the IRS, from exercising any rights it may have with respect to the transactions that are the subject of the application.

The DOL implemented the final version of the VFC Program effective April 29, 2002. The final version covers 15 prohibited transactions, expanding the interim program, which covered 13. In November 2002, the DOL finalized class exemption PTE 2002-51, which exempts plans participating in the VFC Program from Code Section 4975 excise taxes for four prohibited transactions:

1. Failure to transmit participant contributions to a plan within prescribed time limits;

2. The plan's making a loan at fair market interest to a party in interest with respect to the plan;

3. Purchase or sale of an asset between a plan and a party in interest at fair market value; and

4. The sale of real property to a plan by the employer and the leaseback of the property to the employer, at fair market value and fair market rental rate.

In addition, the IRS stated it would not seek to impose excise taxes for *any* of the VFC program prohibited transactions so long as the requirements for the class exemption were met. [Ann 2002-31, 2002-19 IRB 908]

Q 9:83.1 May an employer that sponsors a plan limit the liability of, or indemnify, service providers?

In Advisory Opinion 2002-08A [Aug 20, 2002], the DOL said that clauses limiting liability and indemnifying service providers were not "per se" violations of ERISA Section 401(a)(1)(B) or Section 408(b)(2), but it noted that any agreement that protects the service provider against fraud or willful misconduct is void against public policy. At a minimum, the fiduciary is obliged to assess comparable services at comparable prices from other service providers who may give a plan greater protection. [DOL Adv Op 2002-08A]

Q 9:86   Is an insurance company a fiduciary under ERISA with regard to 403(b) assets that are under its authority or control?

The answer depends on the nature of the investment vehicles under which the Section 403(b) assets are maintained.

The Supreme Court, in *John Hancock Mutual Life Insurance Company v. Harris Trust and Savings Bank* [114 S Ct 517 (1993)], examined this issue by looking at the definition of *plan assets*. It decided that resolution of this issue depends upon whether, with regard to such assets, the investment risk is to be borne by the insurance company itself or by the plan participants. In affirming the decision of the Second Circuit, the Court narrowly construed the "guaranteed benefit policy" exclusion. The Court wrote that where an insurance company allocates investment risk to itself, the exclusion applies. Thus, the insurance company would be beyond the reach of the fiduciary rules with regard to those assets in connection with which it provides guaranteed benefit payments or a fixed rate of return. On the other hand, the Court held that with respect to those assets in connection with which the insurance company provides no guaranteed benefit payments or fixed rates of return, the insurance company is a fiduciary under ERISA. Therefore, certain assets held in an insurance company's general account could be considered plan assets, and the insurance company would, with respect to such assets, be an ERISA fiduciary. Such assets would also be subject to ERISA's prohibited transaction rules.

The DOL published PTE 95-60 in response to *Harris Trust*, so as to permit insurance companies to go forward with arm's-length transactions that involve general account assets arising from contracts issued to ERISA covered plans. The Small Business Job Protection Act of 1996 subsequently amended ERISA Section 401, adding a new Section 401(c), requiring the Secretary of Labor to issue regulations to clarify the status of plan assets held in an insurance company's general account. Section 401(c) directs the Secretary of Labor to issue regulations applicable to policies issued on or before December 31, 1998, to provide guidance for the purpose of determining, in cases where an insurance company issues one or more policies to or for the benefit of an employee benefit plan (and such policies are supported by assets of the insurance company's general account), which assets of the insurance company (other than plan assets held in its separate accounts) constitute plan assets for purposes of ERISA and the Code.

The DOL published a proposed regulation late in 1997 and a final regulation in January 2000. The final regulation provides conditions, which include extensive disclosure requirements, under which an insurance company would not be deemed a fiduciary with regard to general account policies (other than guaranteed benefit policies, the assets of which are not considered plan assets in any event) issued on or before December 31, 1998. Pursuant to Congress's amendment to Section 401 of ERISA, the relief provided in the regulation applies only to nonguaranteed benefit policies issued on or before December 31, 1998. All general account contracts issued on or after January 1, 1999, that are not guaranteed benefit policies will be subject to ERISA's fiduciary provisions.

In its decision on remand in *Harris Trust and Savings Bank v. John Hancock Mutual Life Insurance Company* [302 F 3d 18 (2d Cir 2002)], the Second Circuit held that where an insurance company is subject to ERISA's general fiduciary duty, this duty did not extend to releasing funds in a manner other than that specified by the contract. ERISA, the court stated, does not explicitly resolve tension that may exist between plan documents and fiduciary obligations imposed on plan administrators, but where parties negotiate the terms of a contract governing a plan, then the administrators, by following the terms of the contract, cannot be in breach of fiduciary duty.

Chapter 10

Distributions

Evan Giller, Esq.
Teachers Insurance and Annuity Association-
College Retirement Equities Fund

Barbara N. Seymon-Hirsch, Esq.
Davis & Harman LLP

The 403(b) tax-sheltered annuity, mutual fund separate account, or church plan retirement account is a tax-deferred vehicle. * While deferral continues, the 403(b) owner enjoys the benefit of tax-free accumulation. A point is reached, however, when this benefit may not continue for 100 percent of the account. Then, minimum distributions are required to commence, or else severe penalties may be imposed. In the case of 403(b) plans, the commencement date may be delayed until as late as age 75 with respect to amounts that were contributed and earned before 1987. When this apportionment is not successfully implemented, distributions of 403(b) accounts must commence under the rule that otherwise applies to post-1986 accumulations under a change in the law under the Small Business Job Protection Act of 1996: no later than the April 1 of the calendar year following the later of (1) the calendar year in which the 403(b) participant attains age 70½ or (2) the calendar year in which the participant retires. In the event of earlier death, distributions may be required to start even sooner. Participants not subject to the age 70½–based required beginning date may continue to apply the somewhat different distribution rules that formerly applied.

---

* Unless otherwise noted, references to a "403(b) contract" will include a 403(b) tax-sheltered annuity, mutual fund separate account, and church plan retirement account.

Ms. Seymon-Hirsch and Mr. Giller would like to thank Bryan Keene, an associate with Davis & Harman LLP, for his significant contributions to this chapter.

In April 2002, the IRS released final and new temporary, proposed regulations governing required minimum distributions. The final and new temporary regulations apply for determining required minimum distributions for calendar years beginning on or after January 1, 2003. However, taxpayers who own a 403(b) tax-sheltered annuity from which annuity distributions are being made may rely upon certain provisions of the regulations proposed in 1987 or 2001 for purposes of determining required minimum distributions. [Notice 2003-2, 2003-2 IRB 257]

Although distributions sometimes may be accelerated and begin sooner than required, a 10 percent penalty may result if the 403(b) participant makes withdrawals before age 59½. Furthermore, distributions are taxable when made, so an earlier distribution date results in an earlier tax liability than would have resulted from a later distribution date.

Following the receipt of a lump-sum or installment benefit from a 403(b) plan, to the extent it is an eligible rollover distribution, the individual receiving this benefit may wish to defer its taxation. One way of doing this is to roll over, by way of a rollover to an IRA, within 60 days of receipt.

Starting in 1993, a further incentive for 403(b) rollovers was added to the tax code: 20 percent mandatory withholding for eligible rollover distributions (ERDs). The only way to avoid this withholding is to have the eligible rollover amount directly rolled over to an eligible retirement plan, unless the participant decides to leave the asset where it is. The withholding will apply if the distribution is made to the participant or spousal beneficiary. This means that, where the amount is distributed to the participant who intends to roll it over within 60 days from the date of receipt (instead of doing a direct rollover), a 20 percent tax will be withheld. Therefore, only 80 percent of the distribution will escape tax by being rolled over within 60 days, unless the recipient finds other money to use to replace the 20 percent that was withheld as federal income tax. If this is not done, the 20 percent withheld will be immediately taxable even though it is to be credited against tax liabilities or received as a refund at a later time.

Requirements Governing Timing and Amount of Benefit Distributions

Q 10:2   What regulations must be followed in order to meet the required minimum distribution rules established in Code Sections 403(b)(10) and 401(a)(9)?

On April 17, 2002, the IRS released final, temporary, and proposed regulations providing guidance on the minimum distribution rules. These regulations replace the prior proposed regulations that were issued on July 27, 1987 [52 Fed Reg 29070] and on January 17, 2001 [66 Fed Reg 3928]. These regulations apply for determining required minimum distributions (RMDs) for calendar years beginning on or after January 1, 2003. For determining RMDs for calendar year 2002, taxpayers could rely on the final and new temporary regulations, the 2001 proposed regulations, or the 1987 proposed regulations.

Distributions for 2001 could be based on either the 2001 proposed regulations or the 1987 proposed regulations. The IRS has said that if required distributions were made for 2001 before the contract or plan adopted the 2001 regulations, the distributions would be treated as if they were made under the 1987 regulations. If the total amount of distributions made under the 1987 regulations equaled or exceeded the amount required under the new regulations, no further distributions were required. If the amount distributed under the prior regulations did not equal the amount required under the new regulations, the amount remaining to be distributed would be calculated using the new regulations. The IRS provided a model amendment for plans to adopt to implement this rule. [Ann 2001-82, 2001-31 IRB 123]

In Revenue Procedure 2003-2 [2003-1 IRB 76], the IRS announced that it will be issuing three transition rules under Treasury Regulations Section 1.401(a)(9)-6T that will apply at least through the end of the calendar year that final regulations are published. First, respecting variable and increasing annuity payments covered under A-1 of the regulation (including Section 403(b) annuities), the transition rule is expected to provide that distributions that satisfy the requirements for variable or increasing payments under the 1987 or 2001 proposed regulations will be deemed to satisfy the requirements of Section 1.401(a)(9)-6T, A-1. The second transition rule is expected to provide that under Section 1.401(a)(9), A-12, a participant's entire interest under an annuity contract can be determined by reference to the dollar amount credited to the employee and without regard to the actuarial value of any benefits provided under the contract (see Q 10:10). The third rule is expected to provide a special effective date for governmental plans.

The IRS has also stated that a distribution in excess of the RMD amount as calculated under the new regulations may be rolled over into an IRA.

Q 10:11   What is the applicable account balance when distributions are being made from an individual account?

The applicable accumulation is the accumulation as of the last valuation date in the calendar year preceding the distribution calendar year reduced (where available) by the grandfathered accumulation (see Q 10:17). Thus, if the distribution calendar year (see Q 10:4) is 2001, and the plan provides for daily valuation, the applicable accumulation is the accumulation value (as reduced by the grandfathered amount) on December 31, 2000.

In addition, in accordance with Treasury Regulations Section 1.401(a)(9)-6T, A-12, the entire interest under an annuity contract includes the actuarial value of any other benefits (such as minimum survivor benefits) that will be provided under the contract. (For a special transition rule, see SQ 10:2.)

Q 10:12   When distributions are being made from an individual account plan to the participant, how is the required minimum distribution amount calculated?

Under the regulations, the required minimum distribution is equal to the quotient obtained by dividing the applicable account balance by the applicable distribution period. In general, the applicable distribution period for distribution calendar years up to and including the employee's date of death is determined by reference to a table found in Treasury Regulations Section 1.401(a)(9)-9, which is provided in Appendix A of this book. This table is utilized whether or not the participant has named a beneficiary and, with one major exception, regardless of the age of that beneficiary (see Q 10:13). The age used to calculate the required amount for purposes of this table is the employee's age as of the employee's birthday in the relevant distribution calendar year. The distribution period under the table is the life expectancy as of the employee's age plus ten years. Thus, under these regulations, the life expectancy is "recalculated" each year for all participants and all beneficiaries.

Under the 1987 proposed regulations, the applicable distribution period was determined by reference to the life expectancies of the participant, and where applicable, a beneficiary. Generally, life expectancies were calculated using the participant's and designated beneficiary's attained ages as of their birthdays in the calendar year in which the participant attained age $70\frac{1}{2}$.

Unless life expectancies were being recalculated, the applicable life expectancy was reduced by one year in each subsequent distribution calendar year. The death of the participant or designated beneficiary did not reduce the applicable life expectancy if life expectancies were not being recalculated. The life expectancy of a participant and a spouse beneficiary, either individually or jointly, could be recalculated, but not more frequently than annually. The life expectancy of a designated beneficiary other than a spouse could not be recalculated. A participant's life expectancy (or the joint life expectancy of a participant and a spouse) was recalculated annually by redetermining their life expectancies in each distribution calendar year using the participant's and spouse's attained ages as of the participant's and spouse's birthdays in each succeeding calendar year in which the recalculation was done. Upon the death of the participant or spouse, the life expectancy of the deceased participant or spouse was reduced to zero in the calendar year following the calendar year of the death. The participant's entire remaining accumulation needed to be distributed by the last day of the year in which the last applicable life expectancy was reduced to zero. [1987 Prop Treas Reg § 1.401(a)(9)-1, E-8]

The plan or contract could specify whether life expectancies were to be recalculated or could allow the participant to choose whether to use recalculation. If the plan or contract was silent or the participant failed to elect, life expectancies were deemed to be recalculated. As of the date of the first required distribution, whatever method of determining life expectancy was in effect was irrevocable and applied to all future years. [1987 Prop Treas Reg § 1.401(a)(9)-1, E-7]

Life expectancies were computed by use of the expected return multiples in Tables V and VI of Treasury Regulations Section 1.72-9. [1987 Prop Treas Reg § 1.401(a)(9)-1, E-1, E-3, E-4]

Q 10:15 If the participant meets the distribution requirements by receiving periodic payments from an annuity contract, what amount must be paid out each year?

Distributions will satisfy the requirements of these rules if they are in the form of periodic annuity payments for the employee's life or for the joint lives of the employee and the beneficiary, or over a period certain. The life annuity may also provide for a period certain. The period certain generally is not permitted to exceed the applicable distribution period (see SQ 10:11) for the employee. However, if the employee's sole beneficiary is the employee's spouse and the annuity provides only a period certain and no life annuity, the period certain may be the longer of the applicable distribution period or the joint life and survivor expectancy of the employee and the spouse. Annuity payments must commence on or before the employee's required beginning date.

Annuity payments must be made at uniform intervals not to exceed one year. The payments must not increase, or they must increase only as follows:

- In accordance with a cost of living index issued by the Bureau of Labor Statistics
- Under certain survivor benefit arrangements where the designated beneficiary dies or is no longer the beneficiary pursuant to a qualified domestic relations order
- To provide cash refunds of employee contributions upon an employee's death
- To pay for increased benefits under the plan

- When an account balance is being annuitized under an insurance company contract, if the total future expected payments exceed the account value being annuitized, the payments may be increased

  —by a constant percentage, applied at least annually

  —to provide a payment upon the death of the employee equal to the excess of the account value being annuitized over the total of payments before the death of the employee

  —as a result of certain dividend payments or other payments that result from certain actuarial gains

[Treas Reg § 1.401(a)(9)-6T, A-4] See SQ 10:2 for a special transition rule.

The minimum distribution requirement will be satisfied if the entire account balance is annuitized in accordance with these rules. If a portion of the account balance is annuitized, the remaining amount in the account must be distributed in accordance with the individual account rules.

If distributions are in the form of a joint and survivor annuity with a nonspouse beneficiary, the payment to the beneficiary is subject to the minimum distribution incidental benefit rules (see Q 10:28).

Distributions After Death of Participant

Q 10:23   How is it determined whether the five-year rule or the life expectancy rule applies to a distribution?

When an employee dies before his or her required beginning date, distribution of the employee's entire interest must be made in accordance with either the five-year rule or the life expectancy rule (see Q 10:21). The regulations provide that if a 403(b) contract does not specify the method of distribution, the distribution must be made in accordance with the following rules:

1. If the employee has a designated beneficiary as of the applicable date, distributions are to be made in accordance with the life expectancy rule.

2. If the employee has no designated beneficiary, distributions are to be made in accordance with the five-year rule.

The contract or plan may adopt a provision specifying either method, or a provision that allows employees or beneficiaries to elect which method will apply. [Treas Reg § 1.401(a)(9)-3] The contract or the underlying plan may contain a provision specifying which of the two methods to use, or it may allow employees and beneficiaries to elect the method to be used. In the event that an election is permitted, it must be made no later than the earlier of (1) December 31 of the calendar year in which distributions would be required to commence in order to satisfy the requirements of the exception to the five-year rule or (2) December 31 of the calendar year that contains the fifth anniversary of the date of the death of the participant. As of that date, the election is irrevocable and applies to all future years. [Treas Reg § 1.401(a)(9)-3, A-4]

If the contract or plan does not contain a provision either designating the option or allowing an election, or if the election is not made, distributions must be made as follows:

1. If an employee has a designated beneficiary, distributions are made in accordance with the life expectancy rule.

2. If the employee has no designated beneficiary, distributions are made in accordance with the five-year rule.

The regulations contain a transition rule that allows a beneficiary who is receiving payments under the five-year rule to switch to the life expectancy rule under certain circumstances. [Treas Reg §§ 1.401(a)(9)-1, A-2(b)(2), 1.401(a)(9)-3, A-4]

Designated Beneficiaries

Q 10:25   When is the designated beneficiary determined?

In general, the employee's designated beneficiary is determined based on the beneficiaries designated as of the September 30 following the calendar year of the employee's death. Thus, if a beneficiary named as of the date of the employee's death disclaims in favor of another beneficiary or receives his or her full distribution under the plan by the September 30 following the year of the employee's death, that person is not taken into account in determining the employee's designated beneficiary for purposes of the required distribution rules. However, if the distributions are in the form of an irrevocable annuity, the designated beneficiary will be determined as of the annuity starting date. [Treas Reg § 1.401(a)(9)-6T, A-10]

Under the regulations, the designated beneficiary was generally determined as of the participant's required beginning date. However, if annuity payments commenced to the participant either on or before the required beginning date, the designated beneficiary was determined as of any date during the 90 days before the date on which the annuity payments commenced. If there was no beneficiary at that time, the distribution period was limited to the participant's life or life expectancy. [1987 Prop Treas Reg § 1.401(a)(9)-1, D-3]

For purposes of calculating the distribution period for distributions beginning after the death of the participant, the designated beneficiary was determined as of the participant's date of death. If there was no designated beneficiary at that time (or if there was a beneficiary who is not a designated beneficiary), distributions were made in accordance with the five-year rule. [1987 Prop Treas Reg § 1.401(a)(9)-1, D-4]

Minimum Distribution Incidental Benefit Requirements

Q 10:29   What are the minimum distribution incidental benefit requirements?

In order for a distribution to satisfy the minimum distribution requirements, the amount or form of the distribution must meet the MDIB requirements as well as the general distribution requirements described previously. In general, the regulations greatly simplified the application of these rules from the prior proposed regulations. A distribution to an employee from an individual account will satisfy the MDIB rules if they follow the requirements described in SQ 10:12, if distributions are being made in the form of a single life annuity to the employee, or if distributions are made in the form of a joint and survivor annuity where the spouse is the employee's sole beneficiary.

However, if the participant's benefit is in the form of a joint and survivor annuity for the lives of the participant and a beneficiary other than the participant's spouse, the MDIB requirements are satisfied only if, after the participant's required beginning date, the periodic amount payable to the beneficiary after the participant's death does not exceed the "applicable percentage" of the periodic amount paid to the participant. The applicable percentage is set out in a table in the regulations. [Treas Reg § 1.401(a)(9)-6T, A-2] It is based on the excess of the age of the participant over the age of the beneficiary as of their attained ages as of their birthdays in a calendar year. For example, if the participant is 20 years older than a nonspouse beneficiary, the periodic payment to the beneficiary on the death of the participant can be no greater than 73 percent of the periodic payment that had been made to the participant. If the employee has more than one beneficiary, the applicable percentage will be the percentage using the age of the youngest beneficiary.

Taxation and Investment in the Contract

Q 10:46   When can the exception for "substantially equal periodic payments" be used?

The exception for substantially equal periodic payments is available only if the participant terminated employment prior to beginning the periodic payments. [IRC § 72(t)(3)(B)] A second requirement is that the payments cannot be substantially modified (other than by reason of death or disability) within a five-year period beginning on the date of the first payment or, if later, at age 59^1/$_2$. [IRC § 72(t)(4)]

IRS Notice 89-25[1989-1CB 662] describes three methods for determining whether payments constitute a series of "substantially equal periodic payments." The first method provides that the annual payment may be calculated in the same way minimum distribution payments under Code Section 401(a)(9) are calculated. The second method provides for the calculation of an annual payment by amortizing the account balance and using a reasonable interest rate, over the life or joint life expectancies of the participant and designated beneficiary, if any. The third method provides for the calculation of an annual payment by dividing the account balance by an annuity factor derived using reasonable mortality factors and interest rates.

In October 2002, the IRS released Revenue Ruling 2002-62 [2002-42 IRB 710], which modifies Notice 89-25 effective for any series of payments commencing on or after January 1, 2003. The rules of Revenue Ruling 2002-62 also may be used for distributions commencing in 2002. Revenue Ruling 2002-62 describes three methods (similar to the three methods described in Notice 89-25) for determining whether payments constitute a series of substantially equal periodic payments.

The first method, referred to as the "required minimum distribution method," provides that the annual payment is determined by dividing the account balance for each year by the number from the "chosen life expectancy table" for that year. Under this method, the account balance, the number from the chosen life expectancy table, and the resulting annual payments are redetermined each year.

The second method, referred to as the "fixed amortization method," provides that the annual payment is determined by amortizing in level amounts the account balance over a specified number of years determined using the chosen life expectancy table and the "chosen interest rate." Under this method, the account balance, the number from the chosen life expectancy table, and the resulting annual payment are determined once for the first distribution year and the annual payment is the same amount in each succeeding year.

The third method, referred to as the "fixed annuitization method," provides that the annual payment is determined by dividing the account balance by an annuity factor that is the present value of an annuity of one dollar per year beginning at the participant's age and continuing for the life of the participant (or the joint lives of the participant and the beneficiary). The annuity factor is derived using a mortality table set forth in Revenue Ruling 2002-62 and the chosen interest rate. Under this method, the account balance, the annuity factor, the chosen interest rate, and the resulting annual payment are determined once for the first distribution year and the annual payment is the same amount in each succeeding year.

For purposes of Revenue Ruling 2002-62, the "chosen life expectancy table" is one of the following:

1. The uniform lifetime table set forth in Revenue Ruling 2002-62;

2. The single life expectancy table in Treasury Regulations Section 1.401(a)(9)-9, A-1; or

3. The joint and last survivor table in Treasury Regulations Section 1.401(a)(9)-9, A-3.

Special rules apply with respect to which table may be chosen. The "chosen interest rate" may be any interest rate that is not more than 120 percent of the federal mid-term rate (determined in accordance with Code Section 1274(d) for either of the two months immediately preceding the month in which the distribution begins). The "account balance" that is used to determine payments must be determined in a reasonable manner based on the facts and circumstances.

Revenue Ruling 2002-62 provides special rules regarding modifications to a series of substantially equal periodic payments. In general, if such a modification occurs, the penalty tax of Code Section 4974(c), plus interest for the deferral period, is recaptured. [IRC § 72(t)(4)] Under all three methods described in Revenue Ruling 2002-62, such a modification will occur if, following the date the account balance is determined under the applicable method, there is (1) any addition to the account balance (other than gains or losses), (2) any nontaxable transfer of a portion of the account balance to another arrangement, or (3) a rollover by the taxpayer of the amount received resulting in such amount not being taxable. However, Revenue Ruling 2002-62 [2002-42 IRB 710] permits a one-time change to the required minimum distribution method that will not be treated as a "modification" to a series of periodic payments. Under this special rule, an individual who begins distributions in a year using the fixed amortization method, the fixed annuitization method, or a method of calculating substantially equal periodic payments commencing before 2003 may in any subsequent year switch to the required minimum distribution method to determine the payment for the year of the switch and all subsequent payments. If a switch to the required minimum distribution method is made, that method must be used in all subsequent years.

Rollovers and Transfers

Q 10:96 How much time does a participant have to complete a rollover?

To the extent a participant does not accomplish a direct rollover, a participant may roll over an eligible rollover distribution within 60 days from the date the distribution is received. For distributions made after 2001, the Secretary of the Treasury may waive this 60-day requirement where the failure to waive the requirement would be against equity or good conscience, including casualty, disaster, or other events beyond the reasonable control of the participant. [IRC § 402(c)(3)(B)]

Effective January 27, 2003, for distributions occurring after December 31, 2001, such a waiver is granted automatically if the failure to complete a rollover within the required 60 days is due solely to an error on the part of a financial institution, if the following conditions are satisfied:

1. The financial institution receives funds on behalf of a taxpayer prior to the expiration of the 60-day rollover period;

2. The taxpayer follows all procedures required by the financial institution for depositing the funds into an eligible retirement plan within the required 60 days;

3. Had the financial institution deposited the funds as instructed by the taxpayer, it would have been a valid rollover; and

4. The funds are deposited into an eligible retirement plan within one year from the beginning of the 60-day rollover period.

[Rev Proc 2003-16, 2003-4 IRB 1]

In other situations, a taxpayer may apply for a hardship exception to the 60-day rollover requirement under normal IRS procedures for requesting private letter rulings. In determining whether to grant a waiver, the IRS will consider all relevant facts and circumstances, including the following:

1. Errors committed by a financial institution (other than those resulting in an automatic waiver, as described above);

2. The taxpayer's inability to complete a rollover due to death, disability, hospitalization, incarceration, restrictions imposed by a foreign country, or postal error;

3. The taxpayer's use of the amount distributed (e.g., in the case of payment by check, whether the check was cashed); and

4. The time elapsed since the distribution occurred.

[Rev Proc 2003-16, 2003-4 IRB 1]

The time for making a rollover also may be postponed in the event of service in a combat zone or in the case of a presidentially declared disaster or a terrorist or military action. [IRC §§ 7508, 7508A; Treas Reg § 301.7508-1; Rev Proc 2002-71, 2002-46 IRB 850]

Under prior law, the 60-day period could not be extended even if the failure to meet the deadline was through no fault of the participant. [Ltr Ruls 9145036, 8548073; Treas Reg § 1.402(c)-2, Q&A 11]

Chapter 11

Loans, Life Insurance, and Plan Termination

Richard A. Turner, Esq.
The Variable Annuity Life Insurance Company

Loans are an important feature in many 403(b) programs. In effect, they give participants an opportunity to borrow from, and then repay, themselves. However, loans should not be permitted to adversely affect the participant's primary goal of retirement savings. As a result, loans are subject to very specific limits on amounts, as well as requirements for repayment. In recent years, the Department of the Treasury has published final regulations that provide significant guidance regarding loans and loan defaults. In addition, loans may be transferred between 403(b) plans in certain circumstances. However, if a material loan term is changed in the transfer, it can become a new loan for many testing purposes.

A 403(b) plan or program may also offer life insurance protection, provided that it is incidental to the primary purpose of retirement savings. In determining whether the life insurance protection is incidental, the same rules that apply to qualified plans generally apply to 403(b) programs. The cost of life insurance protection is taxable to the participant each year. The IRS released guidance in 2001 that revised the method for quantifying that cost. Death benefits from the life insurance policies are generally taxable to the beneficiary to the extent of the policy's cash value on the date of death, less the previously reported cost of insurance and any other unrecovered investment in the contract. The amount of the death benefit that exceeds the cash value will be excluded from income as proceeds from life insurance.

Plan terminations present some unique issues in the context of 403(b) plans. If the Employee Retirement Income Security Act of

1974 (ERISA) does not apply, in many cases plan termination can be a relatively simple matter of halting contributions. Individual employees can often keep their annuity contracts, certificates, or custodial accounts intact. If the employees have not separated from service, those contracts, certificates, and accounts would still be subject to withdrawal restrictions, which would be imposed by the investment product. In an ERISA plan, however, determining when and how a plan may be terminated is complicated by the combination of Internal Revenue Code withdrawal restrictions and ERISA requirements, which can create uncertainty as to when a plan termination has been effected.

Loans

Q 11:1   May loans be offered in 403(b) programs?

Yes. Loans may be offered from an annuity or life insurance contract that qualifies under Code Section 403(b) and will be treated as being made from the employer's 403(b) plan. [IRC § 72(p)(5); Treas Reg § 1.72(p)-1, Q&A 2] The IRS has also ruled privately that a custodial account under Code Section 403(b)(7) may offer loans. [See also Sen Comm Notes, TAMRA 1988]

A number of requirements must be satisfied, however, in order to prevent a loan from being a taxable distribution to the participant—either as an actual distribution or as a "deemed distribution"—at the time it is made. (These requirements apply also to contracts that met the requirements of Section 403(b) but that have since failed to satisfy those requirements.) [Treas Reg § 1.72(p)-1, Q&A 2(e)]

Note. Reference will be made throughout this chapter to Treasury Regulations Section 1.72(p)-1. Reference will also be made to amendments to that regulation, which will be effective for assignments, pledges, and loans made on or after January 1, 2004, but do not apply to loans made under an insurance contract that is in effect on December 31, 2003, if the insurance carrier is required to offer loans to contract holders that are not secured (other than by the participant's or beneficiary's benefit under the contract).

If the 403(b) plan is subject to the Employee Retirement Income Security Act of 1974 (ERISA), a loan from the plan (including a loan under the terms of an annuity contract held under the plan) will be treated as a prohibited transaction, subjecting the fiduciary(ies) to potential liability, unless the loan program has at least been authorized by a written provision in the plan. In addition, either the plan or a loan program authorized by the plan must satisfy specific ERISA requirements, including the following:

- Making loans available to all participants and beneficiaries on a reasonably equivalent basis;
- Not making loans available to highly compensated employees, officers, and directors in greater amounts than for other employees;
- Charging a reasonable rate of interest that provides the plan with a return commensurate with the interest rates charged by persons in the business of lending money for loans that would be made under similar circumstances; and
- Adequately securing the loan so that it may be reasonably anticipated that loss of principal or interest will not result from the loan.

[ERISA §§ 406(a)(1)(B), 408(b)(1); 29 CFR 2550.408b-1]

Also, if the ERISA 403(b) plan is subject to qualified joint and survivor annuity and qualified preretirement survivor annuity rules, married participants must obtain spousal consent for loans over $5,000 if the total accrued benefit subject to security is greater than $5,000. [ERISA § 205(c)(4)]

Loans as Distributions

Q 11:3 If a loan is not treated as an actual distribution, under what circumstances can the loan still be taxable as a deemed distribution when it is issued?

If a loan is not considered an actual distribution when it is made, it will still be taxable if it is a deemed distribution. A loan (or a portion thereof) will be a deemed distribution to the participant unless it satisfies certain requirements:

1. The loan must be evidenced by a legally enforceable agreement. [Treas Reg § 1.72(p)-1, Q&A 3] The agreement must be in writing, unless it is in an electronic medium that satisfies specific requirements or in another form approved by the IRS. The agreement only needs to be signed if a signature is required for the agreement to be enforceable under applicable law; and

2. The agreement must clearly identify an amount borrowed, a loan term, and a repayment schedule, each of which satisfies applicable requirements. [Treas Reg § 1.72(p)-1, Q&A 3] An agreement maintained in an electronic medium will not qualify as a legally enforceable agreement, under (1) above, unless the electronic medium:

   a. Is reasonably accessible to the participant or beneficiary;

b. Is reasonably designed to preclude any individual other than the participant or beneficiary from requesting a loan; and

c. Provides the participant or beneficiary with a reasonable opportunity to review and to confirm, modify, or rescind the terms of the loan before the loan is made.

It is generally expected that the IRS and the Department of the Treasury will issue proposed regulations regarding electronic signatures and related issues in the near future.

If the loan exceeds applicable dollar or percentage limits (see SQ 11:7), only the excess portion of the loan will be a deemed distribution, provided that all other requirements are satisfied.

A deemed distribution is taxable to the participant but is not treated as an actual distribution for the purposes of Code Section 403(b)(11), which identifies the withdrawal restrictions for 403(b) annuities. [Treas Reg § 1.72(p)-1, Q&A 12]

> **Note.** Presumably a deemed distribution is also not an actual distribution for the purposes of Code Section 403(b)(7). However, with respect to 403(b) investments, this provision of the regulation refers only to Code Section 403(b)(11). Whether any particular meaning, either favorable or unfavorable for loans from 403(b)(7) custodial accounts, is intended is unclear.

If part or all of a loan is a deemed distribution when the loan is issued, that amount will be reportable on Form 1099R. It may not be rolled over to an eligible retirement plan. Withholding will apply unless it is waived. [Treas Reg § 1.72(p)-1, Q&A 12; IRC § 3405(b)] A portion of the deemed distribution may be nontaxable if the contract contained after-tax amounts. [Treas Reg § 1.72(p)-1, Q&A 11; IRC § 72(e)(8)]

See Q 11:23 for the treatment of loans that are not repaid according to their terms.

Limitations on Amounts

Q 11:7 Are there limits on the amount of nontaxable loans that may be made from the plan to a participant?

Loans are subject to the stated limits, if any, in the plan and in the underlying investment. Apart from the plan and the investment, however, loans from 403(b) plans are limited by a 50/50 rule: they generally cannot exceed the lesser of:

1. $50,000; or

2. 50 percent of the present value of the participant's nonforfeitable accrued benefit under the plan.

[IRC § 72(p)]

In a large number of 403(b) programs, all contributions are 100 percent vested (i.e., nonforfeitable), so the second limit is typically 50 percent of the participant's account balance. See SQ 11:8 and Q 11:9 for rules where a participant owns more than one contract or participates in more than one plan.

If a portion of the participant's contract or account is pledged as collateral for a loan, these limits will be applied only to the actual amount loaned. This is true regardless of whether the loan is made directly from the account or from the annuity issuer with a security interest in a portion of the account. Therefore, if the collateral exceeds the amount loaned, the excess collateral is not counted against these limits. [Treas Reg § 1.72(p)-1, Q&A 1]

$50,000 limit. The $50,000 limit was one of the first limits on plan loans. It restricted the amount that could be borrowed at any time. However, before Congress further refined this limit, nothing prevented a participant from repaying a loan in full and then reborrowing the same money. Participants were thus able to maintain continuous tax-free access to a significant portion of their pre-tax retirement savings.

To curb this perceived abuse, as part of the Tax Reform Act of 1986 (TRA '86) Congress added a one-year lookback rule, which remains in effect today. [Tax Reform Act of 1986, Pub L No 99–514 § 1133 (1986)] The lookback in effect reduces the $50,000 limit by the largest outstanding loan balance during the past 365 days, to determine the maximum new loan. Since the lookback is a moving window, the old potential for gaming is effectively gone.

50 percent limit. A participant may not borrow more than 50 percent of the nonforfeitable account balance in his or her 403(b) plan. The 50 percent limit will not be violated if the loan does not exceed the lesser of (1) $10,000 or (2) 100 percent of his or her vested account balance. [IRC § 72(p)(2)(A)(i)] Thus, under the Code requirements, a participant with a vested account value of $10,000 may borrow his or her entire account balance.

However, care should be taken when applying this special rule to smaller accounts in 403(b) plans that are subject to the requirements of Title I of ERISA. Loans from ERISA 403(b) plans must be adequately secured if they are to avoid being considered prohibited transactions. [DOL Reg § 2550.408b-1(f)] The adequate security rule will not allow more than 50 percent of the participant's vested account balance to be used as collateral for the loan. To comply with this rule, loans made or renewed after October 18, 1989, are not permitted to exceed the 50 percent limit, even with smaller account values where the $10,000 floor would apply, unless outside collateral is obtained to secure the excess over 50 percent. Unlike the Code, ERISA takes into account any collateral in excess of the amount loaned for purposes of applying the 50 percent limit.

Loans secured by employee deductible contributions (made in years before 1987) are treated as taxable without regard to IRS loan limitations.

These limits apply at the time a loan is taken. Events that occur after a loan is taken and cause the loan to exceed 50 percent of the participant's vested account balance do not disqualify an existing loan (although they will affect the employee's ability to take additional loans). [IRC § 72(p)(2)(A); DOL Reg § 2550.408b-1(f)(2)] For example, a participant's account may be partially invested in variable annuities or mutual funds, which can fluctuate in value. Also, a participant might take a permitted withdrawal while the loan is outstanding. Neither of these subsequent events should disqualify a previously issued loan even if, following the event, the loan exceeds 50 percent of the employee's vested account balance.

> **Example 11-1.** Rebecca Smith is a participant in an ERISA 403(b) plan that has both employer contributions and employee deferrals, all of which are 100 percent vested. Her annuity account balance is $18,000. Her maximum nontaxable loan is $10,000 (the greater of 50 percent of her account balance or $10,000). However, if she borrows the entire $10,000, the loan will not be "adequately secured" under the ERISA rules, and thus she will need to provide at least $1,000 of additional collateral for the loan. She will want to check her plan and her 403(b) annuity to see whether the use of outside collateral is permitted, since in most 403(b) arrangements it is not.

Q 11:8   How do these limits apply if the participant has more than one 403(b) annuity?

To apply the IRS loan limits, all of an employee's contracts and accounts in an employer's 403(b) plan or program are treated as one annuity. [IRC § 72(p)(2)(D)] If an employee had a separate 403(b) annuity from a previous employer and if that annuity was not transferred into the current employer's plan, then the other annuity should qualify for a separate set of loan limitations.

If an employee has multiple 403(b) annuities within an employer's plan, he or she may total the value of the annuities and borrow 50 percent of the total, up to $50,000 (as adjusted), in any combination from the annuities. [Treas Reg § 1.403(b)-1(b)(4); Ltr Rul 8742008] This may be important if one or more of the participant's 403(b) investments do not allow loans. Of course, the ability of the participant to borrow larger amounts from any one contract also depends on the terms of the plan and of the contracts. It should also be noted, however, that aggregating two small plan accounts may reduce the amount the participant can borrow from either of the plan accounts, because the $10,000 floor may no longer apply.

> **Note.** Plan sponsors or product issuers who request information from a participant regarding loans from other plans should be entitled to rely on the information that the participant provides, unless they know that information is not correct. This is the position articulated in the preamble to Treasury Regulations Section 1.72(p)-1 (as amended by TD 9021, Dec 3, 2002).

> **Example 11-2.** ABC Corporation, a charitable organization, has established an ERISA 403(b) plan that consists solely of employer discretionary contributions and also allows employees to defer a portion of their salary to annuities in a separate non-ERISA 403(b) program. Both the ERISA plan and the non-

ERISA program allow nontaxable loans, and neither accepts outside collateral.

Josh, a relatively new ABC employee, has vested account balances in the ERISA plan and the non-ERISA program of $9,000 and $11,000, respectively. Josh took a loan of $8,500 from his salary deferral 403(b) annuity contract under the non-ERISA program. Then he applied to the ERISA 403(b) plan for a loan. When the administrator of the ERISA 403(b) plan saw on Josh's loan application that he already had an $8,500 loan from his non-ERISA annuity, the plan loan was limited to $1,500.

Why? Josh's ERISA plan vested balance, by itself, would seem to justify a loan of up to $4,500 (the ERISA 50 percent limit without outside collateral; the IRS limit, if this were a non-ERISA 403(b) annuity, would be $9,000). However, aggregation of the two 403(b) annuities results in a maximum nontaxable loan total of $10,000, and Josh has already borrowed $8,500.

The Code's aggregation rule will not override the ERISA adequate security requirement. Thus, a participant's vested balance in a non-ERISA 403(b) annuity should not be counted to satisfy the ERISA 50 percent limit.

The reverse situation holds more promise. Using the Code's aggregation rule, one could count a participant's nonforfeitable account balance in an employer's ERISA 403(b) plan to determine the maximum nontaxable loan from the participant's non-ERISA 403(b) annuity under the Code's 50 percent limit.

Q 11:10   Should a participant's vested interest in a public employer's eligible Section 457 deferred compensation plan be counted in applying the loan limits to plans of that employer?

Since the passage of the Small Business Job Protection Act of 1996 [Pub L 104–188] (SBJPA), there has been considerable debate over whether loans are now permitted under governmental 457(b) plans, with such debate fueled by a favorable reference in the legislative history to the SBJPA. [HR Conf Rep No 104–737, at 250 (1996)] In proposed regulations published recently for Section 457(b) plans, the IRS appears to have concluded in favor of such loans and at least their permissive coverage by Section 72(p). [Prop Treas Reg § 1.457-6(f), 67 Fed Reg 30826 (May 8, 2002)] It should be noted that it is still possible for the IRS to take a different position in the final regulations. However, the affirmative answer regarding loans in eligible governmental deferred compensation plans is also referenced in the preamble to the amendments to Treasury Regulations Section 1.72(p)-1 [67 Fed Reg 71824]. If loans from these plans are permitted, and the loans are subjected to the requirements of Section 72(p), it would appear clear that such plan balances should also be counted when applying the limits of Section 72(p) to loans, plans, or arrangements sponsored by the employer.

Q 11:11   How do the loan limits apply when a new loan is used to repay or refinance an existing loan?

Whenever a loan is replaced with another loan, that replacement is considered a refinancing. [Treas Reg § 1.72(p)-1, Q&A 20, as revised in the corrections to final regulations published in 68 Fed Reg 9532 (Feb 28, 2002)] A refinancing can include a loan transfer (see Q 11:29) when any terms of the original loan are being changed. Whether a transfer involves the transfer of the original loan or the replacement of the original loan by a new loan will likely depend on the circumstances. In the event of a refinancing, the loans (old and new) must satisfy the amount limitations in the Code, based on the account value at the time of the refinancing. How those limits apply, however, depends on whether the repayment period has been lengthened beyond the maximum allowable period for the original loan (which period may be greater than the actual remaining loan term).

If the repayment period has not been lengthened beyond the original loan's maximum allowable repayment period, the refinanced loan is tested as a single loan for purposes of applying the loan limitations. If the repayment period has been lengthened beyond the original loan's maximum allowable repayment period, the original loan must be counted twice in applying the loan limitations —once as part of the new loan and again as the original loan—*unless* the new loan payments are sufficient to repay the original loan over the maximum allowable repayment period for the original loan. [Treas Reg § 1.72(p), Q&A 20]

> **Note.** It is acceptable to reamortize a loan at a new interest rate when, for example, a participant takes advantage of falling interest rates to reduce the required loan payment. In addition, if the remaining loan term is shortened, the original loan is counted only once.

> **Example 11-3.** Denise Sanchez received a loan of $19,000 from her 403(b) annuity nine months ago. Her quarterly payments are $1,161.98. The current loan balance is $16,607. Her nonforfeitable account balance is $122,000. She wants to take a new loan of $35,000, repayable in quarterly installments over five years, and use a portion of the loan to repay her existing outstanding loan.

> To pay off the additional loan amount over 60 months would require quarterly repayments of $1,124.86, based on the interest rate under her loan agreement. If her quarterly payments for the remaining portion of the original loan term (51 months) are at least $2,286.84 ($1,161.98 for the original loan, plus an additional $1,124.86 for the additional loan amount), then the new loan will be treated as two separate loans, and the maximum new loan is $47,607 ($50,000 − $2,393, where $2,393 represents the difference between her maximum loan in the last 12 months and her current loan balance). If her quarterly payments for the first 51 months of the new loan are less than $2,286.84, then both the old loan and the total new loan will be considered to be outstanding at the time the new loan is taken, and the loan

limit will be $31,000 ($50,000 – $2,393 – $16,607), resulting in $4,000 of the new $35,000 loan being treated as a deemed distribution.

Example 11-3.1. Donald Burns received a 15-year principal residence loan under the terms of his ERISA 403(b) annuity contract nine years ago. The current loan balance is $30,000, and Donald's account balance is $90,000. Donald's largest outstanding loan balance in the past 12 months is $34,000. He wants to take advantage of lower interest rates provided on new loans and borrow an additional $15,000. He replaces his original loan with a single $45,000 loan, repayable in level quarterly installments over five years. Donald's new loan term does not exceed the maximum allowable loan term for the original loan. As a result, the original loan is only counted once, as part of the new loan, in applying the loan limitations, and his new loan satisfies the loan limits.

Q 11:12   May a participant take more than one loan?

Yes, subject to any limits imposed by the plan or the underlying investment. The 2002 amendments to Treasury Regulations Section 1.72(p)-1, when they were in proposed form, would have limited a participant to two loans from a 403(b) plan in any year. The limitation on the number of loans was removed when the amendments were published in final form. [See 67 Fed Reg 71823]

Q 11:12.1   May plan loans be extended using a credit card?

The preamble to the 2002 amendments to Treasury Regulations Section 1.72(p)-1 indicates that because no limit is imposed on the number of loans that a participant may take, there is "no section 72(p) barrier to credit card loans that otherwise meet the requirements of that section." [See 67 Fed Reg 71823] The preamble does not (and could not), however, attempt to address any plan or ERISA issues that might arise, or any issues that might arise under state insurance law with respect to such loans under an annuity contract issued under the plan.

Repayment Requirements

Q 11:17   May repayment be suspended during a leave of absence?

In some cases, this level amortization can be suspended for up to a year, if permitted by the plan or the contract, in the event of a leave of absence. However, the suspension is allowed only if the participant's pay during the leave (after reduction for income and employment tax withholding) is insufficient to make the scheduled loan payments. [Treas Reg § 1.72(p)-1, Q&A 9] It appears that this exception applies only if the loan agreement so provides. Otherwise, a missed payment would trigger taxation of the entire loan (see Q 11:25). If this "leave of absence" exception is used, the loan must still be repaid within not more than five years (or longer, for a principal-residence loan). Repayment after the leave of absence can be accomplished by either:

1. Making larger payments after the leave, to repay the loan within the period previously established; or

2. Making payments not less than the regularly scheduled payments, and repaying the entire remaining loan balance within the maximum period allowed for loans of that type.

Suspension of repayment may also be permitted during a period when the participant is performing services in the uniformed military services. [IRC § 414(u)] The suspension applies only if the plan so provides. Upon suspension, the loan repayment period may be extended up to the loan's maximum repayment period at the time the loan was issued, plus the length of the suspension period.

> **Example 11-3.2.** When Janet Hirsch entered the uniformed military service, she had an outstanding loan under her 403(b) annuity contract. She had taken the loan a year earlier, for a two-year repayment period. Janet returned from military service two years later. Upon her return, the maximum permissible repayment period for her annuity contract loan (assuming no additional plan limitations) was four years. The maximum repayment period initially was five years, three years longer than the original repayment period. Two of the five years remained when Janet returned from uniformed military service. Including the two years of military service, Janet has a maximum repayment period of four years.

In the wake of the terrorist attacks of September 11, 2001, the IRS has also issued a list of deadlines for time-sensitive acts that may be postponed in future guidance under Code Sections 7508 and 7508A, relating to acts required of individuals serving in the armed forces or in support of such armed forces in combat and taxpayers affected by a presidentially declared disaster. [Rev Proc 2001-53, 2001-47 IRB 506] Among those deadlines listed are the repayment requirements under Code Section 72(p). This IRS pronouncement does not by itself extend a repayment deadline; however, it does indicate that the IRS may extend such a deadline in the future. The IRS subsequently provided relief under Code Section 7508A, including relief for certain affected participants with loans. If the last day to perform an act, including the making of a loan payment, fell within the period from September 11, 2001, and November 30, 2001, then the deadline for performing that act was extended by 120 days. [IRS Notice 2001-68; 2001-47 IRB 504]

Q 11:18 What is the maximum term of a plan loan?

The loan agreement must require repayment within five years unless the loan proceeds are used to acquire a dwelling unit that will, within a reasonable time, be used as the participant's principal residence. [IRC § 72(p)(2)(B)]

Principal-residence loans need not be secured by the principal residence. However, see Q 11:15 regarding the deductibility of interest on a principal-residence loan.

No specific repayment period is required for principal-residence loans; however, the loan repayment period must be a reasonable term, which may be at least 15 years. [See Example, Treas Reg § 1.72(p)-1, Q&A 8]

Consequences of Failure to Repay

Q 11:28   If a participant's account includes a loan that has been defaulted but not foreclosed, offset, or repaid, can the participant take an additional nontaxable loan?

Yes, but only if there is an agreement between the employer, the participant, and the plan providing for repayment of the loan by way of payroll deduction. [Treas Reg § 1.72(p)-1, Q&A 19, as revised by corrections under 68 Fed Reg 9532] The payroll-deduction requirement would be waived if the loan were secured by additional collateral held outside the plan. Termination of the mandatory payroll deduction before the new loan is repaid would result in taxation of the entire outstanding balance of that loan. For purposes of this requirement, it would not seem to matter whether the prior defaulted loan had been foreclosed, offset, or repaid before the termination of the payroll deduction.

Transfers

Q 11:30   May a participant loan be transferred to a 403(b) annuity as part of a rollover from another 403(b) annuity or from a non-403(b) plan (such as a 401(a), 403(a), 401(k), or governmental 457(b) plan)?

Yes. [Treas Reg § 1.401(a)(31)-1, Q&A 16; Treas Reg § 1.403(b)-2, Q&A 2] The IRS has recognized such a transfer between two employer-sponsored 401(k) plans in one private ruling that suggests the IRS may be willing to consider a transfer of a promissory note as part of an otherwise valid rollover. In Letter Ruling 9729042, the IRS concluded that a transfer of a promissory note to a new obligee, along with a change in repayment frequency (from weekly to semi-monthly) would not be taxable to the participant and would not cause the loan to be treated as a new loan for testing purposes (see SQ 11:32). The ruling addressed a rollover between two 401(k) plans. Assuming exactly the same circumstances, it would be reasonable to expect any IRS position favoring such a rollover to be applied in the same fashion to a rollover between 403(b) annuities.

Q 11:31   Must a 403(b) arrangement allow transfers or rollovers to another 403(b) arrangement?

Revenue Ruling 90-24 [1990-1 CB 97] does not require either 403(b) plans or 403(b) investments to make or accept trustee transfers requested by an employer, a participant, or a beneficiary. However, a refusal to permit the transfer must be consistent with other applicable laws as well as with the terms of the contract (in the case of an annuity contract). There is no legal requirement that an obligee agree to distribute and transfer a loan in a rollover distribution.

Q 11:32   If the participant transfers a loan, will it be treated as a new loan?

Generally, the loan should not be treated as a new loan unless a substantive term is changed in the transfer that would cause the transfer to be a renegotiation, extension, renewal, or revision of the original loan. If such a substantive term is changed, then it will be treated as a new loan as of the date of the transfer. [TRA '86 § 1134(e); Ltr Rul 8950008]

In the course of a loan transfer, it can be important to be aware of the precise terms of the existing loan in order to avoid potential problems with qualifying the transferred loan as a new loan. Several factors may be different between the existing and the proposed new loan structure, including the charging and crediting of interest, as well as the repayment frequency and repayment methodology.

If the terms of the original promissory note are transferred intact, so that the transfer consists solely of a change of obligee (the party to which the payments are to be paid), then there would not appear to be a basis for considering the loan to be a new loan for purposes of applicable Code limitations and requirements. That would be consistent with the approach taken under TRA '86, for determining whether an existing loan would become subject to new TRA '86 requirements. However, if a substantive term is changed in the transfer, such as the interest rate or the repayment term, for example, the loan may be subject to retesting under applicable requirements. Whether it also becomes a new loan for determining whether the refinancing rules in the proposed regulation would apply appears to be an open question. See SQ 11:11 for a discussion of the rules applicable to refinanced loans.

If a transferred loan is treated as a new loan because a substantive term is changed, the loan still might not be taxable upon transfer. Whether it is taxable will depend on whether the new loan, and the associated account, can satisfy the current loan limitations. See SQ 11:11 for a discussion of the rules set out in the regulations. In addition, if a previously valid loan term (e.g., five years) is shortened in the transferred loan, this change, while making it a new loan, should not by itself cause the loan to be taxable.

If the loan being transferred was a principal-residence loan, it could continue to be a principal-residence loan only if:

1. The loan was considered a transferred loan; or
2. The loan was considered a new loan for testing purposes, but still satisfied the tracing rules applicable to principal-residence loans (see Q 11:19).

Life Insurance

Correction of Defects under the IRS VCT Program

Q 11:47   If a plan fails to satisfy the incidental benefit requirement, may this defect be corrected in one of the self-correction or IRS-approved correction alternatives now available to 403(b) programs?

Yes, it may, provided that the other requirements of the selected program are met. If for any participant the premiums for life insurance exceed the limits and violate the incidental benefit requirements, this can cause that participant's annuities to cease to qualify under Section 403(b). Such a defect might be corrected by the employer, or might be included in a submission under the IRS Voluntary Correction of Tax-Sheltered Annuity Failures. [Rev Proc 2002-47, 2002-29 IRB 133]

Chapter 12

Beneficiary Designations

Peter J. Gulia, Esq.
CitiStreet Retirement Services

Making a beneficiary designation is an important part of estate planning. While a 403(b) benefit will not pass by a will, a beneficiary designation affects the individual's overall estate plan. This chapter focuses on a participant's use of his or her valuable right to name a beneficiary and explains some of the opportunities and limitations in making a beneficiary designation, including marriage and family rights that restrain a beneficiary designation. In addition, this chapter includes some basic information concerning estate and inheritance taxes. Many people assume that they lack sufficient wealth for estate tax issues to be of concern, but that assumption often is incorrect.

This chapter uses the popular expression *probate* to refer to property that is transferred through a court-supervised administration or succession and *nonprobate* to refer to property that is transferred or contract rights provided without such an administration. This chapter uses the term *payer* to refer to a trustee, custodian, insurer, plan administrator, or other person responsible to decide or pay a claim under a governmental plan.

Making a Beneficiary Designation

Q 12:1   Is a 403(b) benefit disposed by a participant's will?

No. A 403(b) annuity contract or custodial account will include a provision by which the participant may designate his or her beneficiary or beneficiaries. The beneficiary designation applies even if the participant's will attempts to state a contrary disposition. [See, e.g., Metropolitan Life Ins Co v O'Donnell, 11 Del Ch 404, 102 A 163, 165 (Del Ch 1917); McCarthy v Aetna Life Ins Co, 92 NY 2d 436, 704 NE 2d 557, 681 NYS 2d 790 (NY Ct App 1998); Riley v Wirth, 313 Pa 362, 169 A 139 (Pa 1933); Equitable Life Assur Soc'y v Stitzel, 299 Pa Super 199, 203, 445 A 2d 523 (Pa Super 1982)] Indeed, if a beneficiary change could be effected by the participant's will, a responsible insurer or custodian would be unwilling to make any payment until a court had determined the correct distribution of a participant's estate or at least had appointed an executor. [See, e.g., Stone v Stephens, 155 Ohio 595, 600–601, 99 NE 2d 766, 25 ALR 2d 992 (Ohio 1951)] Although such a conclusion results simply from applying the terms of the 403(b) contract, some states for convenience include an explicit provision in the probate statute. [See, e.g., Massachusetts General Laws Chapter 167D, § 30; New York Estates, Powers and Trusts Law § 13-3.2; 20 Pennsylvania CS § 8704; see generally Uniform Probate Code §§ 1-201(4), 6-101(a)(3), 6-104, 6-201] Even without a statute, courts have held that a will cannot override a beneficiary designation. [Moss v Warren, 43 Cal App 3d 651, 117 Cap Rptr 796 (1974); Strohsahl v Equitable Life Assurance Soc'y of United States, 71 NJ Super 300, 176 A 2d 814 (Chancery Div 1962); Cook v Cook, 17 Cal 2d 639, 111 P 2d 322 (1941)]

To the extent that a 403(b) arrangement is not subject to the Employee Retirement Income Security Act of 1974 (ERISA), state law may supplement the contract's or account's provisions concerning the manner of making a beneficiary designation. For instance, New York law requires that a beneficiary designation be signed. [New York Estates, Powers and Trusts Law § 13-3.2]

To the extent that a 403(b) arrangement is subject to ERISA, only the plan's provisions govern a beneficiary designation. [ERISA § 514]

Q 12:2   Who may make a beneficiary designation?

Ordinarily, only the participant may make a beneficiary designation. However, a 403(b) contract may permit a beneficiary to name a further contingent beneficiary if the 403(b) participant had not designated all of the 403(b) benefit. [See Ltr Rul 199936052 (June 16, 1999)(concerning an IRA)]

Such a provision can cause the 403(b) benefit that remains undistributed at each beneficiary's death to be subject to federal estate tax and state inheritance tax, notwithstanding that the same benefit was previously taxed upon the participant's death. [IRC § 2041(a)(2); Treas Reg § 20.2041-1(b)] A federal estate tax may be postponed if the beneficiary names his or her spouse as the succeeding beneficiary and that spouse has power to take the entire remaining benefit. [IRC § 2056; Ltr Rul 199936052 (June 16, 1999)]

A more typical 403(b) contract provision for a situtation in which there is no other designated beneficiary provides any undistributed benefit to the personal representative of the participant's estate (see Q 12:7). Although the participant's estate may have been closed before this time, the estate may be reopened for subsequent administration upon the discovery of property that was not disposed by the previous administration. [See generally, Uniform Probate Code § 3-1008]

> **Practice Pointer.** A prudent participant would make a complete beneficiary designation that contemplates all possibilities. A participant who does not wish to specify the alternate takers could create a trust, which could include a power of appointment for a beneficiary to name a further beneficiary.

Q 12:2.1 Why should a participant read a beneficiary designation form?

Plan administrators, custodians, and insurers design beneficiary designation forms anticipating the possibility that a participant might give incomplete or ambiguous instructions. For example, many forms provide that if a participant has not specified how to divide his or her retirement account, the account will be divided among all beneficiaries in equal shares.

A beneficiary designation form might include other "gap-fillers" or "default" provisions, some of which might be surprising to a participant. For example, a beneficiary designation form might provide that a beneficiary change for an account will change the beneficiary for every account with the provider that is classified under the same Internal Revenue Code (Code) subsection. Some retirement plans provide that the beneficiary designated under a pension or life insurance plan be named the "default" beneficiary (see Q 12:7). Because such provisions might frustrate the participant's intent, a participant should complete with care his or her beneficiary designation form.

Q 12:6 Does the doctrine of substantial compliance apply to an ERISA plan?

If a plan is governed by ERISA, the doctrine of substantial compliance should apply only if the plan administrator in its discretion decides to use such a concept to aid its own interpretation or administration of the plan.

To determine the beneficiary under an ERISA plan, a court should hold that any state's doctrine of substantial compliance is preempted. [ERISA § 514; see Egelhoff v Egelhoff, 532 US 141, 121 S Ct 1322, 69 USLW 4206 (2001); see, e.g., Phoenix Mutual Life Ins Co v Adams, 30 F 3d 554 (4th Cir 1994); Continental Assurance Co v Davis, 24 EBC (BNA)2273, 2000 WL 1141434, 2000 US Dist LEXIS 810 (ND Ill Aug 11, 2000); Metropolitan Life Ins Co v Hall, 9 F Supp 2d 560 (D Md 1998); Fortis Benefits Ins Co v Johnson, 966 F Supp 987 (D Nev 1997); First Capital Life Ins Co v AAA Communications Inc, 906 F Supp 1546 (ND Ga 1995)] However, two federal courts have held that a state's common-law doctrine of substantial compliance supplements an ERISA plan's provisions. [BankAmerica Pension Plan v McMath, 206 F 3d 821, 24 EBC (BNA) 1686, (1999); *cert denied* 121 S Ct 358 (2000); Peckham v Gem State Mutual of Utah, 964 F 2d 1043 (10th Cir 1992)] In the absence of findings by the plan administrator, the Fourth Circuit found that a state's doctrine of substantial compliance may be replaced by a federal common-law doctrine of substantial compliance. [Phoenix Mutual Life Ins Co v Adams, 30 F 3d 554 (4th Cir 1994)] Although two of three federal circuits considering the question have held that ERISA does not necessarily preempt a state's doctrine of substantial compliance, the author's view is that ERISA preempts any such law relating to an ERISA plan. [ERISA § 514]

> **Practice Pointer.** Unless a plan provision is contrary to ERISA, an ERISA plan administrator must administer a plan according to the plan's documents. [ERISA § 404(a)] Therefore, if a plan states that any doctrine of substantial compliance will not apply, the plan administrator must interpret and administer the plan without using such a doctrine.

Further, if a plan grants the plan administrator discretion in interpreting or administering the plan, a court will not interfere with the plan administrator's decision unless it was an abuse of discretion. [See Firestone Tire & Rubber Co v Bruch, 489 US 101(1989); Nelson v EG&G; Energy Measurements Group Inc, 37 F 3d 1384 (9th Cir 1994); see, e.g., Clouse v Philadelphia Elec Co, 787 F Supp 93, 15 EBC (BNA) 1347 (ED Pa 1992)]

Q 12:8   Does a divorce revoke a beneficiary designation?

Whether a divorce revokes a beneficiary designation turns on (1) whether ERISA or state law governs the retirement plan, (2) which state's law (if any) applies, and (3) what that state's law (when applicable) provides.

If the 403(b) arrangement is not part of an ERISA plan, state law may apply. In many states, a divorce will not revoke a beneficiary designation that names the ex-spouse. [In the Matter of the Declaration of Death of Dominick Santos Jr, 282 NJ Super 509, 660 A 2d 1206 (1995); Hughes v Scholl, 900 SW 2d 606 (KY 1995); Stiles v Stiles, 21 Mass App Ct 514, 487 NE 2d 874 (1986); O'Toole v Central Laborers' Pension & Welfare Funds, 12 Ill App 3d 995, 299 NE 2d 392 (1973); Gerhard v Travelers Ins Co, 107 NJ Super 414, 258 A 2d 724 (Chancery Div 1969)] Some states have statutory provisions that attempt to provide that a divorce or annulment has the effect of making the former spouse not a beneficiary except as otherwise specified by a court order. [See, e.g., Minn Stat Ann § 524.2-804 (Westlaw 2003); see generally Uniform Probate Code § 2-804(b)] Even when the relevant state has such a statute, it may not apply if the contract or account has contrary provisions, and many contracts include a provision that a divorce or anything other than a beneficiary change form accepted by the insurer or custodian has no effect on the beneficiary designation. In any case, state law will protect a payer that pays the beneficiary of record unless the payer has received a court order restraining payment or at least a written notice that states a dispute about who is the lawful beneficiary. [See, e.g., 20 Pennsylvania CS § 8704; see generally Uniform Probate Code §§ 2-804(g), 2-804(h)]

For a 403(b) arrangement that is part of an ERISA plan, ERISA preempts all state laws. [ERISA § 514] Therefore, only the plan's terms will govern whether a divorce or other circumstance has any effect on the plan beneficiary designation. [ERISA §§ 404(a), 514; Egelhoff v Egelhoff, 121 S Ct 1322, 69 USLW 4206 (2001); Boggs v Boggs, 520 US 833, 117 S Ct 1754, 138 L Ed 2d 45, 65 USLW 4418, 21 EBC (BNA) 1047, Pens Plan Guide (CCH) ¶23934N (1997), *reh'g denied*, 138 L Ed 2d 1043, 66 USLW 3128 (1997)]

Practice Pointer. A plan sponsor should consider whether it might be helpful for a plan to expressly state that any annulment, divorce, marital separation, or other event or circumstance has no effect under the plan.

Practice Pointer. After a divorce, a participant should remember to change or confirm his or her beneficiary designation.

Q 12:10   Who is taxed on the 403(b) distribution set aside for the care of a pet animal?

If a 403(b) distribution is paid to a pet's caretaker who does not serve as a trustee, the distribution is that individual's income.

If a 403(b) distribution is paid to a trustee who serves under a valid trust, the distribution is the trust's income. A valid pet trust that is legally unenforceable will nevertheless be treated as a trust for federal income tax purposes.

The pet trust is subject to federal income tax at the rates that apply to a married individual who files a separate return. Although a trust normally has a deduction in the amount of trust distributions, "since the amounts of income required to be distributed . . . and amounts properly paid, credited, or required to be distributed under [the relevant Internal Revenue Code sections] are limited to distributions intended for beneficiaries, a deduction under those sections is not available for distributions for the benefit of a pet animal. Similarly, such distributions are not taxed to anyone. . . ." [Rev Rul 76-476, 1976-2 CB 192] These rules are consistent with the idea that trust income generally should not be taxed more than once, but should be taxed.

Using Trusts

Q 12:11 Can a participant own his or her 403(b) contract in a living trust?

No. Because a living trust can be revoked or amended, the trust declaration or agreement could not ensure that during the participant's lifetime the 403(b) benefit will be used only for the participant's benefit. The rights under a 403(b) contract must be nonforfeitable for the participant. [IRC § 403(b)(1)(C)]

Practice Pointer. There is no particularly good reason to put a 403(b) contract into a living trust. A 403(b) contract already is nonprobate property that will pass according to its beneficiary designation.

Q 12:12 Can a trust be a beneficiary of a 403(b) contract?

Yes. A participant may name a trust as beneficiary of a 403(b) contract or account. The trust must be legally in existence (or completed such that it would be legally in existence upon the trustee's receipt of money or property) before the participant makes the beneficiary designation.

To make a correct beneficiary designation, the participant should designate the trustee, as trustee of the trust, as beneficiary. Even if that is not done, insurers and custodians should treat a designation of the trust as though it were a designation of the duly appointed and then-currently serving trustee of the trust.

A beneficiary of a trust will not be a designated beneficiary for the purpose of extending life expectancy when measuring minimum distribution and incidental benefit requirements unless the trust meets specified requirements and certain information is certified to the plan administrator (if any). [Treas Reg § 1.401(a)(9)-1, Q&A D-5] (See chapter 10.)

Family Rights That Restrain a Beneficiary Designation

Q 12:16 May a non-ERISA 403(b) participant make a beneficiary designation that does not provide for his or her spouse?

Usually yes. To the extent that a 403(b) contract is not subject to ERISA or to any plan provision, an insurer or custodian will, in the absence of any court order or written notice of a dispute, give effect to a participant's beneficiary designation.

If the participant's spouse did not receive his or her share provided by state law, any distributee may be liable to the participant's executor or surviving spouse to the extent that state law provides for a spouse's elective share to be payable from nonprobate property. [See, e.g., New York Estates, Powers, and Trusts Law § 5-1.1; see also La Rev Stat Ann §§ 23:638, 23:652; La Civ Code Ann art 1505; TL James & Co v Montgomery; 332 So 2d 834 (La 1976); see generally Uniform Probate Code § 2-204 (1998)]

In Louisiana, a plan administrator may follow a participant's beneficiary designation. [La Rev Stat §§ 23:638, 23:652] A distributee who receives benefits under a nongovernmental and non-ERISA 403(b) arrangement must account for and pay over benefits to the participant's surviving spouse to the extent that payment is necessary to satisfy the spouse's community property rights and usufruct. [TL James & Co v Montgomery, 332 So 2d 834 (La 1976)] A distributee who receives benefits under a retirement plan of "any public or governmental employer," is not subject to the claims of forced heirs. [La Civ Code Ann art 1505]

Different law may apply for members of a native American tribe. [Jones v Meehan, 175 US 1 (1899); see also Davis v Shanks, 15 Minn 369 (1870); Hasting v Farmer, 4 NY 293 (1850); Dole v Irish, 2 Barb 639 (1848)] However, a native American tribe's law usually applies between or among members of the tribe and often cannot be enforced against persons outside the tribe.

Q 12:17 Can a participant make a beneficiary designation that does not provide for his or her child?

In the United States, only Louisiana and Puerto Rico have a forced kinship provision in favor of descendants and other heirs. [See La Rev Civil Code, art 1493–1495; PR Laws title 31 § 2362, §§ 2411–2463] Therefore, a participant usually may disinherit his or her children. In some jurisdictions, a family allowance may be required for the surviving spouse or, if there is no surviving spouse, the decedent's children. [See generally Uniform Probate Code § 2-403]

In Louisiana, a plan administrator may follow the participant's beneficiary designation. [La Rev Stat §§ 23:638, 23:652] A distributee who receives benefits under a nongovernmental (and non-ERISA) plan or arrangement must account for and pay over benefits to the participant's surviving spouse to the extent that payment is necessary to satisfy the spouse's community property rights and usufruct and to the participant's children or forced heirs to the extent that payment is necessary to satisfy their légitime. [TL James & Co v Montgomery, 332 So 2d 834 (La 1976)] A distributee who receives benefits under a retirement plan of "any public or governmental employer" is not subject to the claims of forced heirs. [La Civ Code Ann art 1505]

Different law may apply for members of a native American tribe. [Jones v Meehan, 175 US 1 (1899); see also Davis v Shanks, 15 Minn 369 (1870); Hasting v Farmer, 4 NY 293 (1850); Dole v Irish, 2 Barb 639 (1848)]

Whether it is called légitime, legitimate portions, or compulsory portions in civil-law nations, family provision or family maintenance in nations following English law, or ahl al-farā'id under the Koran, in most nations other than the United States of America, an individual is limited in his or her right or privilege to "disinherit" his or her children. [See, e.g., Egypt, Law of Testamentary

Dispositions of 1946, Law of Inheritance of 1943; England and Wales, Inheritance (Provision for Family and Dependants) Act 1975; India-Pakistan, Muslim Family Laws Ordinance of 1961]

Practice Pointer. A retirement plan participant who resides in a nation other than the United States of America should consult an expert lawyer before he or she makes a beneficiary designation that does not provide for his or her spouse and children.

ERISA Survivor Benefits

Q 12:17.1 What benefits must an ERISA plan provide to a participant's spouse?

For a distribution that begins before a participant's death, a plan must, unless an exception applies, provide a qualified joint and survivor annuity (see SQ 12:17.2). [ERISA § 205(a)(1), 205(b)]

Ordinarily, a defined contribution plan that is not governed by ERISA funding standards need not provide a qualified joint and survivor annuity (QJSA) as long as a participant does not elect that his or her retirement benefit be paid as a life annuity. [ERISA § 205(b)(1)(C)(ii)]

Practice Pointer. If a plan provides a life annuity as a normal form of benefit, a plan sponsor may amend the plan to provide that every annuity is an optional form of benefit or to eliminate every annuity option. Such an amendment is not a cutback of accrued benefits. [ERISA § 204(g)(2)(B); Treas Reg § 1.411(d)-4, Q&A-2(e)] Once the amendment is effective, the plan need not provide a QJSA unless (if the plan permits) a participant affirmatively chooses it or chooses a different life annuity and fails to deliver a qualified election.

Caution. Some practitioners suggest designing or amending a plan to preclude annuity options. Moreover, some suggest that a plan not provide any form of benefit beyond a single sum. Although nothing in ERISA restrains a plan sponsor from making such a provision or amendment, a plan sponsor might consider whether an absence of some options would make it difficult or impossible to obtain favorable treatment under state income tax laws. [See, e.g., NY Tax Law §§ 612, 617-a; 72 PS § 7303; 61 Pa Code § 101.6(c); Bickford v Commonwealth, 533 A2d 822 (Pa 1987)]

For a distribution that begins after a participant's death, a plan must provide a qualified preretirement survivor annuity (see SQ 12:17.3) or an alternate survivor benefit (see SQ 12:17.4). [ERISA § 205(a)(2), 205(b)]

Q 12:17.2 What is a qualified joint and survivor annuity?

A qualified joint and survivor annuity (QJSA) is an annuity for the participant's life with a survivor annuity for his or her surviving spouse's life. The periodic payment of the survivor annuity must be no less than 50 percent (and no more than 100 percent) of the payment during the joint lives of the participant and his or her spouse. A QJSA is the actuarial equivalent of an annuity only on the participant's life. [ERISA § 205(d)]

Q 12:17.3   What is a qualified preretirement survivor annuity?

For a defined contribution plan, a qualified preretirement survivor annuity (QPSA) is the annuity that results from using not less than half the participant's vested account balance to buy an annuity for the surviving spouse's life. [ERISA § 205(e)(2)]

Q 12:17.4   What is an alternative survivor benefit?

A defined contribution plan that is not governed by ERISA funding standards may omit both a QJSA and a QPSA if the plan (in addition to meeting other conditions) provides that, absent a qualified election (see SQ 12:17.5), the benefit that remains after a participant's death belongs to the participant's surviving spouse. [ERISA § 205(b)(1)(C)]

Q 12:17.5   What is a qualified election?

A Section 403(b) plan governed by ERISA may include a provision that assures a participant's surviving spouse some retirement income after the participant's death and must include a provision that assures a survivor benefit if the participant dies before plan distributions begin. [ERISA § 205] A plan must permit a participant to "waive" one or more of these benefits. [ERISA § 205(c)(1)(A)] To do so, the participant must deliver to the plan administrator a qualified election. [ERISA § 205(c)(2)] Ordinarily, such an election has no effect unless the participant's spouse consents to the election. [ERISA § 205(c)(2)(A)] Also, a participant's qualified election must meet several form, content, and procedure requirements.

Q 12:17.6   What must a spouse do to consent to a participant's qualified election?

In addition to meeting other form, content, and procedure requirements, a spouse's consent to a participant's election (see SQ 12:17.5) must

1. Be in writing;
2. Name a beneficiary that cannot be changed without the spouse's consent or expressly consent to the participant's beneficiary designations (without further consent); and
3. Acknowledge the effect of the participant's election.

[ERISA § 205(c)(2)(A)(i)]

Further, a consent has no effect unless "the spouse's consent . . . is witnessed by a plan representative or a notary public[.]" [ERISA § 205(c)(2)(A)(iii)] A premarital agreement cannot serve as a spouse's consent.

The courts have held that a plan administrator must comply with these requirements. [See, e.g., McMillan v Parrott, 913 F 2d 310 (6th Cir 1990); Lasche v George W Lasche Basic Retirement Plan, 870 F Supp 336, 338, Pens Plan Guide (CCH) ¶ 23905L (SD Fla 1994)]

Q 12:17.7   May a spouse's guardian sign the spouse's consent?

Yes. Even if the electing participant is the spouse's guardian, he or she may give the spouse's consent. [Treas Reg § 1.401(a)-20, Q&A-27] However, a guardian must act in the best interests of his or her ward. A guardian serves under a court's supervision and must account for his or her actions in court. Further, some guardianship decisions require a court's approval before the guardian implements the decision. [See, e.g., Uniform Probate Code § 206] It may be difficult to persuade a court that turning away money is in a surviving spouse's best interest. Although a participant may suggest making an irrevocable designation naming a trust for his or her spouse's benefit as the plan beneficiary, most retirement plans do not permit an irrevocable beneficiary designation.

Q 12:17.8   Does a notary witness an acknowledgment or an affidavit?

The text of ERISA Section 205 is ambiguous concerning whether a plan representative or notary need witness only the spouse signing his or her acknowledgment that he or she signed the consent or must witness the spouse's signing of the consent. [ERISA § 205(c)(2)(A)(iii)] An acknowledgment would be consistent with ERISA's provisions concerning the form of a survivor benefit explanation and spouse's consent and a plan administrator's fiduciary duty to administer the plan. [ERISA §§ 205, 404(a)(1)] Likewise, an acknowledgment would be consistent with a plan administrator's procedure of furnishing the form on which a spouse may sign his or her consent. But the IRS's model-form clause for the witness suggests that the model-form consent is an affidavit. [Notice 97-10, 1997-1 CB 370]

Q 12:17.9   Who is a plan representative?

ERISA does not define its use of the term *plan representative.* [ERISA §§ 3, 205] Nor does the legislative history of the Retirement Equity Act of 1984 explain what Congress meant by a plan representative. [S Rep No 98-575 to accompany HR 4280, 98th Cong, 2d Sess (1984), *reprinted in* 1984 USCCAN 2547, 2560]

Many practitioners assume that a person is a plan representative for the limited purpose of administering a plan's provisions required or permitted by ERISA Section 205 if the plan administrator has authorized the person to witness a spouse's consent.

In a case that involved facts and forms typical of a retirement plan's service arrangements, a federal court found that the litigants who asserted that a spouse's consent had been witnessed did not offer enough evidence even to allege that a securities broker-dealer's employee was a plan representative. [Lasche v George W Lasche Basic Retirement Plan, 870 F Supp 336, 339, Pens Plan Guide (CCH) ¶ 23905L (SD Fla 1994)]

Q 12:17.10 Who is a notary?

ERISA does not define its use of the term *notary public.* [ERISA §§ 3, 205] Nor does the legislative history of the Retirement Equity Act of 1984 explain what Congress meant by a notary public. [S Rep No 98-575 to accompany HR 4280, 98th Cong, 2d Sess (1984), *reprinted in* 1984 USCCAN 2547, 2560]

Many practitioners assume that Congress intended to describe a person state law recognizes as one whose certificate that he or she witnessed an acknowledgment will be recognized as conclusive evidence that the acknowledgment was made. Usually, a recognized official's certificate that he or she witnessed an acknowledgment is conclusive evidence that the acknowledgment was made. [See generally Uniform Acknowledgment Act §§ 9–10] In most states, an acknowledgment may be made before a judge, court clerk, recorder of deeds, or notary. [See generally Uniform Acknowledgment Act §§ 2–3] In New Jersey, for example, a lawyer, if he or she is a licensed attorney, may certify an acknowledgment or affidavit. [NJSA § 41:2-1]

Q 12:17.11 How may a person present in a foreign nation make an acknowledgment?

When a person is not present in the United States, his or her acknowledgment may be made before a United States ambassador, consul, consular officer, or consular agent. [22 USC §§ 4215, 4221; see also Succession of Justus, 48 La Ann 1096, 20 So 680 (La 1896); Jermann v Tenneas, 44 La Ann 620, 11 So 80 (La 1892); Andrews v Chapman, 10 Rob 188 (La 1845); Ferrers v Bosel, 10 Mart (os) 35 (La 1821); Savage v Birckhead, 20 Pick 167 (Mass 1838); Scanlon v Wright, 13 Pick 523 (Mass 1833); St. John v Croel, 5 Hill 573 (NY 1843); In re Mitzkel's Estate, 36 Misc2d 671, 233 NYS2d 519 (NY Sur 1962)] A consular officer must officiate and perform a notarial act that an applicant properly requests. [22 US § 4215; see also In re Mitzkel's Estate, 36 Misc2d 671, 233 NYS2d 519 (NY Sur 1962); see generally Uniform Acknowledgement Act § 4(1)]

Further, most state laws recognize an acknowledgment made before a judge, court clerk, or notary of the nation where the acknowledgment is made. [See generally Uniform Acknowledgement Act § 4(2)–(3)] It is unclear, however, whether a plan administrator would adopt such a rule. [ERISA §§ 404(a)(1)(D), 514(a)]

Q 12:17.12   How may a person in military service make an acknowledgment?

A person who is

1. A member of the armed forces;
2. A former member of the armed forces entitled to retired or retainer pay and legal assistance, or the dependent of an active or former member if the dependent is entitled to legal assistance;
3. A person "serving with, employed by, or accompanying the armed forces outside the United States"; or
4. A person subject to the Uniform Code of Military Justice outside the United States

may make his or her acknowledgment, affidavit, deposition, or other statement that calls for a notarial act before a military officer described below. [10 USC §§ 1044, 1044a(a)(1)–(4)]

The following persons may officiate and certify a notarial act:

1. A judge advocate or reserve judge advocate;
2. A civilian attorney who serves as a legal assistance attorney;
3. An adjutant, assistant adjutant, or personnel adjutant, whether on active or reserve duty; or
4. A person designated by another statute or by a regulation of any of the armed forces.

[10 USC § 1044a(b)(1)–(4)]

Further, most state laws recognize an acknowledgment that a person serving in any of the armed forces or his or her dependent, even if not entitled to military legal assistance, makes before a commissioned officer. [See generally Uniform Acknowledgement Act § 10.1] It is unclear, however, whether a plan administrator would adopt such a rule. [ERISA §§ 404(a)(1)(D), 514(a)]

Q 12:17.13   Must a notary be independent of the participant?

Yes. Although nothing in ERISA Section 205 requires that a witness to a spouse's consent be independent of the electing participant, at least two courts have interpreted the statute to include such a requirement:

> [T]he district court focused on the fact that the notary public before whom Mr. Jensen had purportedly signed the document was Mrs. Jensen herself—a circumstance that the court concluded would render the document ineffective as a spousal waiver. The court explained its thinking thus: "Generally, it is considered contrary to public policy for a notary to take an acknowledgement of an instrument to which he or she is a party. [citation omitted] [C]ongress, through the [Retirement Equity Act], wanted a spouse to carefully consider a decision to waive retirement benefits without pressure from the other spouse and so imposed

the requirement that the waiver be witnessed by a plan representative or a notary. To permit a spouse to act as notary to an instrument concerning their own benefits would appear to undermine this congressional intent."

[Howard v Branham & Baker Coal Co, No 91-5913, 968 F 2d 1214 (Table), 1992 WL 154571 slip op at 3 (6th Cir July 6, 1992) (unpublished disposition), *quoting and affirming* No 90-00115 (ED Ky) (unpublished order); *accord* Lasche v George W Lasche Basic Retirement Plan, 870 F Supp 336, 339, Pens Plan Guide (CCH) ¶ 23905L (SD Fla 1994)]

The federal courts' view is consistent with state laws concerning when a notary properly may officiate and the legal effect of a notary's certificate that he or she witnessed an acknowledgment. [1 Am Jur 2nd Acknowledgments § 16]

Q 12:17.14 Must a plan representative be independent of the participant?

Yes. Although nothing in ERISA Section 205 requires that a witness to a spouse's consent be independent of the electing participant, at least one Federal court has interpreted the statute to include such a requirement. A plan administrator who was the same person as the electing participant could not, even though he was a plan representative (or even if he was the only plan representative), witness his spouse's consent. [Lasche v George W Lasche Basic Retirement Plan, 870 F Supp 336, 339, Pens Plan Guide (CCH) ¶ 23905L (SD Fla 1994)]

Practice Pointer. If a lawyer or financial planner who advises a participant about making a beneficiary designation that would provide for anyone other than the participant's spouse knows that the participant also is a plan administrator, trustee, or other fiduciary, the lawyer or planner should advise the participant to ask his or her spouse to sign the consent in the presence of an independent notary. Failing to give that advice might be malpractice.

Because ERISA permits a plan administrator to rely on a spouse's consent witnessed by a notary, it seems unlikely that a federal court would find that it could be prudent for a plan administrator to rely on a spouse's consent witnessed only by the interested participant or someone who is subordinate to the interested participant. [ERISA §§ 205(c)(6), 404(a)(1)]

Q 12:17.15 What should a plan administrator do if it relied on a notary's false or incorrect certificate?

If a plan administrator acted according to ERISA's fiduciary duties when it decided to accept a spouse's consent, the consent (or purported consent), even if not properly witnessed, nonetheless discharges the plan from liability to the extent of the payments made before the plan administrator knew that the consent did not meet the requirements of ERISA Section 205 and of the plan. [ERISA § 205(c)(6)] If the plan administrator acted according to ERISA's fiduciary duties, it is not liable to the spouse. [ERISA § 404(a)(1)] Of course, the plan administrator must promptly correct or stop payments once it knows that a spouse's consent was not properly witnessed.

If a plan incurs an expense because the plan administrator relied on a notary's certificate, the plan's fiduciary may be under a duty to evaluate whether it is in the plan's best interest to pursue a claim or lawsuit against the notary. [ERISA § 404(a)(1)] A notary is responsible for damages caused by his or her negligent performance of his or her duties. [John D Perovich, Annotation, Liability of Notary Public or His Bond for Negligence in Performance of Duties, 44 ALR 3d 555 (1972); Kenneth W Biedzynski, 58 Am Jur 2d Notaries Public (Liability for Notarial Acts—Negligent Acknowledgment) § 60 (2002)]

Common-Law Marriage

Q 12:23   How does common-law marriage affect a beneficiary designation under an ERISA plan?

If a participant has a spouse, an ERISA plan may provide that some or all of a 403(b) benefit belongs to a spouse (see Q 12:14).

If a couple resides, previously resided, or even traveled in a state that recognizes common-law marriage (see Q 12:21), the couple may be married, notwithstanding the absence of any ceremony or writing. A recognized common-law marriage is no less a marriage than a ceremonial marriage. [See 5 CFR § 630.1202]

> **Example 12-2.** Harold and Wendy lived together in Alabama. Harold never made any beneficiary designation under his employer's ERISA-governed 403(b) plan. The plan provides that a surviving spouse is entitled to the participant's account. After Harold's death, Wendy calls the human resources office to ask about this plan benefit, and the manager tells Wendy that the employer has no record that Wendy is Harold's spouse. Wendy files the plan's claim form and attaches to it an affidavit that states facts that, if correct, would constitute a common-law marriage under Alabama law. Because the employer, acting as plan administrator, does not receive any contrary information, it decides that Wendy is Harold's surviving spouse. The plan administrator instructs the custodian to pay the full benefit as Wendy requested.

> **Practice Pointer.** A plan administrator must act as an expert when deciding plan claims. [ERISA § 404(a)(1)] Therefore, a plan administrator should obtain expert legal advice to evaluate any individual's claim that he or she is the common-law spouse of a participant.

Q 12:24   How does common-law marriage of a same-sex couple affect a beneficiary designation?

If a participant has a spouse, state law may provide that some or all of a 403(b) benefit belongs to a spouse (see Q 12:14). If a couple resides, previously resided, or even traveled in a state that recognizes common-law marriage, the couple may be married, notwithstanding the absence of any ceremony or writing. Many states recognize common-law marriage (see Q 12:21).

Most people assume—and at least one court has held—that common-law marriage does not apply to a couple in which both persons are of the same gender. [DeSanto v Barnsley, 328 Pa Super 181, 476 A 2d 952 (1984)] However, such a discrimination may be unconstitutional or contrary to federal civil rights law, and therefore of no effect. [See U.S. Const art IV sec 1 & Fifth Amendment; Saenz v Roe, 526 US 489, 119 S Ct 1518, 143 L Ed 2d 689, 67 USLW 4291, 61 Soc Sec Rep Serv 75, 1999 US LEXIS 3174 (1999); Romer v Evans, 517 US 620, 116 S Ct 1620, 134 L Ed 2d 855, 64 USLW 4353, 70 Fair Employ Prac Cases (BNA) 1180 (1996); Loving v Virginia, 388 US 1 (1967)]

If a same-sex couple reside in a state other than the state in which they married, a federal statute states that the current state need not recognize the marriage established in the other state: "No State . . . shall be required to give effect to any public act, record, or judicial proceeding of any other State . . . respecting a relationship between persons of the same sex that is treated as a marriage under the laws of such other State . . . , or a right or claim arising from such relationship." [28 USC § 1738C] It is unclear whether this statute is the law, because it may be unconstitutional. [See US Const art IV sec 1 & Fifth Amendment; Saenz v Roe, 526 US 489, 119 S Ct 1518, 143 L Ed 2d 689, 67 USLW 4291, 61 Soc Sec Rep Serv 75, 1999 US LEXIS 3174 (1999); Romer v Evans, 517 US 620, 116 S Ct 1620, 134 L Ed 2d 855, 64 USLW 4353, 70 Fair Employ Prac Cases (BNA) 1180 (1996)]

Thus, a participant in a non-ERISA plan or program who is part of a same-sex couple and wants to name a beneficiary other than his or her same-sex spouse should seek expert legal advice.

A marriage of a same-gender couple will not be recognized in applying ERISA's rights for a spouse. "In determining the meaning of any Act of Congress . . . , the word 'marriage' means only a legal union between one man and one woman as husband and wife, and the word 'spouse' refers only to a person of the opposite sex who is a husband or a wife." [1 USC § 7]

Q 12:25   How does a Vermont civil union of a same-sex couple affect a beneficiary designation?

If a participant was a party to a Vermont civil union, state law might provide that, after the participant's death, some or all of a plan benefit must be provided to the other party to the civil union to the extent necessary to provide such a spouse his or her property rights (see SQ 12:16).

Vermont law provides that same-sex couples must have the opportunity to obtain the same benefits and protections afforded by Vermont law to married opposite-sex couples. [Vermont Const chapter I art 7; Baker v Vermont, 744 A 2d 864, 1999 Vt LEXIS 406 (1999)] Under Vermont statute, the same-sex parties to a civil union have the same benefits, protections, and responsibilities as are provided for spouses in any other marriage. [15 VSA §§ 1201(2), 1204(a)] This rule applies whether the source of law is statute, administrative regulation, court rule, policy, common law, or any other source of civil law. [15 VSA § 1204(a)] Further, a party to a civil union is included in any definition or use of the term "spouse" as that term is used in any Vermont law. [15 VSA § 1204(b)]

Vermont law provides that a surviving spouse has a right to at least one third of his or her spouse's personal estate. [14 VSA §§ 401–402] A court has power to enter an order relating to nonprobate property, such as a retirement plan benefit, when necessary to give effect to a surviving spouse's property rights. [14 VSA § 1721]

Thus, a participant who is a party to a Vermont civil union and wishes to name a beneficiary other than his or her spouse should seek expert legal advice.

Q 12:26   What happens if a participant has two spouses?

Although most Americans assume that a person cannot have two legitimate spouses at the same time, this is not necessarily so if that person married in another nation. While a state may choose not to recognize a marriage that it finds contrary to its strong public policy, a state may give deference to the customs and laws of another nation. California, for example, has held that a decedent could have more than one spouse for inheritance purposes. [Estate of Dalip Singh Bir, 83 Cal App 2d 256, 188 P 2d 481 (1948) (More than 50 years before the decedent's death in California, two women had married him in the Punjab Province of British India "according to the law and manner of the Jat community"); see also Sousa v Freitas, 10 Cal App 3d 660, 89 Cal Rptr 485 (1970)] However, a court might find that a relationship or status that is recognized under another nation's law or custom is not the same kind of relationship or status that the U.S. state recognizes as marriage.

Community Property

Q 12:27   What is community property?

Community property is a term of art that lawyers use to refer to a regime that treats each item of property acquired by either spouse of a married couple during the marriage and while the couple are domiciled in a community property state (see SQ 12:28) as owned equally by each spouse. Each spouse's ownership exists presently, notwithstanding that the other spouse currently may hold title to or have control over the property. Generally, a 403(b) arrangement is community property to the extent earned during the marriage and while the participant was domiciled in a community property state. Although it is sometimes difficult to evaluate when a retirement plan interest was "earned," a typical community property regime will treat a 403(b) contract right as earned during the marriage to the extent that contributions were made while the participant was married and domiciled in a community property jurisdiction. In Wisconsin, the nonparticipant's community property right in a retirement plan or deferred compensation plan (including a 403(b) contract) terminates on the nonparticipant's death if the nonparticipant's death occurs before the participant's death. [Wis Stat Ann §§ 766.31(3), 766.62(5)]

In a separate-property system (which applies in 41 states and all U.S. territories and possessions other than Puerto Rico), an item of property normally belongs to the individual who has title to it, paid for it, earned it, or otherwise acquired it. Although any property owned by a married individual may become subject to equitable distribution upon a divorce or other marital dissolution, the property belongs completely to the individual who owns it until a court makes an order. (For more information on domestic relations orders, see chapter 13.)

The community property regime "first obtained recognition in written form in 693 A.D., in Visigothic Spain[.]" [William Quiby deFuniak, 1 Principles of Community Property § 2 at 4 (1943); see also William A. Reppy Jr. & Cynthia A. Samuel, Community Property in the United States 1-1-1-10 (2000); see generally Paul Due, *Origin and Historical Development of the Community Property System*, 25 La L Rev 78 (1964)]

Q 12:28 Which states are community property states?

Arizona, California, Idaho, Louisiana, Nevada, New Mexico, Puerto Rico, Texas, Washington, and Wisconsin are community property jurisdictions.

Community property law varies considerably from state to state. For example, if all 403(b) contributions were made before the participant was married but investment earnings accrued after the marriage, some states would classify the entire 403(b) arrangement (including investment earnings) as separate property, while others might classify those investment earnings that accrued after the marriage as community property.

Wisconsin is the only state to have adopted the Uniform Marital Property Act recommended by the National Conference of Commissioners on Uniform State Laws. [Wis Stat §§ 766.001–766.97 (1986)]

Alaska gives its married residents a choice of whether to use a separate property regime or a community property regime. The separate property regime applies unless the married couple agree to use a community property regime. If the couple choose community property, they may use a written community property agreement or a community property trust to vary some of the state law provisions that otherwise would govern their community property. [Alaska Stat § 34.77.020 *et seq* (Westlaw 2000)]

Q 12:29   May community property law be applied to nonspouses?

Maybe. In a state that applies community property law to determine the property rights of married persons but does not recognize common-law marriage, a court might apply community property law to protect the expectations of a nonspouse in a relationship that, in a judge's view, resembled marriage. Arizona, California, and Louisiana provide community property rights to a putative spouse, but not to a meretricious nonspouse. [Stevens v Anderson, 75 Ariz 331, 256 P 2d 712 (Ariz 1953); Calif Civil Code § 4452; La Civil Code Ann arts 117–118] Washington appears to apply community property law even to meretricious spouses. [Connell v Francisco, 127 Wash 2d 339, 898 P 2d 831 (Wash Sup 1995); Warden v Warden, 36 Wash App 693, 676 P 2d 1037 (1984); but see Creasman v Boyle, 31 Wash 2d 345, 196 P 2d 835 (Wash 1948)]

Other legal theories for adjusting the property rights of putative spouses or meretricious spouses include express or implied contract, partnership, and unjust enrichment.

Q 12:30   How does community property law affect payment of benefits under a 403(b) plan that is subject to ERISA?

Not at all. ERISA preempts state laws that relate to a 403(b) plan that is subject to ERISA. [ERISA § 514]

Instead, ERISA provides its own rules designed to protect a spouse [ERISA § 205] (see chapter 9 on survivor annuity requirements) or surviving spouse [ERISA § 205] (see chapter 9 on death benefit beneficiary designations) or to accept a court order that divides a participant's benefit to provide a benefit for the participant's spouse or former spouse. [ERISA § 206(d)(3)] (See chapter 13 on qualified domestic relations orders.)

Premarital Agreements

Q 12:33   Can a premarital contract waive a right to a non-ERISA Section 403(b) benefit?

Yes. Even if a surviving spouse is entitled to an elective share or community property or other protective rights under state law, an expertly prepared premarital or postnuptial agreement (see SQ 12:35, Qs 12:36–12:37) should be sufficient to eliminate or waive those rights. [See generally Uniform Probate Code § 2-207] Along with other requirements, a premarital agreement must be in writing and signed by the parties and must be acknowledged by the parties in the presence of a notary public or similar officer. [See, e.g., NY Domestic Relations Law § 236B(3)]

In some circumstances, it may be difficult to enforce the terms of a premarital agreement. At least one court has held that an offset against contract rights in recognition of a surviving spouse's receipt of retirement benefits (that were not provided by the premarital agreement) could be an ERISA violation, notwithstanding that the person applying the offset had no connection to any ERISA plan. This was so because the offset had the effect of "discriminating" against the spouse because she exercised her right to a benefit under an ERISA plan. [See, e.g., Mattei v Mattei, 126 F 3d 794, 21 EBC (BNA) 1745, Pens Plan Guide (CCH) ¶23937W (1997) (construing ERISA § 510)]

Postnuptial Agreements

Q 12:35   What is a postnuptial agreement?

A postnuptial agreement is an agreement made between two persons who already are spouses concerning property rights that arise from their marriage. Typically, a postnuptial agreement provides that one or both of the spouses waive one or more of the property rights that a spouse otherwise would have. A postnuptial agreement can waive a spouse's right to a share of the other's estate. Within limits required by public policy and basic fairness, a postnuptial agreement can specify what property division will apply if the marriage ends in divorce.

Generally, a postnuptial agreement must be written. In New York, a postnuptial agreement must be in a writing signed by the parties and must be acknowledged by the parties in the presence of a notary public or similar officer. [See, e.g., NY Domestic Relations Law § 236B(3)]

Many state statutes or court decisions add additional requirements meant to ensure basic fairness. Typically, each party should fully disclose his or her financial circumstances to the other. Further, the better practice is for each party to get the advice of a lawyer of his or her choosing. Some states require that the postnuptial agreement be fair and equitable. [See, e.g., Pacelli v Pacelli, 319 NJ Super 185 (NJ Super Ct 1999)]

In Minnesota, a postnuptial agreement is valid only if:

1. Each spouse has a net worth of at least $1.2 million;

2. Each spouse has the advice of a lawyer of his or her choosing; and

3. The couple stays married for at least two years.

[Minn Stat § 519.11]

A postnuptial agreement is void if it was signed under the threat of a divorce. [See, e.g., In re Sharp's Estate, 11 D&C 3d 371 (Pa Common Pleas 1979)]

Tenancy by the Entirety

Q 12:39 Why might an individual want to own property in a tenancy by the entirety?

Because neither spouse alone can dispose of the property (see Q 12:38), a tenancy by the entirety may provide useful protection against the claims of creditors. For example, if only one of the two spouses is bankrupt, the bankruptcy trustee generally cannot reach property held in a tenancy by the entirety. [See, e.g., Blodgett v US, 161 F 2d 47 (8th Cir 1947); but see 11 USC § 110] For a detailed explanation of creditor protections that may arise from tenancy by the entirety, see Lewis D. Solomon & Lewis J. Saret, Asset Protection Strategies at §§ 7.2–7.7 (New York: Aspen Publishers, 1999).

However, a 403(b) participant may not need the protection that a tenancy by the entirety ownership, when available, could provide. A benefit under an ERISA plan is not subject to the claims of the participant's creditors (other than the plan itself). [29 USC §§ 1056(d)(1), 1144; ERISA §§ 206(d)(1), 514] Likewise, a benefit under an ERISA plan is excluded from the participant's bankruptcy estate. [11 USC § 541(c)(2), 29 USC §§ 1056(d)(1), 1144; ERISA §§ 206(d)(1), 514; Patterson v Shumate, 504 US 753, 112 S Ct 2242, 119 L Ed 2d 519 (1992)] Depending on state law, a non-ERISA 403(b) contract may or may not be subject to the claims of the participant's creditors. Likewise, a non-ERISA 403(b) benefit may or may not be excluded from the participant's bankruptcy estate. [11 USC § 541(c)(2); see, e.g., In re Johnson, 191 BR 75 (Bankr MD Pa 1996) (tax-deferred annuity excluded from bankruptcy administration)]

For either ERISA or non-ERISA 403(b) benefits, a federal tax lien supersedes any ERISA, plan, or contract restraints. [IRC §§ 6321, 6331; Treas Reg§ 1.401(a)-13(b)(2)] A federal tax lien may attach to a taxpayer's property rights in a tenancy by the entirety, even if the taxpayer's spouse is not a debtor. [United States v Craft, 535 US 274, 122 S Ct 1414, 2001-USTC ¶ 50,361 (2002)]

Finally, a married individual may prefer tenancy by the entirety ownership simply because it reflects his or her beliefs about the nature of marriage.

Disclaimers

Q 12:43 What is the effect of a disclaimer?

If a beneficiary makes a legally valid disclaimer that the plan administrator, insurer, or custodian accepts, the benefit will be distributed as though the beneficiary/disclaimant had died before the participant's death.

Q 12:45   Can a beneficiary's executor or agent disclaim?

If a plan permits a beneficiary to disclaim a plan benefit, whether that power can be exercised only by the beneficiary personally or by the beneficiary's executor, personal representative, guardian, or attorney-in-fact as a fiduciary depends on the plan's language. Unless the plan document states that a power to disclaim can be exercised by an executor, personal representative, guardian, or attorney-in-fact, only the beneficiary personally may exercise the power to disclaim. [R Scott Nickel, as Plan Benefit Administrator of the Thrift Plan of Phillips Petroleum Co v Estate of Lurline Estes, 122 F 3d 294, 21 EBC (BNA) 1762, Pens Plan Guide (CCH) ¶ 23937U (5th Cir 1997)]

For a Section 403(b) contract not held under any plan, it is unclear whether a similar result would apply under state law. In some states, a personal representative may disclaim an interest and the disclaimer relates back to the disclaimant's death or even to the death of the person making the disclaimant a beneficiary. [See, e.g., Texas Probate Code § 37A; Rolin v IRS, 588 F 2d 368 (2d Cir 1978) (applying New York law)]

Even if a fiduciary has power under applicable law to make a disclaimer, such a disclaimer might not be a qualified disclaimer for federal tax purposes.[Compare Ltr Ruls 200013041, 9615043, 9609052 (disclaimer recognized) with Ltr Rul 9437042 (disclaimer not recognized); see also Rev Rul 90-110, 1990-2 CB 209 (disclaimer by trustee not a qualified disclaimer)]

Government Claims

Q 12:47   Is a 403(b) contract counted as an asset for Medicaid eligibility?

A Section 403(b) benefit probably is counted as an "available resource" for Medicaid eligibility purposes to the extent that the patient or his or her spouse currently has a legal right to get payment under the 403(b) contract and the plan (if any). [42 USC § 1396a-p] A participant may wish to consider not selecting as his or her beneficiary a person likely to need Medicaid benefits if a more appropriate beneficiary designation can be made. A beneficiary should not make a disclaimer unless he or she first gets his or her lawyer's advice that doing so will not be a federal health care crime. [See 42 USC § 1320a-7b(a)(6)]

Q 12:50   When will the IRS file a levy on a participant's 403(b) benefit?

If a participant has not yet severed from employment or attained age $59^1/_2$, the IRS usually will not file a levy on the participant's 403(b) benefit. The IRS will levy on a participant's 403(b) benefit only if he or she has been unusually abusive. A levy on retirement savings requires the approval of an IRS supervisor. [Internal Revenue Manual ¶ 5.11.6.2]

Unclaimed Property

Q 12:52   Is a non-ERISA plan or contract subject to unclaimed property law?

Yes. Each of the fifty states (and the District of Columbia and U.S. possessions) has a law regulating abandoned or unclaimed property.

For example, a typical unclaimed property law requires any person in possession of intangible property that is unclaimed by its owner for a period of a specified number of years to transfer that property to the custody of the state. [See, e.g., 765 IL CS 1025]

If a state's law is based on either uniform act, a "[state] government or political subdivision, public corporation, public authority, . . . trust, . . . or any . . . legal . . . entity" is subject to the unclaimed property law. [Revised Uniform Disposition of Unclaimed Property Act § 1(g) (1995); Uniform Disposition of Unclaimed Property Act § 1(g) (1981)]

Q 12:53   When is a retirement plan benefit considered abandoned?

The "waiting period" that sets up a legal presumption that property is abandoned or unclaimed varies by state law. But under typical laws, the waiting period starts when the benefit "became payable or distributable." [See Revised Uniform Disposition of Unclaimed Property Act §§ 7–9 (1966); Uniform Disposition of Unclaimed Property Act §§ 7–9 (1954)] Under many retirement plans, a benefit usually is paid within a month from the date that the benefit became distributable. Therefore, as a practical matter, many plan administrators and payers start the waiting period on the check date.

Tax-Oriented Estate Planning

Q 12:55   What is the federal estate tax?

The federal estate tax is a tax on the right to transfer property upon death. This tax is imposed on a decedent's taxable estate, which includes nonprobate property and rights. The tax rates begin at 18 percent and go as high as 50 percent. [IRC § 2001 (c)] An unlimited marital deduction allows an individual to transfer any amount to his or her surviving spouse (if the spouse is a U.S. citizen) without federal estate tax at that time, but tax may apply when the survivor dies. [IRC § 2056] A tax credit allows an individual to transfer about $1 million for 2003 without federal estate tax. [IRC § 2010 (b)]

Q 12:56   What is a state death transfer tax?

In addition to the federal estate tax, every state except Nevada imposes some form of death transfer tax. An estate tax is a tax on the privilege of transferring property from a decedent. An inheritance tax is a tax on the privilege of receiving property from a decedent, including even property that the decedent did not own at the time of his or her death. Unlike the federal estate tax law, which has a marital deduction, an inheritance tax or a state estate tax may apply when the beneficiary is the decedent's spouse. In 37 states and the District of Columbia, the amount of the state death transfer taxes is the maximum amount for which the state death transfer tax credit is available under federal estate tax law. [See IRC § 2011] In the other states, the state death transfer taxes may be greater. Only Connecticut, Louisiana, New York, North Carolina, Tennessee, and Puerto Rico have a state or local gift tax.

Q 12:58 Is a 403(b) arrangement subject to state death tax?

An explanation of the death tax for the individual states is beyond the scope of this chapter. Some states tax a Section 403(b) benefit for death transfer tax purposes according to rules similar to those of the federal estate tax. A few states may have exemptions or exclusions for a retirement benefit that was already in payout status before the participant's death. In several states, the tax may vary based on the relationship of the beneficiary to the participant/decedent.

Q 12:59 Does a beneficiary designation of the spouse qualify for the marital deduction?

Yes. As long as the spouse is the only person who can benefit, at least until his or her death, a beneficiary designation of the spouse qualifies for the marital deduction. [IRC § 2056; Ltr Rul 1999360527]

Who Can Give Advice

Q 12:65 May a financial services representative give advice about a beneficiary designation?

A financial services representative may give practical advice about how to fill in the beneficiary information requested by the application for an annuity or life insurance contract or a custodial account. He or she must not give advice about the legal effect of a beneficiary designation.

Except when done by a properly admitted lawyer, giving legal advice, even for free, is a crime in every state of the United States. Even if the nonlawyer explicitly states that he or she is not a lawyer, it is still a crime to give legal advice.

Of course, any criminal punishment is in addition to the nonlawyer's liability to his or her "client" for any inappropriate advice. Courts have not hesitated to impose liability on a nonlawyer for giving incorrect or even incomplete advice. [Buscemi v Intachai, 730 So 2d 329 (Fla App 1999) (nonlawyer financial planner who gave legal advice could be held liable for failure to do so properly), *review denied,* 744 So 2d 452 (Fla 1999); Banks v District of Columbia Dep't of Consumer & Regulatory Affairs, 634 A 2d 433 (DC 1993); Cultum v Heritage House Realtors, Inc, 694 P2d 630 (Wash 1985); Bowers v Transamerica Title Ins Co, 675 P2d 193 (Wash 1983); Webb v Pomeroy, 655 P 2d 465 (Kan Ct App 1982); Biakanja v Irving, 49 Cal 2d 647, 320 P 2d 16 (Cal 1958)] A nonlawyer will be held to the same standard of care and expertise as a lawyer. [Williams v Jackson Co, 359 So 2d 798 (Ala Civ App 1978), *writ denied,* 359 So 2d 801 (1978); Wright v Langdon, 274 Ark 258, 623 SW 2d 823 (Ark 1981); Biakanja v Irving, 49 Cal 2d 647, 320 P 2d 16 (Cal 1958); Ford v Guarantee Abstract & Title Co, 553 P 2d 254 (Kan 1976); Torres v Fiol, 110 Ill App 3d 9, 65 Ill Dec 786, 441 NE 2d 1300 (1982); Latson v Eaton, 341 P 2d 247 (Okla 1959); Bowers v Transamerica Title Ins Co, 675 P 2d 193 (Wash 1983); Mattieligh v Poe, 57 Wn 2d 203, 356 P 2d 328 (1960). See also Correll v Goodfellow, 125 NW 2d 745 (Iowa 1964); Brown v Shyne, 151 NE 197 (NY 1926)] This duty, even for a nonlawyer, includes the duty to have and use specialist expertise, or to refer one's "client" to an appropriate specialist.

A nonlawyer plan administrator also will be liable for incorrect or incomplete advice. Although a lawsuit against a plan administrator or other ERISA fiduciary grounded on state-law claims, such as negligent misrepresentation or negligent communication, is preempted [Griggs v E I DuPont de Nemours & Co, 237 F3d 371 (4th Cir 2001); Farr v US West, Inc, 151 F 3d 908 (9th Cir 1998)], a plan administrator's incorrect statement might be a breach of its fiduciary duty to furnish accurate and non-misleading information. [See Griggs v E I DuPont de Nemours & Co, 237 F3d 371 (4th Cir 2001)]

Many 403(b) plan participants believe they cannot afford legal advice. Although a financial services representative should urge a participant to obtain expert legal advice, it may be impractical to avoid participants' questions asked in the course of filling out a 403(b) application. Perhaps it is not the unauthorized practice of law to furnish widely known general information that does not involve applying the law to a specific factual situation.

Practice Pointer. If a participant expresses a desire to make a beneficiary designation that would provide anything less than 100 percent of his or her death benefit for his or her spouse, a nonlawyer financial planner should urge the participant to seek the advice of an expert lawyer.

Q 12:67 Does the lawyer who draws up an individual's will need to know about the individual's beneficiary designation under a 403(b) contract?

Yes. Professor John Langbein, an authority on the law of wills, trusts, and estates, observed that many Americans die with several wills—maybe one that was written in a lawyer's office and a dozen others that were filled out on standard forms. For most people, those forms—beneficiary designations—dispose of far more money and property than the will does. [John H Langbein, The Nonprobate Revolution and the Future of the Law of Succession, 97 Harvard L

Rev 1108 (Mar 1984); Michael Carrico, Public Knowledge and Attitudes about Property Distributions at Death and Will Substitutes in Indiana, American Bar Foundation Research Journal (1984); See also Carrico, Uniform "Super Will" Legislation Project, 14 Probate & Property 45 (1986)]

Making a beneficiary designation under a 403(b) contract is an important part of estate planning. Although a Section 403(b) benefit will not pass by a will (see SQ 12:1), the Section 403(b) beneficiary designation does affect an individual's overall estate plan. A participant should make sure his or her lawyer knows the beneficiary designation the participant made under each 403(b) contract and should ask for the lawyer's advice about whether to consider changing any beneficiary designation.

Common Mistakes

Q 12:68 What are some of the common mistakes people make with beneficiary designations?

Because people enroll in retirement plans or Section 403(b) contracts quickly, they sometimes make beneficiary designations that are less than carefully considered. Following are some common mistakes.

1. Failing to coordinate a beneficiary designation's provisions with those made in other non-probate designations, trusts, and a will. Although a beneficiary designation's provisions need not be the same as those of a participant's will or other dispositions, if they are different, the participant should understand why he or she has made different provisions and whether they are likely to add up to a combined result that he or she wants.

2. Failing to consider whether a beneficiary designation is consistent with tax-oriented planning. A participant might have had a lawyer's advice about how to leave his or her estate, including both probate and non-probate property, to achieve a desired tax outcome. Making a beneficiary designation without considering its effect on the participant's tax-oriented plan could result in an unanticipated tax.

3. Making a beneficiary designation that a plan administrator, insurer, or custodian will refuse to implement. For example, a participant might try to make a beneficiary designation that refers to terms that may be used in a will or trust but are precluded by his or her Section 403(b) plan or contract. A plan administrator's interpretation of the beneficiary designation without the offending terms might result in a disposition quite different from what the participant intended.

4. Not naming specific beneficiaries—for example, writing "all my children, equally" or describing a class. When a beneficiary designation refers to information that is not in a retirement plan's or Section 403(b) contract's records, a plan administrator, insurer, or custodian may

decide that the participant did not make a beneficiary designation, or it may allow a claimant an opportunity to name every person in the class and prove that there are no others. Since it is difficult to prove the nonexistence of an unidentified person, even the opportunity to correct the participant's beneficiary designation would result in significant frustration and delay.

5. Neglecting to use a beneficiary's Social Security number or taxpayer identification number, especially for a daughter.

   Example. Harold Smith had three children—John, Catherine, and Alice. He named them his beneficiaries using only their given names. By the time of Harold's death many years later, John and Alice had married. John had no special difficulty claiming his benefit. But Alice, who had changed her surname to Carpenter, was required to submit proof that she is the same person as Alice Smith. Because an identifying number assigned by the Social Security Administration or the IRS is unique, this difficulty could have been avoided had Harold put Alice's Social Security number on the beneficiary designation form.

6. Naming a minor as a beneficiary without considering who the minor's guardian would be. For example, a divorced participant might not want to name his or her young child as a beneficiary if doing so might have the effect of putting money in the hands of the child's other parent, the participant's former spouse. Instead, the participant might name a suitable trustee or custodian.

7. Naming a child as a beneficiary without considering his or her prudence.

   Example. Philip names his daughter, Britney, as beneficiary of his custodial account. When Philip dies, Britney is age 19, and no longer a minor under applicable law. Although Britney should use the funds to pay her $25,000 sophomore year college tuition, she buys a new car and then neglects to pay the second car insurance premium. When the uninsured car is stolen, Britney has nothing left from her father's gift.

   A participant who wants to benefit his or her child should consider the child's maturity and decide whether to appoint a suitable trustee to manage the child's benefit.

8. Forgetting to give a copy of the beneficiary designation to the beneficiary. A plan administrator, insurer, or custodian has no duty or obligation to contact a participant's beneficiaries to invite them to submit a claim. Indeed, many service providers specifically avoid doing so because such a communication might invite fraudulent claims. A beneficiary might not claim a benefit if he or she is unaware that he or she is a beneficiary. Likewise, the beneficiary might have difficulty claiming the benefit if he or she does not know the name of the plan administrator, insurer, or custodian.

9. Naming one's estate as the beneficiary. Some participants think that naming their estate as beneficiary is a way to avoid inconsistency in their

estate plan. Although such a beneficiary designation might serve to avoid inconsistency, it has disadvantages. For example, amounts paid or payable to an executor or personal representative for the estate are available to a decedent's creditors. Further, a benefit's "run" through an estate might, because of accounting and timing differences, result in a larger income tax than the tax that would have resulted if the recipient had received the benefit directly. [IRC §§ 1, 72, 641–691]

10. Failing to make a beneficiary designation at all. A participant who has difficulty making up his or her mind about a beneficiary designation is unlikely to have read a plan's summary plan description or a Section 403(b) contract's terms carefully enough to understand the effect of the plan's or contract's default provision (see Q 12:7).

    Practice Pointer. A planner might suggest that the risks of failing to make a beneficiary designation outweigh the risks of a less than perfectly considered beneficiary designation. In those circumstances, a planner might remind the participant that a typical plan or contract allows a participant to change his or her beneficiary designation at any time.

11. Forgetting to review one's beneficiary designation. A participant should review his or her beneficiary designations on a periodic basis and whenever there is a significant change in his or her family or financial status.

    Example. Martha names her husband, John, as her beneficiary under an ERISA plan. Although Martha wants to make sure that their children, Peter and Maria, will be provided for, she trusts her husband to take care of the whole family. When Martha and John divorce some years later, Martha neglects to change her beneficiary designation. After Martha's death, John submits his claim to the plan administrator. The plan administrator follows the plan's terms, which do not revoke a beneficiary designation because of a participant's divorce (see SQ 12:8). The plan pays John, and he spends the money without considering the needs of Peter and Maria.

The common mistakes described above are only some of the many errors plan participants may make. Although a Section 403(b) benefit is meant to be consumed mostly during a participant's retirement years, the participant's death may occur before retirement. Therefore, a participant should exercise his or her valuable right to name a beneficiary and exercise that right wisely.

Chapter 13

Qualified Domestic Relations Orders

Peter J. Gulia, Esq.
CitiStreet Retirement Services

Although a 403(b) arrangement is intended to provide retirement benefits primarily for a participant, domestic relations law in all states recognizes interests in retirement plans and arrangements as property subject to division upon the dissolution of a marriage. ERISA and the Internal Revenue Code include provisions designed to create a workable regime to permit retirement plans and 403(b) arrangements to meet those marital property expectations. ERISA requires a plan governed by ERISA to permit a qualified domestic relations order. The Internal Revenue Code provides that a payment to a spouse or former spouse under a qualified domestic relations order is the alternate payee's (rather than the participant's) income. The federal law tries to balance a nonparticipant alternate payee's right to receive a retirement benefit with the plan administrator's need for administrative efficiency and certainty.

Overview

Q 13:2   What kind of 403(b) plan must accept a QDRO?

If a 403(b) plan is subject to Title I of ERISA, it must accept a QDRO. [ERISA § 206(d)(3)(A)]

A 403(b) plan that is a governmental plan, or a church plan that has not elected to be covered under ERISA, is not required by ERISA to accept a QDRO. If, however, ERISA does not apply, state law is not preempted, and a domestic relations court may use its contempt powers to compel the plan administrator to accept a QDRO. For some governmental plans, the plan administrator may have sovereign immunity that protects against monetary liability from its decision to refuse a court order. A church plan might have constitutional grounds to refuse a court order that would interfere with the free exercise of its religious doctrine or church management. [See generally Basich v Board of Pensions, Evangelical Lutheran Church in Am and Basich v Evangelical Lutheran Church in Am, No C8-95-882 and No CX-95-883, 19 EBC (BNA) 2231, 540 NW 2d 82 (Minn App 1995), *review denied* (unpublished order), Minn Sup Ct (Jan 25, 1996) *cert denied,* 117 S Ct 55, 136 L Ed 2d 18 (1996)]

If a 403(b) arrangement is not under a plan, the insurer or custodian is not required by ERISA to accept a QDRO, but it usually will accept an order (if it is determined to be a QDRO). Also, an insurer or custodian may accept a court order that is not a QDRO to the extent required by applicable state laws.

Q 13:7   May a QDRO be used to pay child support?

Yes. A QDRO is a DRO that provides for an alternate payee and meets form requirements. [ERISA § 206(d)(3); IRC § 414(p)(1)(A)] A DRO includes an order that "relates to the provision of child support[.]" [ERISA § 206(d)(3)(B)(ii)(I); IRC § 414(p)(1)(B)(i)] Several court decisions have recognized the use of a QDRO to pay child support. [See, e.g., In re Marriage of LeBlanc, 944 P 2d 686 (Colo App 1997); Rohrbeck v Rohrbeck, 318 Md 28, 566 A 2d 767 (Md 1989); Baird v Baird, 843 SW 2d 388 (Mo 1992); Arnold v Arnold, 154 Misc 2d 715, 586 NYS 2d 449 (NY 1992); Stinner v Stinner & Bethlehem Steel Corp, 523 A 2d 1161 (Pa 1987)]

If a child's custodial parent is the participant's spouse or former spouse, receiving child support payments from an insurer or custodian following a QDRO might be disadvantageous to the custodial parent if he or she (rather than the child) is the alternate payee. Child support payments received are not income. [IRC §§ 71, 215; Blair v Commissioner, TC Memo 1988-581 (Tax Court 1988)] However, an alternate payee who is the participant's spouse or former spouse is, for federal income tax purposes, the distributee of a QDRO distribution. [IRC § 402(e)(1)(A)]

Practice Pointer. If a custodial parent uses a QDRO to collect child support payments, his or her lawyer should make sure that the court order specifies that the child (rather than the custodial parent) is the payee.

In the Department of Labor's (DOL's) view, "[I]f an alternate payee is a minor or is legally incompetent, [a QDRO] can require payment to someone with legal responsibility for the alternate payee (such as a guardian or a [person] acting in loco parentis in the case of a child, or a trustee acting as an agent for the alternate payee)." [DOL-PWBA, QDROs, The Division of Pensions Through

Qualified Domestic Relations Orders, Q1-9 (1997); see also 100th Cong, 1st Sess, General Explanation of the Tax Reform Act of 1984 at 222]

Caution. The DOL's view, explained in its QDRO booklet, is not administrative law. Further, the DOL has no authority concerning the federal income tax effect of payments under a DRO or a QDRO.

Requirements of a Qualified Domestic Relations Order

Q 13:10   What makes a court order a QDRO?

A QDRO is a court order that

1. Is made under a state's domestic relations law or community property law (see below);
2. Relates to the provision of property rights, alimony, or child support to a spouse (or former spouse), child, or other dependent of the participant;
3. Specifies each plan to which the order applies;
4. Specifies the name and last known mailing address of the participant;
5. Specifies the name and last known mailing address of the alternate payee;
6. Recognizes, creates, or assigns to an alternate payee a right to receive all or a portion of the participant's benefit under a 403(b) arrangement;
7. Specifies the fixed or determinable amount of the participant's account balance payable to each alternate payee;
8. Specifies the number of payments or the period to which the order applies;
9. Does not require any 403(b) plan or arrangement to provide additional vesting;
10. Does not require any 403(b) plan or arrangement to provide additional benefits;
11. Does not require any 403(b) plan or arrangement to provide any form of benefit not otherwise provided under the plan (if any) and 403(b) arrangement; and
12. Does not require any 403(b) plan or arrangement to pay to an alternate payee benefits that are required to be paid to another alternate payee under a previously determined QDRO.

[ERISA §§ 206(d)(3)(B), 206(d)(3)(C), 206(d)(3)(D); IRC § 414(p)(1)–(3); Treas Reg § 1.401(a)-13(g)(iii)(A)]

Planning Pointer. A QDRO must be a court order. A private agreement between spouses is not a DRO. A court judgment, decree, or order is required. [See Stinner v Stinner & Bethlehem Steel Corp, 523 A 2d 1161 (Pa 1987)]

The DOL has clarified that state domestic relations law includes community property law only insofar as such law is ordinarily applied to determine alimony, child support, and property division in domestic relations proceedings. [DOL ERISA Adv Op 90-46A]

A QDRO cannot require a plan to pay a joint and survivor annuity for the life of the alternate payee and his or her later spouse or beneficiary. [IRC § 414(p)(4)(A)(iii)]

When directed to a governmental plan, a DRO is treated as a QDRO for federal income tax purposes, even if the DRO does not meet many of the QDRO requirements. [IRC § 414(p)(11)]

Q 13:11   Is a court order to refrain from changing a beneficiary a QDRO?

Usually not. In a divorce proceeding, a domestic relations court sometimes makes (or is deemed to have made) an order that restrains one or both of the divorcing parties from taking actions that could frustrate the court's ability to divide property between the parties. For example, a court might order a participant to refrain from changing his or her beneficiary designation under any retirement plan or account, including a 403(b) contract.

Unless such an order specifies a payment to an alternate payee and meets the other requirements of the QDRO rule (see SQ 13:10), it is not a QDRO. If an order is not a QDRO, the 403(b) plan administrator, insurer, or custodian has no obligation to act following the order.

> **Example 13-2.** In their divorce proceeding, a domestic relations court ordered JoAnn and Kenneth not to dispose of or transfer any marital assets while the proceeding was pending. In violation of this order, Kenneth changed the beneficiary designation under an ERISA plan from JoAnn to his children by a previous marriage. After Kenneth's death, the plan benefit was properly payable to the designated beneficiaries. Because the domestic relations court's order was not a QDRO, ERISA preempted it.

[See, e.g., Central SE & SW Areas Pension Fund v Howell, 227 F 3d 672 (6th Cir 2000)]

Even if a court order relates to a non-ERISA 403(b) plan or contract (and thus is not preempted), a plan administrator, insurer, or custodian need not follow an order if it was not named in the court proceeding, served with legal process, and afforded a court hearing. Further, to comply with a 403(b) contract's anti-alienation provision, an insurer or custodian must make a reasonable effort to resist a court order that is not a QDRO.

Q 13:15 What should a plan administrator do when a court order is ambiguous?

If an order is ambiguous, the order is not a QDRO. To be a QDRO, an order must clearly specify all of the required elements (see SQ 13:10). [IRC § 414(p); ERISA § 206(d)(3)]

If a plan administrator is in doubt about how to give effect to a court order, it is very likely that the order is not a QDRO.

Because many divorce lawyers submit defective orders, a plan administrator often is tempted to treat a defective order as a QDRO. Because a plan administrator's effort to correct or resolve a defect might adversely affect one of the parties, yielding to this temptation can lead to further litigation.

In *Hullett,* the federal courts upheld a plan administrator's decision that a defective order was a QDRO. [Hullett v Towers Perrin Forster & Crosby Inc, 38 F 3d 107, 18 EBC (BNA) 2340, Pens Plan Guide (CCH) ¶ 23901Q (1994)] In the author's opinion, the court erred in this decision by applying Pennsylvania law rather than ERISA, by finding in dicta that the district court could review *de novo* the plan administrator's decision that the domestic relations order was a QDRO, and by remanding to the district court rather than the plan administrator for "fact finding" to resolve the ambiguous provisions of the order determined to be a QDRO. Perhaps this expensive litigation could have been avoided had the plan administrator properly decided that the order was not a QDRO.

Q 13:16 May a QDRO direct payment to the alternate payee's lawyer?

No. A QDRO cannot create or recognize a right for any person other than an alternate payee. [ERISA § 206(d)(3)(B)(i); IRC § 414(p)(1)(A)] An alternate payee cannot be anyone other than a spouse, former spouse, child, or other dependent of the participant. [ERISA § 206(d)(3)(k); IRC § 414(p)(8)] Therefore, a QDRO may not direct payment to the alternate payee's lawyer. [See Johnson v Johnson, Pension Plan Guide (CCH) ¶23,957T (NJ Super Ct 1999)]. A QDRO may direct payment to an alternate payee in an amount that reflects attorneys' fees within the child support ordered. [See Trustees of the Directors Guild of Am v Tise, 234 F 3d 415 (9th Cir 2000)]

A court order other than a QDRO has no effect regarding an ERISA plan. [ERISA § 514(b)(7)] Although for a non-ERISA 403(b) arrangement it is possible to use a court order other than a QDRO, it is unlikely that the participant's lawyer will allow the alternate payee's lawyer to do so—a court order other than a QDRO results in tax on the participant (see Q 13:44).

Q 13:17 Can a QDRO provide for a spouse in a same-sex couple?

Maybe. Even when recognized under applicable state law, a marriage of a same-sex couple will not be recognized in applying either ERISA or the Code. "In determining the meaning of any Act of Congress . . . , the word 'marriage' means only a legal union between one man and one woman as husband and wife, and the word 'spouse' refers only to a person of the opposite sex who is a husband or a wife." [1 USC § 7]

Another approach may accomplish the desired effect, however. That is, a QDRO may provide for a dependent of the participant. [ERISA § 206(d)(3)(B)(ii)(I); IRC § 414(p)(1)(B)(i)] If the participant provides sufficient support for his or her spouse in a same-sex couple, the nonparticipant may be a dependent. [See IRC § 152]

Even if a QDRO is effective to permit a distribution to a participant's same-sex spouse, it might not shift income tax to the alternate payee. Only an alternate payee who is the participant's spouse or former spouse as the United States Code defines that term is treated as a distributee. Any other distribution, even if paid under a valid QDRO, is treated as a distribution to the participant. Further, a QDRO distribution paid to an alternate payee who is not the participant's spouse or former spouse (as the United States Code defines that term) cannot be rolled over. [IRC §§ 402(c), 402(d)(4)(J), 402(e)(1)(A); Notice 89-25, 1989-1 CB 662, Q&A 4]

If an alternate payee is a nonspouse for federal income tax purposes, the plan administrator or payor must "withh[o]ld from the [QDRO] distribution as if the . . . participant were the payee." [Notice 89-25, 1989-1 CB 662, Q&A 3] The participant may make his or her withholding certificate on IRS Form W-4P.

Q 13:18   What is the importance of *earliest retirement age*?

A QDRO cannot require a plan to pay an alternate payee until the participant's earliest retirement age. [IRC §§ 414(p)(3)(A), 414(p)(4)(A)] For such purpose, *earliest retirement age* means the earlier of

1. The first date that the participant is entitled to a distribution; or
2. The later of
   a. The date the participant attains age 50, or
   b. The earliest date the participant could receive a distribution if the participant separated from service.

[IRC § 414(p)(4)(B); ERISA § 206(d)(3)(E)(ii)]

> **Example 13-4.** Susan has a 403(b) annuity contract that imposes no distribution restrictions other than those required by Code Section 403(b)(11). Susan divorces Tom when both of them are in their early 30s. If Susan continues to work for her employer, a QDRO cannot order a payment to Tom until Susan reaches age 50. If, however, Susan quits her job or is fired, a QDRO could require that Tom be paid immediately.

The rule that precludes a distribution to the alternate payee until the participant's earliest retirement age (unless the plan expressly specifies otherwise) is strictly construed. [Dickerson v Dickerson, 803 F Supp 127, 15 EBC (BNA) 2630 (ED Tenn 1992); Stott v Bunge Corp, 800 F Supp 567 (ED Tenn 1992)] Whether a defined contribution plan should permit a QDRO distribution before the participant's earliest retirement age is a plan design choice.

Q 13:19 Can a plan permit payment to an alternate payee before the participant's earliest retirement age?

Yes. A plan may permit payment to an alternate payee before the participant's earliest retirement age. [Treas Reg § 1.401(a)-13(g)(3); HR Conf Comm Rep on PL 99-514 (Tax Reform Act of 1986), 99th Cong, 2d Sess at II-858 (1986); Ltr Rul 8837013]

> **Practice Pointer.** Some plan sponsors choose to permit an immediate distribution to an alternate payee, believing that to do so is simpler than keeping a court order "open" for many years while waiting for the participant to reach retirement. Other plan sponsors decide that it is inappropriate to pay an alternate payee before the participant becomes entitled to receive a distribution. Further, such a provision might lead to fraud.

Q 13:20 Can an order made after the participant's death be a QDRO?

Maybe. For a defined benefit plan, an order made after the participant's death, even if the order "relates back" to the time of an earlier court order for state law purposes, is not a QDRO because such an order would "require the plan to provide increased benefits (determined on the basis of actuarial value)." [ERISA § 206(d)(3)(D)(ii); Robichaud v Samaroo, 193 F 3d 185, 23 EBC (BNA) 1761, 1999 US App LEXIS 23221 (3d Cir, Sept 24, 1999); but see Payne v GM/UAW Pension Plan, 1996 WL 943424 (ED Mich 1996)]

However, the same benefit soundness concerns typically are not involved with a defined contribution plan that permits a participant to designate any beneficiary to receive his or her undistributed account. As long as the participant's account has not been distributed and the order does not interfere with the rights of a surviving spouse, an order made after the participant's death may nonetheless be a QDRO. Of course, a domestic relations order must meet all of the QDRO requirements (see SQ 13:10).

The unpleasantness and expense of needless litigation can be avoided if the alternate payee's lawyer obtains an appropriate order before the participant's death and prepares that order to state that the former spouse is deemed the participant's surviving spouse to the extent of any distribution or benefit required under the order.

Special Provisions

Q 13:21 Can a QDRO provide survivor benefits to the alternate payee?

Yes. A QDRO may provide that an alternate payee who is a former spouse of the participant be treated as the participant's surviving spouse for all or some purposes of the ERISA survivor annuity rules. [ERISA § 206(d)(3)(F); IRC § 414(p)(5); Treas Reg § 1.401(a)-13(g)(4)] If used, such a provision would have the effect of wholly or partly depriving the participant's current spouse of survivor benefits to which he or she otherwise might become entitled. [ERISA § 206(d)(3)(F)(i); IRC § 414(p)(5)(A); Treas Reg §§ 1.401(a)-13(g)(4)(iii)(B), 1.401(a)-13(g)(4)(iii)(C)] If the former spouse who is treated as a current spouse dies before the participant's annuity starting date, the participant's actual current spouse is treated as the current spouse, except as otherwise provided by another QDRO. [Treas Reg § 1.401(a)-13(g)(4)(iii)(C)]

In the absence of an express statement in a QDRO that the former spouse will be treated as the participant's surviving spouse, a preretirement survivor annuity is payable to the participant's current spouse, even if that means that the former spouse receives no payment (because the participant died before becoming entitled to receive retirement benefits). [Dugan v Clinton, No 86-C-8492, 1987 WL 24805 (not reported) (ND Ill 1987)] Therefore, if a divorce practitioner is not certain that a QDRO distribution will be paid immediately, he or she should make sure that the court order states that the alternate payee is the surviving spouse, at least to the extent of the amount owing to the alternate payee. Also, a court order could compel the participant to designate his or her former spouse as beneficiary.

Bankruptcy

Q 13:46 Does a participant's bankruptcy affect an alternate payee's right to a 403(b) plan's payment?

No. A property settlement debt incurred in a divorce proceeding is nondischargeable. [11 USC § 523(a)(15)] Also, although a bankruptcy may impair a participant's obligation other than a divorce property settlement, a participant's bankruptcy does not affect a plan administrator's obligations. [See, e.g., In re Gendreau, 122 F 3d 815, 21 EBC (BNA) 1533, Pens Plan Guide (CCH) ¶23936M, Bankr L Rep ¶77,497 (9th Cir 1997), *cert denied*, 66 USLW 3475 (1998); see also In re McCafferty, 96 F 3d 192 (6th Cir 1996)] However, a participant's bankruptcy might impair the participant's obligations other than a property settlement debt. [See, e.g., In re Ellis, 72 F 3d 628 (8th Cir 1995); Bush v Taylor, 912 F 2d 989 (8th Cir 1990), *vacating prior opinion* at 893 F 2d 962 (8th Cir 1990)]

Practice Pointer. If there is a significant risk that the participant might become bankrupt, his or her spouse or former spouse should prefer (in the absence of other factors) a QDRO over a personal obligation that might be discharged in bankruptcy.

Practice Pointer. The attorney for the non-participant should work promptly to have the QDRO completed. In the absence of a QDRO, the courts have discharged bankrupt participants from responsibility for meeting marital-property expectations. [See, e.g., In re Varrone, 269 BR 475 (Bankr D Conn 2001); In re King, 24 BR 69 (Bankr D Conn 1997)]

Chapter 14

Tax Aspects of Church Plans

Danny Miller, Esq.
Ice Miller

David W. Powell, Esq.
Groom Law Group, Chartered

Church retirement plans described in Section 403(b) are generally retirement income account programs described in Code Section 403(b)(9). This chapter discusses the requirements that must be met by a Section 403(b)(9) retirement income account plan or program. Because a church retirement income account plan will almost always want to be exempt from the requirements of ERISA, this chapter also discusses the requirements for being treated as an ERISA exempt church plan. Finally, because the reader may wish to consider the advantages and disadvantages of a Section 403(b)(9) church retirement income account plan compared to a church Section 401(a) qualified plan, a general discussion of the requirements applicable to the latter type of plan has been provided (along with a discussion of a few miscellaneous church retirement plan issues).

Church Retirement Income Accounts

Q 14:6   Can retirement income account assets be commingled with other church assets?

The assets of a retirement income account may be commingled in a common fund with other church assets for investment purposes, but that part of any common fund that equitably belongs to any retirement income account must be separately accounted for and cannot be used for, or diverted to, any purposes other than the exclusive benefit of the employee and his or her beneficiaries. The other church assets with which retirement income account assets can be commingled are assets devoted exclusively to church purposes (e.g., a church endowment fund) and the assets of other church retirement and employee benefit programs (e.g., a Section 401(a) qualified plan). [TEFRA Comm Rep; see Ltr Ruls 19937052, 9645007, and 9123046. See also Ltr Ruls 200229050 (church permitted to commingle assets of 401(a) and 403(b) plans with church endowment funds), 200242047 (permitting commingling of assets of 403(b) plans, qualified plans, and IRAs)]

Special Definitions and Rules for 403(b) Church Plans

Q 14:10.1   Are there any special minimum distribution rules applicable to a 403(b) church plan?

Yes. On April 17, 2002, the IRS issued final regulations relating to required minimum distributions (RMDs) from 403(b) plans. These final regulations included special provisions for church retirement income accounts. The final regulations provide that annuity payments from 403(b)(9) church retirement income accounts may satisfy the requirements applicable to annuity payments issued by insurance companies, even if the payments are not made through a commercial insurer. This rule permits church retirement income accounts that "self-annuitize" to provide annuity payments without the need to purchase annuity contracts from commercial insurers. [Treas Reg § 1.403(b)-3, A-1(c)(3)]

Q 14:12.1   How does a minister's housing allowance affect contributions to a 403(b) plan?

A minister may be eligible to exclude all or a portion of his or her compensation from income to the extent that the compensation is eligible to be treated as a housing allowance under Code Section 107. Even though a minister's housing allowance may be excludable from income, it can still be counted as compensation for purposes of the plan's definition of that term used in determining retirement benefits. [Rev Rul 73-258, 1973-1 CB 194] The IRS there ruled that a minister's housing allowance can be counted as compensation for purposes of determining the amount of compensation on which contributions to a 401(a) qualified plan can be based. Although the IRS has not ruled on this issue in the context of a 403(b) plan, it is probable that the same conclusion would be reached with respect to determining the amount of compensation on which contributions to a 403(b) plan can be based.

However, although a 403(b) plan can include a minister's housing allowance in its plan definition of compensation, any such housing allowance that is excludable from income under Code Section 107 cannot be counted as compensation (or includible compensation) used for purposes of calculating contribution limits under Code Section 415. [Ltr Rul 200135045] Thus, in performing contribution limits testing, the excludable housing allowance will reduce the amount of a minister's includible compensation.

Miscellaneous Church Plan Provisions

Q 14:37 Are retirement payments made to retired clergy considered to be compensation with respect to which a tax-excludable housing allowance can be claimed?

Retirement payments made from the national retirement program of a church or convention or association of churches are entitled to be treated as a tax-excludable housing allowance, subject to the requirements of Code Section 107. [Rev Rul 75-22, 1975-1 CB 49; Rev Rul 63-156, 1963-2 CB 79] The IRS has not ruled on whether retirement payments made to retired clergy outside of a national denominational retirement plan (e.g., made directly through a local church) are eligible for exclusion under Code Section 107, but the principle of Revenue Ruling 63-156 would seem to be applicable in such a case. Whether this principle would also be extended to payments made from IRAs is not clear.

In 2002, Congress passed legislation to clarify the amount of housing allowance that can be excluded from income under Code Section 107. The Clergy Housing Allowance Clarification Act of 2002 [Pub L No 107-181, 116 Stat 583, was signed into law on May 20, 2002, and provides that the amount of excludable clergy housing allowance is limited to the fair rental value of the clergyperson's housing. This clarification should also apply to any housing allowance with respect to retirement distributions to eligible clergy from a 403(b) plan.

Chapter 15

Section 457 Plans

Henry A. Smith, III, Esq.
Smith & Downey

Internal Revenue Code Section 457 provides the rules on taxation of nonqualified deferred compensation arrangements between a state or local government or a nongovernmental, nonchurch tax-exempt organization and an individual who performs services for such an entity. This chapter examines both types of Section 457 plans: so-called eligible and ineligible plans. This chapter also examines which deferred compensation plans of governmental and tax-exempt entities are covered by Code Section 457 and the requirements that must be met by eligible plans under Code Section 457. The tax consequences to participants in eligible and ineligible plans under Code Section 457 are discussed, as well as the applicability of the Employee Retirement Income Security Act of 1974 (ERISA) to Section 457 plans. The changes made to the eligible plan rules by the Small Business Job Protection Act of 1996 (SBJPA) and the Economic Growth and Tax Relief Reconciliation Act of 2001 (EGTRRA) are discussed in detail, as are the IRS's proposed regulations under Code Section 457, which were issued in May 2002.

Overview

Q 15:3 What are the two types of Section 457 plans?

The first type of Section 457 plan is an *eligible deferred compensation plan.*
Eligible plans must meet specific requirements contained in Code Section 457. If
those requirements are met, participants may defer taxes on their elective
deferrals and any employer contributions under the plan (and earnings on those
deferrals and contributions) until amounts are paid or made available to them.
Although technically a nonqualified plan, an eligible plan resembles a tax-
qualified plan in that as long as the plan meets the requirements of Code
Section 457, plan participants are not taxed on their plan interests until they
actually receive plan distributions, even if they are fully vested in those interests
and even if, in the case of a governmental eligible deferred compensation plan,
those interests are funded.

The second type of Section 457 plan is an *ineligible deferred compensation
plan.* Ineligible plans are deferred compensation plans of governmental and
nonchurch tax-exempt employers that do not meet the Section 457 requirements
for eligible plans and resemble, in some ways, the nonqualified plans of for-
profit employers. Unlike participants in an eligible plan, participants in ineligible plans are taxed on their elective deferrals and any employer contributions
under the plan when those amounts cease to be subject to a substantial risk of
forfeiture. Earnings on ineligible plan contributions, like earnings on eligible
plan contributions, are taxed when amounts are paid or made available under
the plan.

Before 1997, eligible plans typically were used to provide deferred compensation to employees only by governmental entities that could not, and still may
not, sponsor tax-sheltered annuity programs under Code Section 403(b) (i.e.,
governmental entities other than certain educational organizations) and tax-
exempt entities that could not, and still may not, sponsor those programs (i.e.,
tax-exempt entities other than Section 501(c)(3) entities), because, among other
reasons, the dollar limit on annual deferrals under an eligible plan was (and still
is for participants age 50 and over) less than the dollar limit on annual deferrals
under more attractive Section 403(b) programs and was offset (through 2001),
dollar for dollar, by deferrals under Section 403(b) programs.

Since 1997, under a change contained in the Small Business Job Protection
Act of 1996 (SBJPA), tax-exempt employers have been able to sponsor 401(k)
plans. Therefore, from 1997 through 2001, eligible plans typically were used
only by governmental entities (which still may not sponsor 401(k) plans, except
for certain grandfathered arrangements) that may not sponsor Section 403(b)
programs, because, among other reasons, for those years the dollar limit on
annual deferrals under an eligible plan was less than the dollar limit on annual
deferrals for 401(k) and 403(b) plans and was offset, dollar for dollar, by
deferrals under 401(k) and 403(b) plans.

Beginning in 2002, the Economic Growth and Tax Relief Reconciliation Act of 2001 (EGTRRA) repealed the dollar for dollar offset of the 457(b) limit by deferrals under 401(k) and 403(b) plans. Therefore, beginning in 2002, most tax-exempt and governmental employers that did not previously maintain eligible plans established eligible plans in order to provide additional deferred compensation opportunities to their eligible employees. (It should be noted that although governmental and "ERISA church" employers may offer eligible plan participation to all their employees, employers governed by the Employee Retirement Income Security Act of 1974 (ERISA) must limit participation in their eligible plans to top-hat group members.)

Furthermore, because of the relatively low dollar limit that applies to eligible plans, even after the EGTRRA increase, entities that use them as part of an executive's deferred compensation package usually supplement them with ineligible plans. Therfore, ineligible plans generally have a much broader application for executive deferred compensation planning than eligible plans.

Q 15:8   May a rabbi trust be used in connection with a Code Section 457 plan?

Yes. A rabbi trust may be used in connection with a plan created under Code Section 457 (see Q 15:37). [Ltr Ruls 9212011, 9211037] The existence of the rabbi trust does not cause the underlying Section 457 plan to be funded and does not alter the tax treatment of plan participants. (It should be noted that proposed legislation would require the IRS to reconsider whether the existence of a rabbi trust causes a nonqualified plan to be funded. [Prop Treas Reg § 1.457-8(a)])

Note. Governmental eligible deferred compensation plans must now have actual trusts, as discussed in Qs 15:15 and 15:37.

Q 15:9   Are arrangements providing for the transfer of property in return for the performance of services subject to the provisions of Code Section 457?

No. Property transfer arrangements governed by Code Section 83 are not deferred compensation plans subject to Code Section 457. Benefits under those plans are not taxed until the time provided in Code Section 83.

For example, a number of tax-exempt employers have recently considered or instituted stock option programs, using mutual fund stock in place of the more typical employer stock, in order to provide executives with a form of not-currently-taxed compensation that is not subject to the limitations on eligible deferred compensation plans or the onerous taxation-on-vesting rules applicable to ineligible deferred compensation plans. However, the May 2002 IRS proposed regulations under Code Section 457 state that vested options granted under these plans after May 8, 2002, will not result in deferral of taxation under Code Section 83, but rather will result in current taxation under Section 457(f). [Prop Treas Reg § 1.457-12]

Eligible Plans

Q 15:16 Who is an *eligible employer?*

An *eligible employer* under Code Section 457 is a state, a political subdivision of a state, an agency or instrumentality of a state or political subdivision, and any other organization that is exempt from tax under Subtitle A of the Code other than churches (as defined). There It should be noted that, especially before the EGTRRA changes enhancing the Code Section 457 rules, being an eligible employer under Code Section 457 was not an advantageous designation, because it subjected the employer to the dollar for dollar offset rule, the Section 457(f) taxation-on-vesting rule, and other restrictions. There is still some controversy concerning whether a Native American tribe is an eligible employer as defined under Code Section 457. [See, e.g., "American Indian Tribes and 401(k) Plans," 95 TNT 132-31]

> **Note.** Subtitle A of the Code includes all organizations exempt from tax under Code Section 501 (i.e., many more tax-exempt organizations than the religious, educational, and charitable organizations that are tax exempt under Code Section 501(c)(3)).

Q 15:18 Is there a maximum amount that may be deferred by or on behalf of a participant under an eligible plan?

Yes. The maximum amount that may be deferred by or on behalf of a participant under an eligible plan for 2002 is the lesser of $11,000 or 100 percent of the participant's includible compensation, subject to rules under Code Section 457(b)(3), which provide for increased limits in certain limited circumstances (see SQ 15:19). This limit increases to $12,000 in 2003, $13,000 in 2004, $14,000 in 2005, and $15,000 in 2006 and thereafter. Prior to EGTRRA, this limit was the lesser of $8,500 or one-third of the participant's includible compensation.

The maximum amount of compensation that any individual participating in more than one eligible plan may defer under all of those plans during any taxable year may not exceed these limits (see Q 15:36). [IRC §§ 457(b)(2), 457(c)(1)]

For years prior to 2002, the maximum amount that a participant could defer under an eligible plan or plans also was required to be reduced by the following:

1. Amounts contributed by or on behalf of the participant under any tax-deferred annuity program for the taxable year (i.e., under a 403(b) plan);

2. Elective deferrals by the participant under any 401(k) plan for the taxable year (except a rural cooperative plan as defined in Code Section 401(k)(7));

3. Elective deferrals by the participant under any simplified employee pension (SEP) for the taxable year (except a rural cooperative plan as defined in Code Section 401(k)(7));

4. Amounts contributed by or on behalf of the individual under any savings incentive match plan for employees (SIMPLE) under Code Section 402(k) for the taxable year; and

5. Deductible contributions by the participant to a plan described in Code Section 501(c)(18), which involves certain trusts created before June 25, 1959, for the taxable year (except a rural cooperative plan as defined in Code Section 401(k)(7)).

The offset to the eligible plan limit for deferrals to other types of plans is repealed by EGTRRA, effective in 2002. [IRC § 457(c)(2)]

If amounts are deferred by or on behalf of a participant in excess of the eligible plan limit, most commentators believe that the excess amounts deferred will be considered to have been deferred under an ineligible plan. Some commentators believe, however, that Code Section 457 may be interpreted to mean that an eligible plan that permits excess deferrals will lose its eligible plan status for all purposes and all deferral amounts (see Q 15:36).

For years prior to 2002, if a participant had amounts contributed under a Code Section 403(b) plan, a 401(k) plan, a SEP, or a Section 501(c)(18) trust for a year and had amounts deferred under an eligible plan in the same year, and the total amounts deferred exceed the eligible plan limits, the excess deferrals were considered made available to the participant in the year of the deferral and subject to taxation. (For those years, if an individual participated in both a Section 457 plan and a Section 403(b) or 401(k) plan, the maximum aggregate deferral was $7,500 (indexed to $8,500 for 2001) increased, if applicable, by the catch-up provision (see SQ 15:19), but in no event in excess of the Section 403(b) or 401(k) limit, as applicable.) [Treas Reg § 1.457-1(b)(2), Exs 5, 6; Ltr Rul 9152026 (Sept 27, 1991)]

Q 15:19 Are the maximum deferral amounts for eligible plans ever increased for a participant?

Yes. During each of the three taxable years ending before the participant reaches normal retirement age, the participant may defer up to the lesser of two times the regular dollar limit (i.e., two times $11,000 in 2002, two times $12,000 in 2003, two times $13,000 in 2004, two times $14,000 in 2005, and two times $15,000 in 2006 and thereafter) or the sum of (1) the regular eligible plan limitation for the year (determined without regard to the special limit) and (2) as much of the maximum deferrals for prior years as have not been used previously (the catch-up provision).

This special catch-up limit is not available to a participant in a governmental eligible plan who takes advantage of the special "age 50 and older" catch-up provision made available under EGTRRA for those plans. Specifically, EGTRRA permits the following special catch-up contributions, in addition to the regular eligible plan dollar limits, for participants age 50 and older in governmental eligible plans: $1,000 in 2002, $2,000 in 2003, $3,000 in 2004, $4,000 in 2005, and $5,000 in 2006 and thereafter.

For purposes of the catch-up provision computation, unused deferrals for previous years may be included only for years after 1978 during which the individual was eligible to participate in the plan for all or any portion of the year.

A participant may elect the catch-up provision only once to apply to all or any portion of the three-year period. For example, if a participant elects to use the catch-up provision only for the one taxable year ending before normal retirement age, and, after retirement, the participant renders services for an eligible employer as an independent contractor, the eligible plan may not provide that the participant may use the catch-up provision for any of the taxable years subsequent to retirement. [IRC § 457(b)(2), (3); Treas Reg §§ 1.457-1(a)(2), 1.457-2(e), (f)]

For purposes of the catch-up provision, *normal retirement age* is the age specified in the plan. If no age is specified in the plan, normal retirement age is the later of the latest normal retirement age specified in the basic pension plan of the eligible employer or age 65. A plan may define normal retirement age as any range of ages ending no later than age 70$^{1}/_{2}$ and beginning no earlier than the earliest age at which the participant has the right to retire under the eligible employer's basic pension plan without the consent of the eligible employer and to receive immediate retirement benefits without an actuarial or similar reduction because of retirement before some later specified age in the eligible employer's basic pension plan. The plan also may provide that in the case of a participant who continues to work beyond the ages specified above, the normal retirement age will be the date or age designated by the participant, but that date or age may not be later than the mandatory retirement age provided by the eligible employer or the date or age at which the participant separates from the service of the eligible employer. [Treas Reg § 1.457-2(f)(4)]

Q 15:26   When must distributions commence under an eligible plan?

Payment of deferred amounts under an eligible plan must commence no later than the later of:

1. 60 days after the end of the plan year in which the participant or former participant attains, or would have attained, normal retirement age (see SQ 15:19); or

2. 60 days after the end of the plan year in which the participant separates from service (see Qs 15:23, 15:24).

[Treas Reg § 1.457-2(i)] (See Q 15:27 for the rules after SBJPA.)

Note. The IRS issued INFO 2001-0099, stating that the Code Section 72(t) penalty on premature distributions from qualified retirement plans and IRAs does not apply to Code Section 457 arrangements.

Q 15:33   Can amounts deferred under an eligible plan be rolled over to an individual retirement account (IRA), a tax-qualified plan, or a tax-sheltered annuity?

Prior to EGTRRA, there was no provision that permitted a rollover to an IRA from an eligible plan. Under pre-EGTRRA law, such a transfer would constitute a taxable distribution and an impermissible IRA contribution. [IRC § 457(a); Treas Reg § 1.457-1(a)(1); Rev Rul 86-103, 1986-2 CB 62; TAM 9121004] For example, the IRS noted in a 1991 ruling that a Section 457 plan is not an exempt trust, as described in Code Section 401(a), and is not treated as such an exempt trust; therefore, the Section 402(a)(6)(F) provision permitting tax-free rollovers of distributions required by a qualified domestic relations order (QDRO) from an exempt trust to an IRA does not apply to any distributions from a Section 457 plan made pursuant to a QDRO (see Q 15:39). [Ltr Rul 9145010]

Similarly, prior to EGTRRA, amounts deferred under an eligible plan could not be rolled over into a tax-qualified retirement plan (e.g., a 401(k) plan, a profit-sharing plan, a money purchase pension plan, or a defined benefit plan) or a Section 403(b) tax-sheltered annuity.

EGTRRA revised these rules to permit rollovers from governmental, but not tax-exempt, employer eligible plans to IRAs, among 401(a) qualified plans, 403(b) plans, and eligible plans, beginning in 2002.

Q 15:40   Has the IRS published any model language or recent regulations concerning eligible plans?

Yes. On July 27, 1998, the IRS published Revenue Procedure 98-41 [1998-32 IRB 7], which provides model amendments that employers that sponsor eligible plans may use to bring their plans into compliance with the changes to Code Section 457 contained in SBJPA and the Tax Reform Act of 1997 (TRA '97). The model amendments contained in Revenue Procedure 98-41 are based on earlier guidance provided by the IRS in Notice 98-8 [1998-4 IRB 6], which discussed the SBJPA and TRA '97 changes to Code Section 457. It is hoped that the IRS will publish similar model language that is intended to assist employers in ensuring that their eligible plans comply with the changes contained in EGTRRA.

In addition, in May 2002, the IRS published extensive proposed regulations under Code Section 457. [Prop Treas Reg §§1.457-1–1.457-12] The proposed regulations contained extensive guidance on the requirements for eligible plans, and two provisions affecting ineligible plans. The comment period for the proposed regulations expired on August 7, 2002. It is expected that the IRS will issue a revised version of the proposed regulations after it has had an opportunity to review the comments received.

Ineligible Plans

Q 15:44 How does a participant in or beneficiary of an ineligible plan treat the compensation deferred under that plan?

Compensation deferred under an ineligible plan is included in the gross income of the participant or beneficiary in the first taxable year in which there is no substantial risk of forfeiture of the rights to the compensation. In other words, participants in ineligible plans are taxed on amounts deferred by them or on their behalf as soon as those amounts become vested, even if those amounts are not then distributed or made available.

Earnings on the compensation deferred under an ineligible plan are includible in gross income when amounts under the plan are paid or made available to the participant or beneficiary. However, the IRS's May 2002 proposed regulations under Code Section 457 suggest that "earnings" for this purpose include only earnings accruing on ineligible plan deferrals after the vesting date for those deferrals. [Prop Treas Reg §§ 1.457-11(a)(2)] (It is unclear under the proposed regulations when fully vested earnings accruing prior to the deferrals' vesting date are taxable.) This position seems to contradict that of the current regulation on this topic, published in 1982. The current regulation suggests that all earnings (regardless of when they accrue) are not taxed until distributions are made under the ineligible plan, and most ineligible plan sponsors have consistently relied on this 1982 regulation. This author hopes that the IRS will withdraw the position on the earnings issue taken in the May 2002 regulations. Sponsors of ineligible plans should consult with counsel about this technical, but operationally important, issue and should monitor carefully developments affecting this issue.

The tax treatment of any amount made available to a participant or beneficiary under an ineligible plan is determined under the extraordinarily complex rules for annuities contained in Code Section 72. [IRC §§ 457(f), 72; Treas Reg § 1.457-3(a); Ltr Rul 8946019]

The application of the ineligible plan rules can be illustrated by the following two IRS rulings. In the first, Letter Ruling 9212006, a school district permitted teachers to defer salary during a four-year period (the deferral period) and to take a paid leave of absence during the year following the deferral period. A teacher would agree to defer 20 percent of salary for each year in the deferral period, and he or she would receive 100 percent of salary during the leave of absence. If the teacher terminated employment during the four-year deferral period, he or she would forfeit any right to the deferred salary and would not be entitled to a leave of absence. If the teacher terminated employment during the leave of absence, he or she would forfeit the right to the remaining monthly payments of salary for the year. The teacher also was required to return to employment for at least one year following the leave of absence. If the teacher failed to return to employment for the full year after the leave of absence, he or she would be required to repay the salary received during the leave of absence.

The IRS determined that the school district was an eligible employer within the meaning of Code Section 457(e)(1) and that the plan was governed by Code Section 457. Because the plan did not limit the amount of deferrals and because it would pay out deferred amounts while the teachers were employed by the school district, however, the IRS determined that the plan was an ineligible plan subject to the rules of Code Section 457(f). Applying those rules, the IRS determined that, because the teacher would forfeit the deferred amounts unless the teacher worked for four years and for an additional year after the leave of absence, the deferred amounts were subject to a substantial risk of forfeiture until paid, for purposes of Code Section 457(f). When paid to the teacher in year 5, however, the deferred amounts were includible in income in accordance with Code Section 72.

In the second ruling, Letter Ruling 9212011, a health care organization exempt from tax under Code Section 501(c)(3) entered into an agreement with an executive that created a supplemental account to which the employer credited 5 percent of the executive's monthly base salary. The executive was not able to make additional contributions to the account. The benefits would vest at the rate of 10 percent per year for ten years, but if the executive terminated employment with the employer at any time within that ten-year period, the executive would forfeit the nonvested portion of his benefits. If the executive did not terminate employment with the employer within ten years, payment of his benefits would commence within 60 days of the date of the executive's termination of employment and would be paid out in equal monthly installments over two years. The benefits could not be assigned, alienated, or encumbered by voluntary or involuntary action. The employer established a rabbi trust for the purpose of holding assets to fund the employer's obligations under the agreement.

The IRS determined that no plan contributions or benefits were taxable to the executive until the executive became vested in those benefits under the terms of the agreement, that the benefits would be includible in income at their value in the year when they were no longer subject to a substantial risk of forfeiture, and that the tax treatment of any amount made available under the agreement would be determined under Code Section 72.

Q 15:45   What have recent IRS private letter rulings concluded concerning the taxation of earnings in ineligible defined compensation plans?

On the issue of the timing of taxation of earnings in ineligible plans, there appears to be a conflict between the current regulation issued in 1982 and the May 2002 proposed regulations. [Prop Treas Reg § 1.457-11(a)(2)] In the past, the IRS has issued several letter rulings [see, e.g., Ltr Rul 9329010] that take the position reflected in the May 2002 proposed regulations. Similarly, Letter Ruling 9444028 appears to confirm the position of the commentators, who believe that the 1982 regulation stands for the proposition that earnings on amounts deferred under the plan, whether earned before or after the vesting date for the deferred amounts, are not taxed until amounts under the plan actually are paid or made available to the participants.

Q 15:51 Is a property transfer arrangement, such as a life insurance based plan or an option plan maintained by a governmental or nonchurch tax-exempt employer, subject to the ineligible plan rules?

No. Code Section 457 is not applicable to arrangements governed by Code Section 83 such as split-dollar life insurance plans or stock option plans. However, the May 2002 proposed regulations under Code Section 457 state that vested options issued by mutual fund stock option plans after May 8, 2002, are not effective to defer taxation under Code Section 83 but instead result in current taxation under Code Section 457. [See Prop Treas Reg § 1.457-12]

Chapter 16

Mergers and Acquisitions

David W. Powell, Esq.
Groom Law Group, Chartered

Mergers and acquisitions are less common in the tax-exempt community than among for-profit corporations. In certain sectors (particularly health care), however, sponsors of 403(b) and 457 plans are increasingly combining with or becoming part of other tax-exempt, governmental, and for-profit employers in a variety of arrangements, including mergers, acquisitions, and privatizations. The new configurations can give rise to many concerns—including plan terminations, severance pay, and distributions—that require unique responses. In addition, the Economic Growth and Tax Relief Reconciliation Act of 2001 (EGTRRA) has added some flexibility to these arrangements but raises some new issues as well.

403(b) Plan Considerations

Q 16:2 What happens if a tax-exempt organization eligible to maintain a 403(b) plan acquires another tax-exempt organization that maintains a 403(b) plan?

When a tax-exempt organization that sponsors a 403(b) plan is acquired by another tax-exempt organization, the acquiror should carefully review the acquiree's plan documents, Form 5500 filings, and other relevant information to determine whether the plan is in compliance with the Internal Revenue Code

(Code) and, if applicable, ERISA. The acquiror will also want to consider whether the design of the acquiree's plan is in accord with its own retirement plan objectives. Depending on the results of those examinations, the acquiror may choose to continue, correct, merge, freeze, or even terminate the acquiree's 403(b) plan (see SQ 16:3, Qs 16:5, 16:9). Whether the acquisition may result in a partial termination and vesting of accounts of affected participants under the acquiree's plan should also be considered.

If the acquiree becomes part of the same controlled group as the acquiror, careful attention should be paid to the impact of controlled group status on the application of nondiscrimination rules, such as the 403(b) plan nondiscrimination safe harbors of IRS Notice 89-23 [1989-1 CB 654], on the continued operation of the plans of either entity. Where transactions involve church or governmental entities, careful attention must also be paid to whether the post-transaction plans will be or will continue to be church or governmental plans in order to be certain which Code or, if applicable, ERISA requirements must be met. [See, e.g., Ltr Rul 9717039]

Where it is found that the acquiree's 403(b) plan has failed to satisfy the requirements of Code Section 403(b), it may be advisable for the plan to be frozen or terminated. Choosing either of those courses will depend on the degree of continuing responsibility that the acquiror wishes to have for the acquiree's plan. The acquiror may want for some reason (often, to meet employee expectations regarding the benefits that will continue to be available) to assume responsibility for the acquiree's 403(b) plan. Once the acquiree's 403(b) plan is corrected to meet the requirements of Code Section 403(b) (e.g., through the Self-Correction Program (SCP) or the Voluntary Correction for Tax-sheltered Annuities (VCT) program under IRS Revenue Procedure 2002-47 [2002-29 IRB 133] (see SQ 16:11)), the acquiror may either merge the acquiree's plan into its own 403(b) plan or simply assume operations of the plan.

In any event, any defects that would cause the acquiree's plan to fail to meet the requirements of Code Section 403(b), such as violations of the nondiscrimination requirements of Code Section 403(b)(12), must be given serious consideration: a merger of plans before appropriate correction that includes a plan that does not meet those requirements might cause the merged plan also to fail to satisfy Code Section 403(b). Other defects that may cause particular contracts not to satisfy Code Section 403(b) may be of concern if found in numerous contracts or in group contracts. [See Examination of 403(b) Plans, Guidelines Promulgated by the IRS, May 1999] Defects that merely cause an inclusion of excess amounts in taxable income, such as violations of the maximum exclusion allowance (MEA) (repealed after 2001) and the Section 415 limit, are presumably of lesser concern because they would not affect the status of the merged plan as a 403(b) plan. Nevertheless, they may, unless corrected, carry significant potential withholding tax or FICA tax liability for the acquiring employer.

Q 16:3   Can an acquiree's 403(b) plan be terminated?

Neither the Internal Revenue Service (IRS) nor the Department of Labor (DOL) has issued guidance on whether an acquiree's 403(b) plan can be terminated. Nonetheless, it should be possible to do so. At a minimum, it would require a corporate action to terminate the plan. [See, e.g., Ann 94–101, 1994-35 IRB 53]

Possibly, by analogy to the process established by the Pension Benefit Guaranty Corporation (PBGC) for terminating a qualified defined benefit plan that offers annuities, the acquiree's 403(b) plan may be terminated by distributing plan assets in the form of individual annuity contracts (or certificates under a group contract) that provide for the applicable distribution restrictions and other requirements of Code Section 403(b) and, in the case of plans subject to ERISA, the applicable spousal consent requirements. [See ERISA § 205] Any Section 403(b)(7) (i.e., mutual fund) monies and Section 403(b)(1) monies attributable to salary reduction contributions must continue to be subject to the applicable withdrawal restrictions. Unlike termination of a 401(k) plan, where it is sometimes possible to make distributions even though a separation from service or other event permitting a distribution under the general rules prohibiting in-service withdrawals has not occurred, termination of a 403(b) plan is not an event that in itself permits distributions earlier than such withdrawal restrictions would otherwise allow. Compare Code Section 403(b)(11) to Section 401(k)(10)(A). Of course, some transactions may result in an actual severance of employment that may in turn permit distribution (see SQ 16:7). If the withdrawal restrictions do allow a distribution, accounts that are subject to ERISA and are valued at less than $5,000 may be distributed without the participant's consent, as long as the 403(b) contract or account also so permits. Participants may be allowed to elect distributions of larger accounts upon a plan termination, if such distributions are permitted under the withdrawal restrictions and spousal consent requirements. The 10 percent excise tax under Code Section 72(t) on early distributions may apply to such distributions if they are not rolled over to another 403(b) plan or individual retirement account (IRA) or, after 2001, a 401(a) or governmental 457(b) plan.

If the acquiror also sponsors a 403(b) plan and is sufficiently convinced that the acquiree's plan has complied with Section 403(b) requirements in the past, the acquiror may allow participants to directly roll over (if a distribution is permitted) or to directly transfer benefits to the acquiror's 403(b) plan, as specified in Revenue Ruling 90-24. [1990-1 CB 97]

Q 16:7   Does acquisition of a 403(b) plan constitute a separation from service or severance of employment that would permit distributions?

By itself, it probably does not. Generally, salary reduction contributions to a 403(b) plan and contributions to a 403(b)(7) custodial account cannot be distributed before one of the following: attainment of age 59$\frac{1}{2}$, separation from service (before 2002), death, disability, or hardship (and no income may be distributed on account of hardship). EGTRRA amended the Code to substitute the term "severance of employment" for "separation from service" after 2001. The legislative history indicates that the purpose of this change was to eliminate the "same desk" rule, regardless of when the severance of employment occurred. [IRC §§ 403(b)(7)(A)(ii), 403(b)(11)] Under the pre-EGTRRA rule, there was little authority on what constituted a separation from service for purposes of a 403(b) plan; however, the concept had been discussed by the IRS in other situations, such as the distribution rules applicable to 401(k) plans and the pre-1993 rules that applied to the rollover of in-service distributions. In rulings in those two contexts, the IRS has generally held that an employee would be considered separated from the service of his or her employer only upon death, retirement, resignation, or discharge, and not when he or she continued in the same position for a different employer as a result of the liquidation, merger, consolidation, change of form, or transfer of ownership of his or her former employer. [Rev Rul 77–336, 1977-2 CB 202; Rev Rul 80–129, 1980-1 CB 86; Rev Rul 81–141, 1981-1 CB 204; Ltr Rul 9443041] This stance was known as the "same desk rule." In at least one letter ruling, the IRS has applied its 401(a) plan rulings regarding the same desk rule to 403(b) plans. [Ltr Rul 8617125]

Thus, under the pre-EGTRRA rule, whether the acquisition of a 403(b) plan sponsor would constitute a separation from service that would permit a distribution depended on the facts of the situation, with particular emphasis on whether the employee under consideration was continuing in the same job. It was also important to consider how the acquisition was treated for other benefits purposes (e.g., under Consolidated Omnibus Budget Reconciliation Act of 1985 (COBRA) health care continuation coverage).

It may be noted that the rules permitting distribution upon separation from service in the context of 401(k) plans had been earlier amended by the Tax Reform Act of 1986 (TRA '86) specifically to permit distributions upon the disposition by a corporation of substantially all of its assets, upon the disposition by a corporation of its interest in a subsidiary, or upon plan termination, if certain additional requirements are met. [IRC § 401(k)(10)] Similar provisions were not added to Code Section 403(b), however, and thus these exceptions to the same desk rule were not available to 403(b) plans.

After EGTRRA, a severance of employment with the common-law employer, such as in an asset acquisition, may be sufficient to permit distributions. This would make it possible for the affected participants to take eligible rollover distributions that might be rolled over to an acquiror's 401(k) plan, for example. However, distributions before age 59^1/$_2$ may still be subject to the 10 percent tax on early distributions under Code Section 72(f). In other cases, for example, where the acquiror may wish to take a transfer of a portion of the acquiror's 403(b) plan attributable to acquired participants into the acquiror's own 403(b) plan, it may be desirable to amend the 403(b) plan to not permit distributions upon severance of employment before age 59^1/$_2$.

Note, however, that the IRS has indicated that even though there may have been a severance of common-law employment, a distribution from the acquiree's plan may not be permitted when there is a transfer of assets and liabilities to a plan maintained by the new employer, or if the new employer assumes the acquiree's plan. [See Notice 2002-4, 2002-2 IRB 298]

Q 16:11 What happens if an acquiree's 403(b) plan is found to have defects?

Many defects of a 403(b) plan may be corrected under the VCT program (see chapter 18). The VCT program, however, can require a time-consuming submission process. Further, under SCP, many operational defects can be corrected without involving the IRS. There is a requirement that corrections be completed by the end of the second year after the year the violation occurred unless the defect was "insignificant" (see chapter 18). [Rev Proc 2002-47, 2002-29 IRB 133] Generally, if the acquiror's 403(b) plan is not also defective, it will often be advisable to keep the acquiror's plan and the acquiree's plan separate until any deficiencies in the acquiree's 403(b) plan are resolved.

Severance Pay and 403(b) Plans

Q 16:12 Could severance pay be deferred under a 403(b) plan as a salary reduction contribution under the law in effect before 1996?

Prior IRS authority indicated that the ability of employees to defer severance pay to a 403(b) plan was significantly limited. Under the law in effect before August 20, 1996 (the effective date of the Small Business Job Protection Act of 1996 (SBJPA)), IRS regulations provided that a salary reduction agreement was effective "only to the extent such amounts are earned by the employee after the agreement becomes effective." [Treas Reg § 1.403(b)-1(b)(3)(i)] In the context of severance payments, the IRS has held that amounts will be treated as earned in the year "when the services are performed which give rise to the employee's entitlement to the terminal pay," not when the severance pay vests. [See GCM 39659 (Sep 8, 1987) (terminal pay based on accumulated leave and service that vested only on retirement or death was considered earned each year in which services were performed, rather than upon vesting)]

The IRS's position on this matter was also articulated in its "Guidelines for Examination of 403(b) Plans" published by the IRS in May 1999. The guidelines similarly apply the "earned when services performed" concept in the analogous context of determining includible compensation for Section 403(b)(2) MEA purposes, which also requires that compensation be earned within the year. [See also Treas Reg § 1.403(b)-1(e)(1)(I)]

It should be noted that neither the regulations nor the guidelines address how to determine how much severance pay was earned in each year—a practical problem with the IRS's position. For example, in the case of a newly established severance pay plan, it is simply unclear whether a portion of severance pay based on years of service performed before the establishment of the plan may be attributable to such earlier years or whether such retroactive amount is considered earned in the year the plan is established.

Interestingly, the IRS has backed away from the "earned" requirement to permit pick-up contributions of severance pay and unpaid leave to governmental plans. [Ltr Rul 200249009]

457 Plan Considerations

Q 16:15 What happens if an employer sponsoring a 457(b) plan is acquired by another tax exempt or governmental employer?

When a tax-exempt organization such as a hospital is merged with another tax-exempt organization or a governmental employer, the acquiree's 457(b) plan may continue to be maintained (and expanded and modified favorably, in the case of a governmental acquiror), but it is advisable to review the terms of the plan to ensure that such terms will apply as intended under the post-merger entity.

Similarly, when a governmental employer maintaining a 457(b) plan is acquired by another governmental employer, the successor employer may continue to maintain the 457(b) plan. However, when a tax-exempt employer acquires a governmental employer's 457(b) plan, the differences between the 457 rules for governmental sponsors and tax-exempt sponsors in funding, distribution election and rollover rules effectively preclude continued operation of the plan by a nongovernmental entity. In such cases, the proposed regulations indicate that the governmental 457(b) plan may be frozen and transferred to continue to be maintained by another governmental entity, or the plan must be terminated, in which case all assets must be distributed as soon as practicable. If the plan is neither transferred nor terminated, the assets will be taxable under Code Section 402(b) or 403(c), and the trust will become a taxable trust. [Prop Treas § 1.457-10(a)(2)]

In the reverse situation, when a tax-exempt employer's 457(b) plan is acquired by a governmental employer, the proposed regulations indicate that Code Section 457(f) and Proposed Treasury Regulations Section 1.457-11 (i.e., the "substantial risk of forfeiture" rules) will apply. [Prop Treas Reg § 1.457-10(a)(2)(i)] However, it is not clear that this cannot be corrected by commencing to comply with the special correction rules for governmental 457(b) plans. [See Prop Treas Reg § 1.457-9]

Special attention should also be paid to whether the plans under the pre- or post-merger entities may be top-hat or church or governmental plans and whether they may gain or lose such status as a result of the merger or acquisition, because retention of non-ERISA status is usually crucial to the compliance of such plans with the Code. In some types of business combinations, such as joint ventures, the status of a plan may not be at all clear, and the facts may require careful evaluation.

Q 16:16 What happens to an acquiree's 457(b) plan if the acquiror is not tax exempt or governmental?

When a tax-exempt organization is acquired by a for-profit organization, important issues arise. First, it should be noted that Code Section 457 does not in fact confer advantages to nonqualified plans of tax-exempt employers (other than perhaps to avoid constructive receipt upon making a payout election, and even that is questionable), but, rather, generally serves to restrict nonqualified deferrals. Thus, there is likely to be little advantage in deferring additional compensation in compliance with the terms of a Section 457(b) plan if the surviving entity is a for-profit corporation. The ordinary rules applicable to nonqualified arrangements not subject to Code Section 457 are likely to be much more beneficial with the exception of the distribution rules; therefore, the creation of a new nonqualified deferred compensation arrangement may be advisable. The Proposed Treasury Regulations state that the acquired 457(b) plan will become subject to the constructive receipt rules of Code Section 451, but do not indicate what the result of that may be. [Prop Treas Reg § 1.457-10(a)(2)(i)]

Where the acquiree's plan was a governmental plan, as noted above, the different rules for governmental 457(b) plans will preclude it from being maintained by a nongovernmental entity without violating numerous Code and ERISA requirements, and the plan should be terminated or frozen or transferred to another governmental entity.

Q 16:17 What should be done with the acquiree's 457(b) plan if the acquiror is not tax exempt or governmental?

The Proposed Treasury Regulations state that a 457(b) plan that is maintained by an employer who is not an eligible employer will become subject to (1) the constructive receipt rules of Code Section 451 if the employer is for-profit entity, or (2) the "substantial risk of forfeiture" rules of Code Section 457(f) if the employer is a governmental entity. As a result, it is likely that most ineligible employers acquiring such plans will wish to terminate the plan and distribute the assets to participants and beneficiaries as soon as practicable. [See Treas Reg § 1.457-10(a)(2)] However, if a for-profit employer determines that the constructive receipt issues can be addressed, although the IRS has issued no guidance on the continued administration of a nongovernmental 457(b) plan when the sponsor is no longer tax exempt, presumably, continuation is permissible provided that the 457(b) plan must continue to operate in a manner exempt from ERISA. Again, it is not possible for a governmental 457(b) plan to be taken over by a nongovernmental sponsor. It will be necessary for the 457(b) plan to be terminated or frozen and transfered, to be maintained by another governmental entity.

Another issue not addressed by the IRS is the consequence of amending an eligible 457(b) plan so that it no longer meets the requirements of Code Section 457(b); for example, by deleting the minimum distribution rules or by providing a new, impermissible form of distribution election. Although arguably the plan may be viewed as no longer subject to Code Section 457, in the absence of a substantial risk of forfeiture, it is possible that the IRS might view such a change as giving rise to immediate taxation of the amounts previously deferred while the entity was subject to Code Section 457.

A different result may occur if the 457 plan sponsored by the tax-exempt sponsor was an ineligible plan. Presumably, additional deferrals of post-merger compensation under what had been a 457(f) plan (i.e., a plan not meeting the requirements of Code Section 457(b) and therefore either treating benefits as subject to a substantial risk of forfeiture or currently taxable) will operate to defer taxation pursuant to the ordinary nonqualified plan rules rather than the rules of Code Section 457(f). Of course, it will always be advisable to review the terms of the ineligible plan to determine whether any changes in plan design may be called for, such as changes in distribution elections. It is unclear whether the deferrals made while the plan was subject to Code Section 457(f) must remain subject to a substantial risk of forfeiture to defer taxation even if the plan is no longer subject to Code Section 457, although the prior and proposed regulations appear to suggest that this is so. [See, e.g., former Treas Reg § 1.457-3(a) and Prop Treas Reg § 1.457-11(a)(1)]

Q 16:18 Can an acquiree's 457 plan be terminated?

If the terms of the plan so permit, an acquiree's 457 plan can be terminated after the acquisition, with distribution as soon as practicable and taxation of benefits to the participants and beneficiaries upon distribution as the result. [Prop Treas Reg § 1.457-10(a)]

Q 16:20 Does the merger or acquisition of a 457(b) plan sponsor constitute a separation from service or severance of employment that would permit distributions?

Before June 7, 2001, probably not. As in the case of 403(b) plans, the same desk rule applied to the merger or acquisition of a 457 plan sponsor (see SQ 16:7). A change in the tax-exempt status of the employer was apparently not a separation from service. [IRC § 457(d)(1)(A)(ii); Ltr Rul 9901014] However, effective June 7, 2001, under EGTRRA, the reference to a "separation from service" in order to permit a distribution was amended to a "severance of employment" for the purpose of eliminating the same desk rule. Thus, upon a change in the common-law employer of the participant, a distribution may be permissible unless the plan terms themselves are more restrictive. [See Rev Proc 2002-47, 2002-29 IRB 133.]

Chapter 18

Tax-Sheltered Annuity Voluntary Correction Programs

Greta E. Cowart, Esq.
Haynes and Boone, LLP

To fill the need for regulatory oversight of tax-sheltered annuities, the Internal Revenue Service announced its Tax-Sheltered Annuity Voluntary Correction (TVC) program in Revenue Procedure 95-24. [1995-1 CB 694] TVC was the first voluntary compliance program designed to help employers make corrections to defects discovered in the administration of their 403(b) plans without disqualifying the plans. The program was extended by Revenue Procedure 96-50 [1996-47 IRB 10] to correction requests filed on or before December 31, 1998. It was extended and substantially modified by Revenue Procedure 99-13. [1999-5 IRB 52] The TVC program was incorporated into the Employee Plans Compliance Resolution System (EPCRS), as restated by Revenue Procedure 2000-16. [2000-6 IRB 518] Revenue Procedure 2001-17 [2001-7 IRB 589] rewrote EPCRS and renamed the correction programs. The TVC program is now the Voluntary Correction of Tax-Sheltered Annuities (VCT) program, and the Administrative Policy Regarding Self-Correction (APRSC) became the Self-Correction Program (SCP). VCT is modeled in most respects on the Voluntary Compliance Resolution program previously instituted for plans qualified under Code Section 401(a).

Early in 1997, the IRS expanded its initiatives encouraging voluntary compliance for 403(b) plans with the release of a field directive inaugurating APRSC. Revenue Procedure 98-22 [1998-12 IRB 11], updated by Revenue Procedure 2000-16 [2000-6 IRB 518], expanded APRSC as part of the EPCRS, which stated that employers may rely on the availability of EPCRS. APRSC was renamed by Revenue Procedure 2001-17 as SCP. Although SCP represents an alternative to the VCT program, it differs from that program: there is no written acceptance of any correction under SCP until the 403(b) plan is audited.

Overview of SCP

Q 18:1   When did the IRS institute SCP, and to which plans does it apply?

On January 7, 1997, the IRS released the Administrative Policy Regarding Self-Correction (APRSC). It replaced the Administrative Policy Regarding Sanctions, which was part of the Internal Revenue Manual and did not apply to 403(b) plans. APRSC applies both to qualified plans under Code Section 401(a)and to 403(b) plans. Before January 7, 1997, IRS agents auditing 403(b) plans had no official basis for excusing a 403(b) plan's minor violations.

On March 23, 1998, the IRS consolidated and updated APRSC with the other correction programs for qualified plans under Code Section 401(a)into the Employee Plans Compliance Resolution System (EPCRS). While EPCRS incorporated APRSC, it did not affect or address VCT.

Revenue Procedures 99-13 and 2000-16 [1999-5 IRB 55; 2000-6 IRB 518] expanded the application of APRSC to 403(b) plans and clarified the acceptable corrections for contributions in excess of the maximum exclusion allowance (MEA) and annual addition limitations. Revenue Procedure 2001-17 renamed APRSC as SCP, but deleted the examples of corrections of contributions in excess of the MEA and annual additions. Revenue Procedure 2001-17 was updated by Revenue Procedure 2002-47. [2002-29 IRB 130]

Q 18:2   Does SCP apply to all 403(b) arrangements?

SCP specifically states that it applies to "403(b) plans." The term *plan* apparently includes two senses of the term: that in the audit guidelines and that under ERISA Sections 3(3) and 402. The audit guidelines refer to all tax-sheltered annuity contracts available with respect to an employer as 403(b) plans.

Q 18:3   How is SCP applied to a 403(b) plan?

SCP is applied at the discretion of the IRS agent auditing the 403(b) plan. He or she is empowered to determine whether a 403(b) plan qualifies for SCP and whether the violations and corrections satisfy the policy's requirements. Although an employer can try to satisfy the SCP requirements, it has no assurance that its corrections are acceptable until the plan is audited and the IRS agent reviews the corrections and approves or rejects them.

Revenue Procedures 98-22, 2000-16, 2001-17, and 2002-47 [1998-1 IRB 723; 2000-6 IRB 518; 2001-7 IRB 589; 2002-29 IRB 130] indicate that "[t]axpayers should be able to rely on the availability of EPCRS in taking corrective actions to maintain the qualified status of their plans"; however, the extent to which taxpayers may rely on this is unclear and will be determined based on the facts and circumstances as well as on each employer's situation and compliance practices and procedures. For example, is reliance misplaced if the policies and procedures are not complete in the view of the IRS agent auditing the 403(b) plan?

Q 18:4   What are the basic eligibility requirements for SCP?

Only operational violations are eligible for correction under SCP. Any violation that requires a plan or contract amendment is ineligible (see Q 18:5). Under SCP, a 403(b) plan can correct its operational violations through prompt self-correction. Insignificant violations may be corrected regardless of when they are discovered. Under SCP as it was originally applied to 403(b) plans, in order for an operational violation to be eligible for SCP, it must not be a violation that solely results in income inclusion. When Revenue Procedure 99-13 expanded APRSC, it permitted a certain self-correction of violations of the MEA and annual addition limitations. [Rev Proc 99-13, 1999-1 CB 409; Rev Proc 2000-16, 2000-6 IRB 518] Revenue Procedure 2001-17 [2001-7 IRB 589] did not include the examples of corrections of MEAs or annual addition excesses as were included in the prior revenue procedures; however, representatives of the Internal Revenue Service have indicated there was no intention to delete those corrections from SCP. Revenue Procedure 2002-47 [2002-29 IRB 130] in section 8, Example 5 added examples of 403(b) plans eligible for SCP because they are insignificant failures in the aggregate.

Both the self-correction and the insignificant defect methods require that the 403(b) plan's violation be an operational violation and that the violation and the plan or arrangement meet the requirements in items 1, 2, and 3 below. If those requirements are met and the violation is caught and corrected before the end of the second plan year following the plan year in which it occurred, it may be corrected under the self-correction methodology (see SQ 18:8, Q18:9), regardless of whether the violation is insignificant. (It should be noted that APRSC originally required correction within the plan year following the plan year in which the error occurred for the self-correction method. This requirement was changed by Announcement 97-12. [1997-7 IRB 55]) If the requirements in items

1, 2, and 3 are met and the violation is not caught and corrected before the end of the second plan year following the plan year in which it occurred, the violation may be corrected only if it is insignificant under the provisions in SCP (see Q 18:11). Revenue Procedure 2001-17 and 2002-47 clarified that for Code Section 401(m) violations the two-year correction period begins to run after the statutory correction period.

In order to be able to use SCP, the employer must meet the following three requirements:

1. *Violation eligibility.*

    a. Under APRSC as originally issued, the violation may not be a violation that can be corrected only by amending the plan. It should be noted that non-ERISA 403(b) plans are not required to have plan documents for tax law purposes; thus, the preceding sentence applies only to 401(a) plans. An operational violation of a tax-sheltered annuity program is a violation that would otherwise result in the loss of the exclusion allowance (e.g., failure to make minimum required distributions), and it is not a demographic or eligibility failure or a failure to purchase annuity contracts or deposit amounts into custodial accounts on behalf of persons who are not employees.

    b. Under Revenue Procedure 99-13, APRSC for 403(b) plans was expanded to permit self-correction of violations of the MEA and annual addition limitation violations in addition to the operational violations described in item 1a above.

2. *Established practices and procedures.* A plan sponsor or administrator must have established practices and procedures (formal or informal) reasonably designed to promote and facilitate overall compliance with Code Section 403(b). SCP is available to 403(b) plans, and it is generally understood that such term would include 403(b) arrangements that are not "plans" for ERISA purposes. Administrators of non-ERISA 403(b) arrangements need to be aware, however, that the implementation of such practices and procedures could be triggers for Department of Labor (DOL) issues regarding plan status under ERISA. That is, establishing certain practices and procedures that make the 403(b) arrangement eligible for SCP may cause the 403(b) arrangement to become a plan for purposes of ERISA. The practices and procedures must have been in place and routinely followed, but, through an oversight or mistake in applying or because of an inadequacy in the procedures, the operational violation occurred. Tax-sheltered annuity plans may need to develop practices and procedures in order to be eligible for SCP.

3. *Correction.* The correction must be a full correction of all violations for all years in which the defects occurred, restoring both current and former participants and beneficiaries to the benefits and rights that they would have had if there had been no violation. The plan itself must also be restored to the position it would have been in if no violations had

occurred. APRSC and SCP differ from their predecessor, the Administrative Policy Regarding Sanctions, in that "full correction" is required for all violations for all years, both open and closed, and not just "to the extent possible." What constitutes full correction is not yet clear for all defects.

Revenue Procedure 99-13 added correction of MEA and annual addition limitation violations to APRSC, but Revenue Procedure 2001-17 continues to exclude from its application eligibility and demographic failures. Contributions in excess of the MEA and annual addition limitation may only be corrected under APRSC or SCP using the distribution method, in which the amounts in excess of the limitations and all earnings thereon must be distributed to the affected participants and beneficiaries and included in their gross income in the year distributed.

Q 18:7   How complete must the compliance practices and procedures be for a 403(b) plan to be eligible for SCP?

The compliance practices and procedures for a 403(b) plan must be as complete as the IRS agent auditing the plan requires for the plan to be eligible for SCP. That means that 403(b) plans must develop compliance practices and procedures that are as complete and thorough as the strictest IRS agent may require to assure that the plan may successfully argue for the application of SCP. An employer not only must develop the compliance practices and procedures but also must implement them in the operation of the 403(b) plan. Revenue Procedures 99-13, 2000-16, 2001-17, and 2002-47 [1999-1 CB 409; 2000-6 IRB 518; 2001-7 IRB 589; 2002-29 IRB 130] make it clear that a plan document is not necessary and also is not sufficient to prove that the employer has established compliance practices and procedures.

Q 18:8   What violations in a 403(b) plan can be corrected through the self-correction method under SCP?

Any operational violation that is eligible, whether or not it is insignificant, may be corrected by the plan sponsor by the end of the second plan year following the plan year in which the violation occurred. Demographic failures and eligibility failures as defined in Revenue Procedures 99-13, 2000-16, 2001-17, and 2002-47 [1999-1 CB 409; 2000-6 IRB 518; 2001-7 IRB 589; 2002-29 IRB 130] are not eligible to be corrected under SCP. The self-correction method is open to any number of eligible operational defects and excess amounts as defined in Revenue Procedures 99-13, 2000-16, and 2002-47, as long as the employer promptly discovers and fully corrects the violation within the specified time period. Thus, the self-correction method gives employers an incentive to constantly monitor their 403(b) plan's compliance with the applicable laws.

Operational violations that may be corrected under APRSC and subsequently SCP after issuance of Revenue Procedures 99-13, 2000-16, 2001-17, and 2002-47 include the following:

1. Failure to satisfy the uniform availability requirement in Code Section 403(b)(12)(A)(ii);

2. Failure to satisfy the actual contribution percentage test under Code Section 401(m);

3. Failure to limit compensation considered to the limitation under Code Section 401(a)(17)($160,000 for 1999, $170,000 for 2000 and 2001, and $200,000 in 2002 and 2003);

4. Failure to comply with the distribution restrictions in Code Section 403(b)(7)or 403(b)(11);

5. Failure to satisfy the incidental death benefit rules of Code Section 403(b)(10);

6. Failure to pay the minimum required distributions under Code Section 403(b)(10);

7. Failure to give employees the right to elect a direct rollover or to give the employees notification of such right as required under Code Section 403(b)(10);

8. Failure to limit elective deferrals to the maximum dollar limit under Code Section 402(g)($10,000 is the basic limit for 1999, $10,500 for 2000 and 2001, $11,000 for 2002, and $12,000 for 2003);

9. Failure involving contributions of allocations in excess of the MEA (for years prior to 2002) or annual addition limitation; and

10. Any other failure to satisfy applicable requirements under Code Section 403(b)that results in the loss of 403(b) status for the plan or the loss of 403(b) status for the custodial accounts or annuity contracts under the plan, provided the violation is not a demographic failure or an eligibility failure as such failures are defined under Revenue Procedures 99-13, 2000-16, 2001-17, and 2002-47.

The failures described in item 9 above may be corrected under SCP only by distributing the excess contribution or allocation adjusted for earnings through the date of distribution to the affected participants and beneficiaries. The other method for correction of MEA or annual addition limit violations (retaining the excess amounts in the account and reducing future contribution limits) is available only if the employer files for correction under the VCT program.

The self-correction method requires that a 403(b) plan's eligible operational violations, insignificant or not, be promptly corrected in full. What constitutes a "full correction" for all the types of eligible operational violations is unclear; few corrections that have been approved through the various compliance programs have been published (see Q 18:5).

Self-correction under SCP is not available for egregious operational failures, eligibility failures, or demographic failures, or for any failure relating to a misuse or diversion of plan assets.

Self-correction is not available to any plan that has received verbal or written notice of an impending examination by the Tax Exempt and Governmental Entities (TEGE) operating division (formerly the Employee Plans (EP) and Exempt Organizations (EO) divisions) or that is currently under such an examination.

Although qualified plans under Code Section 401(a) must have a determination letter or its equivalent for nonindividually designed plans, similar requirements are not imposed on 403(b) plans. Tax-sheltered annuity plans can obtain a private letter ruling on their qualification, but many do not do so. Even though SCP does not state that a private letter ruling is required for a 403(b) plan, such a ruling does provide assurance that the form of the 403(b) plan is in compliance with applicable laws.

Q 18:10   What is the insignificant defect method of correction?

If a violation is not corrected by the end of the second plan year following the plan year in which the violation occurred (see Q 18:9), it may still be eligible for SCP if it is considered to be insignificant given all of the facts and circumstances. The factors considered in determining whether a violation is insignificant for purposes of SCP include, but are not limited to, the following:

1. The number of violations that occurred during the period being examined (a type of violation that affects more than one participant is not considered to have occurred more than once);

2. The percentage of plan assets and contributions involved in the violations;

3. The number of years in which the violations occurred;

4. The number of participants affected by the violation considered in relation to the number of participants in the plan;

5. The number of participants affected as the result of the violation relative to the number of participants who could have been affected by the violation;

6. Whether the plan sponsor made corrections before the plan was examined (APRSC was originally issued as a field directive to guide IRS agents auditing plans; it was incorporated in EPCRS in Revenue Procedure 98-22 and renamed SCP in Revenue Procedure 2001-17 [2001-7 IRB 589], where it is more readily available to employers and practitioners); and

7. The reason for the violations (e.g., errors in transcription, transposition of numbers, minor errors in arithmetic).

The fact that more than one violation occurred in a single year will not automatically disqualify a plan from SCP if the violations in the aggregate are insignificant. Further, if a violation occurs in more than one year, it will not automatically be considered significant. In an example set forth in SCP, a tax-sheltered annuity plan had three different violations affecting three persons in a tax-sheltered annuity plan with 200 participants, and those violations were said to be insignificant. The violations included a failure to make minimum distributions, an impermissible hardship withdrawal, and an excess elective deferral (a contribution in excess of the Section 402(g) limit).

Any correction under the insignificant defect method also must be fully corrected and must place the participant and the plan in the same position they would have been in had there been no violation. Revenue Procedures 98-22 and 2002-47 [1998-12 IRB 11; 2002-29 IRB 130] provides correction principles and examples.

The correction principles state that a qualified failure is not corrected unless full correction is made with respect to all participants and beneficiaries and for all taxable years (whether or not the taxable year is closed). All of the terms of the plan as they existed at the time of the failure are considered when determining whether full correction was made. Because many 403(b) arrangements do not have plan documents, this may be a difficult factor to consider for full correction determination of 403(b) arrangements. The following principles guide whether a correction is a full correction under EPCRS:

- Full correction requires restoration of benefits to what the plan position would have been if there had been no failure, including restoration of current and former participants and beneficiaries to the benefits and rights they would have had if the failure had not occurred.

- The correction should be reasonable and appropriate for the failure, and any standardized correction under the Standardized Voluntary Compliance Program (SVP) renamed Voluntary Correction Standard (VCS) is deemed to be a reasonable and appropriate correction for that particular failure. [Rev Proc 94-62, 1994-2 CB 778] (SVP or VCS is available only to qualified plans under Code Section 401(a).) The correction should resemble a correction already provided for in the Code, the income tax regulations, or other generally applicable guidance. Any correction relating to a nondiscrimination failure should provide benefits for non-highly compensated employees. The correction should keep the plan assets in the plan, except to the extent the Code, regulations, or other guidance generally applicable, requires distribution. The correction should not violate any other applicable requirement.

- Corrective allocations under a defined contribution plan are addressed and provide guidance for defined contribution plans; however, this portion of the guidance provides little guidance for 403(b) plans because failure to follow the plan document is not a violation for a 403(b) plan. Thus, the corrective contributions described in Revenue Procedures 2001-17 and 2002-47 provide little guidance for 403(b) plans.

Special exceptions to full correction are enumerated in Revenue Procedure 2002-47:

- If it is not possible to make a precise calculation or if the probable difference between the approximate and the precise restoration of the participant's benefit is insignificant and the administrative cost of determining precise restoration would exceed the probable difference, full correction is not required.

- If the total corrective distribution due a participant or beneficiary is $50 or less, the corrective distribution is not required if the reasonable direct cost the employer would incur in processing the distribution would exceed the amount of the distribution.

- If the correction requires locating lost participants (current or former) or beneficiaries to provide additional benefits and those persons cannot be located after mailing to the last known address and using the IRS letter forwarding program [Rev Proc 94-22, 1994-1 CB 608] or the Social Security Administration Reporting Service, then the plan is not considered to have failed to correct a failure that is due to the inability to locate the person. However, if the individual is later located, the additional benefits must be provided at that time.

- If corrected by submission under VCP, then for any overpayment to a participant or beneficiary of $100 or less, the Plan Sponsor is not required to pursue repayment.

Also note the following:

- Any additional distributions must be properly reported.

- The IRS indicated that it may provide additional rules regarding appropriate correction methods.

How the IRS will apply SCP is yet to be determined. The development of literature showing cases in which SCP is applied is very limited because the nature of the program requires the cases resolved under SCP in audits to be kept confidential. [Rev Proc 2001-17, § 6.09] Its application will be developed by individual agents in consultation with the Closing Agreement Program Coordinator for the area in one of the six areas, according to reported IRS memoranda accompanying SCP. The areas reported their SCP results to the IRS National Office, which will compile and distribute the results among the districts. Such sharing of information should assist in leveling the application of SCP among the key districts. It is not clear if this will continue under Revenue Procedure 2001-17.

Overview of the VCT Program

Q 18:12 What is the purpose of the VCT program?

The Voluntary Correction of Tax-Sheltered Annuities (VCT) program was developed by the IRS National Office in response to requests from practitioners and employers for a way to correct the violations found in 403(b) plans.

Similar in concept to the Voluntary Compliance Resolution (VCR) program, the VCT program's stated purpose is to "permit an employer who offers a tax-sheltered annuity plan under Section 403(b) to voluntarily identify and correct defects in the plan." [Rev Proc 95-24, 1995-1 CB 694, § 1.01] It offers a sponsoring employer a means of correcting defects it has identified in its 403(b) program without losing the tax exclusion and exemption applicable under Code Section 403(b). The TVC program as initially introduced was similar to the Walk-in Closing Agreement Program (Walk-in CAP) in its sanction calculation. The VCT program now permits anonymous applicants in all areas.

Revenue Procedure 99-13 [1999-1 CB 409] changed the TVC program not only by expanding the scope of violations covered but by moving the administration of the TVC program to the Key Districts. Revenue Procedure 2001-17 [2001-7 IRB 589] changed the TVC program into the VCT program and moved its administration into four areas.

Q 18:13   How did the VCT program come into being?

Based on experience gained in the Audit Closing Agreement Program (Audit CAP) applicable to qualified pension plans, the IRS established three voluntary compliance programs under which employers can voluntarily identify defects in a plan qualified under Code Section 401(a), propose a correction, and work with the IRS to maintain the qualified status of the plan. The first of these was originally named the VCR program, under which the employer proposes a correction for an identified defect and pays a correction fee. The VCR program was generally used to correct operational defects in a qualified plan under Code Section 401(a) and has now been replaced with the Voluntary Correction of Operational Failures (VCO) or the Voluntary Correction Program (VCP).

The second program, originally the Walk-in CAP and now the VCP, allows a plan sponsor with plan form defects or egregious operational defects that are not eligible for the VCR or VCO program to pay a limited sanction and correct both operational and form defects by filing with the IRS Key District CAP Coordinator or the appropriate area office for VCP for the district or area in which the plan sponsor resides.

The third program, originally the Standardized Voluntary Compliance Program (SVP) and now the Voluntary Correction Standardized (VCS) program, is one in which the qualified plan sponsor voluntarily can identify and correct certain defects using a correction method specified by the IRS in Revenue Procedure 94-62, 2001-17, or 2002-47. [1994-2 CB 778; 2001-7 IRB 589; 2002-29 IRB 130] The plan sponsor then files the SVP or VCS request with the IRS National Office or the VCS request with the appropriate area and receives a correction statement on an expedited basis because a standard correction method was used for one of the specified defects.

Based on the success of the three voluntary programs and the requests received from practitioners, the IRS identified a similar need for 403(b) plans and established the TVC, now called the VCT program.

Q 18:14   How long is the TVC or VCT program scheduled to remain in effect?

The TVC program originally was an experimental, temporary program that was put into effect on May 1, 1995, and originally scheduled to expire on October 31, 1996. The program was extended through December 31, 1998. [Rev Proc 96-50, 1996-47 IRB 10] The TVC program, like its predecessor, the VCR program, was made permanent when the IRS issued Revenue Procedure 99-13 [1999-1 CB 409] on February 1, 1999. The VCT program is also permanent under Revenue Procedures 2001-17 and 2002-47. [2001-7 IRB 589; 2002-29 IRB 130]

The IRS has requested public comments regarding the format and operation of the VCT program, as well as the types of eligible defects and the permissible correction methods. It did the same with the VCR program. Indeed, the VCR program, which also started as an experimental program, became permanent after the IRS had a chance to evaluate its success and determine its necessity. Although the initial response to the TVC program was limited, the number of TVC filings has increased but has not yet approached the large number of filings in the VCR program. Hesitation to file may in part be the result of uncertainty regarding the outcome under the original TVC program, lack of historical data for the 403(b) arrangements, concern that entering the VCT program may require the employer to take corrective actions and assume future responsibilities that may change a non-ERISA plan into an ERISA plan, or uncertainty regarding who is responsible for the 403(b) arrangement.

Q 18:15   Why is a TVC or VCT program needed?

When the TVC program was introduced, the time was ripe for a correction program for 403(b) plans. Because 403(b) plans are not required to meet the qualification requirements of Code Section 401(a), employers maintaining such plans are not eligible to use the VCR or VCP program, the SVP or VCS, or the Walk-in CAP or VCP. Yet the IRS noted that such voluntary compliance programs are effective administrative tools and that such a program for 403(b) arrangements would enhance those arrangements' efficient administration. Practitioners and employers maintaining 403(b) programs requested a voluntary correction program similar in design to CAP and the VCR program. The interest in a voluntary correction program for 403(b) plans increased as a result of the publication of large closing agreements, including 403(b) plan issues from the Coordinated Examination Program (CEP). The IRS's audit of 403(b) programs independently of CEP also provides an incentive for investigating voluntary correction programs.

Q 18:16   How does the VCT program operate?

As with the VCR or VCO program, the sponsor of a 403(b) program (or the employer offering the 403(b) arrangement) wishing to take advantage of the VCT program must voluntarily identify all operational defects discovered in the 403(b) arrangement, as well as all demographic failures, all eligibility failures, and all amounts contributed in excess of the MEA or annual addition limitations; must propose corrections for the identified defects; and must describe possible improvements in its administrative procedures that would prevent similar defects from occurring again. Unlike the original VCR program, under the original TVC program the employer calculated the tax that would have been owed on the violation in open years as part of calculating the maximum sanction amount. Under the VCT program, the sanction is based upon set fee schedules by type of defect and number of employees and by calculating the amount of contributions in excess of the MEA and annual addition limitations and multiplying the excess amounts by 2 percent. If the IRS agrees with the employer's proposed correction, the 403(b) arrangement will receive a correction statement from the IRS setting forth the applicable corrections, conditions, and the amount of sanction owed under the original TVC program. Under the revised VCT program the same procedure will generally be followed, but the sanction is based on the presumed sanction, the set fee, or the calculated fee from the schedules in Revenue Procedures 99-13, 2000-16, 2001-17, and 2002-47 for the errors for most correction statements. [1999-1 CB 409; 2000-6 IRB 518; 2001-7 IRB 589; 2002-29 IRB 130]

As part of its submission under the VCO or former VCR program, an employer will be required to pay a flat correction fee, determined by the size of the employer. That practice is similar to the requirements of the original TVC program. The correction or user fee was used under the original TVC program as a credit against the sanction required in the correction statement and also serves as a minimum sanction. The correction or user fee is used as a credit against the amount calculated as the potential maximum sanction amount in the original TVC program. In the VCT program, the sanction is determined based on the type of violation(s) and the number of employees, but there is no user fee associated with the submission.

The original TVC program borrowed the calculation of the tax effect of the violation from the Walk-in CAP. The employer was required to calculate the tax effect as the maximum sanction amount (see Qs 18:19–18:21, 18:23–18:26; SQ 18:22). The ultimate sanction amount paid under the original program was negotiated with the IRS based on the maximum sanction amount applicable and the violations and other equities of the case (see Q 18:19). Under the VCT program, the sanction is not calculated in the same manner, but is based on the type(s) of errors and the number of employees and begins with the presumed amount from the applicable schedule but may range between a high and a low amount. Only the sanction for contributions in excess of the MEA and the annual addition limitations require calculation of the excesses and the sanction.

Correction Fees and Sanctions

Q 18:18   What fees or penalties is an employer required to pay as part of the correction of defects under the VCT program?

1. *Under the Original TVC Program*

   The minimum correction fee under the TVC program for an employer is determined by the number of its employees. The fee is paid with the initial TVC submission as a user fee and is applied as a credit against the negotiated sanction.

   The minimum correction fees (or user fees) are as follows:

Number of Employees	Fee
Fewer than 25	$ 500
At least 25 but no more than 1,000	$ 1,250
More than 1,000 but fewer than 10,000	$ 5,000
10,000 or more	$10,000

   The amounts are similar to the user fees charged under the original VCR program.

   The cost of making corrections and the complexities attendant to making full correction are concerns for tax-exempt organizations considering making a submission to the original TVC program. In addition, the original TVC program, in a requirement borrowed from the Walk-in CAP, imposes a sanction amount up to a maximum of 40 percent of the tax the IRS could apply to the identified defects. Payment of a sanction may be a major concern for public schools or tax-exempt organizations operating with limited funds even if they have the funds to make all of the necessary corrections.

2. *Cost of Correction Under the VCT Program as Revised by Revenue Procedures 99-13, 2000-16, 2001-17, and 2002-47*

   The fee is calculated based on the type of failure(s) and the number of employees based on the following schedules:

   VCT Program Operational Failures Alone

Number of Employees	Fee
Fewer than 25	$ 500
At least 25 but no more than 1,000	$ 1,250
More than 1,000 but fewer than 10,000	$ 5,000
10,000 or more	$10,000

   Fees for Excess Amounts Alone

   Contributions in excess of the MEA and annual addition limits.

The total fee is the fee as calculated by starting with the fee for an operational failure alone in the plan and adding 2 percent of all of the contributions in excess of the MEA or annual addition limitation.

Fees for Demographic Failures or Eligibility Failures Alone

The fee for either a demographic failure or an eligibility failure is based on the schedule below. It is expected that in most instances the fee will be the presumptive amount.

Demographic and Eligibility Features
VCT Program

Number of Employees	Fee Range	Presumptive Fee
0–10	$500–$4,000	$ 2,000
11–25	$500–$8,000	$ 4,000
26–50	$1,250–$8,000	$ 4,000
51–100	$1,250–$12,000	$ 6,000
101–300	$1,250–$16,000	$ 8,000
301–1,000	$1,250–$30,000	$15,000
More than 1,000 and fewer than 10,000	$5,000–$70,000	$35,000
Over 10,000	$10,000–$70,000	$35,000

Number of Employees	Fee Range	Presumptive Amount
10 or fewer	$500 to $4,000	$ 2,000
11 to 50	VCT fee for a plan of this size for operational failure shown above up to $8,000	$ 4,000
51 to 100	VCT fee for a plan of this size for operational failure shown above up to $12,000	$ 6,000
101 to 300	VCT fee for a plan of this size for operational failure shown above up to $16,000	$ 8,000
301 to 1,000	VCT fee for a plan of this size for operational failure shown above up to $30,000	$15,000
Over 1,000	VCT fee for a plan of this size for operational failure shown above up to $70,000	$35,000

Fees for Multiple Types of Failures

When multiple failures occur, the fee is calculated as described below.

Failures	How to Calculate the Fee
Multiple operational failures	Use the fee for operational failures
Multiple demographic/eligibility failures	Use the fee schedule for demographic and eligibility failures

Failures	*How to Calculate the Fee*
Combination of operational and demographic/eligibility failures, use the fee schedule for demographic and eligibility failures	–
Operational failures with correction of MEA and annual addition limitation violations by retaining such excess amounts in the 403(b) plan and reducing future contributions	Add the fee calculated for an operational violation for the plan to 2 percent of the amount of contributions in excess of the MEA and annual addition limitations
Demographic/eligibility failures and operational failures, including contributions in excess of the MEA and annual addition limitations that are corrected by retaining such excess amounts in the 403(b) plan and reducing future contributions	Begin with the fee for the plan from the schedule of fees for demographic and eligibility failures and add to this amount 2 percent of the excess amounts

Egregious Failures

The fee for egregious failures is the maximum fee applicable to the plan plus 40 percent of the total sanction amount with no presumptive amount from any schedule applying. The total sanction amount is the maximum amount payable for the violation under Audit CAP. The total sanction amount would be the tax calculated for the violation in the same way that the maximum sanction would have been calculated under the original TVC program, only without applying the 40 percent maximum.

Q 18:22   Because the sanction in the VCT program is now based on classifications of failures, how are the failures classified?

The failures that are eligible for correction under VCT are the following.

Demographic failures:

1. Failure of the 403(b) plan to satisfy the requirements of Code Section 401(a)(4)(the prohibition on discrimination in favor of HCEs);
2. Failure of the 403(b) plan to satisfy the minimum participation requirements of Code Section 401(a)(26)(now repealed for defined contribution plans); or
3. Failure of the 403(b) plan to satisfy the minimum coverage test of Code Section 410(b).

Eligibility failures:

1. A plan of an employer that is not eligible to maintain a 403(b) plan (i.e., it is not tax exempt under Code Section 501(c)(3)or it is not a public educational organization under Code Section 170(b)(1)(A)(ii));

2. A plan's failure to satisfy the nontransferability requirements of Code Section 401(g);

3. A failure to initially establish or maintain a custodial account as required by Code Section 403(b)(7); or

4. A failure to purchase initially or subsequently either an annuity contract from an insurance company (unless grandfathered under Revenue Ruling 82–102 [1982-1 CB 62]) or a custodial account from a regulated investment company utilizing a bank or an approved nonbank custodian.

Excess amounts:

Excess amounts are amounts contributed in excess of the MEA or annual addition limitations.

Operational failures:

1. Failure to make salary reduction elections uniformly available to all employees able to contribute $200 or more per year (excepting part-time employees working fewer than 20 hours per week and certain students);

2. Failure to satisfy the actual contribution percentage test;

3. Failure to limit compensation to the maximum dollar limit under Code Section 401(a)(17)(currently $200,000);

4. Failure to comply with the distribution restrictions in Code Section 403(b)(7)or 403(b)(11);

5. Failure to satisfy the incidental benefit rules of Code Section 403(b)(10);

6. Failure to pay the minimum required distributions under Code Section 403(b)(10);

7. Failure to give employees the right to elect a direct rollover under Code Section 403(b)(10), including the failure to give a meaningful notice of such right;

8. Failure to limit elective deferral contributions to the maximum dollar limit under Code Section 403(b)(1)(E) ($10,500 in 2001, $11,000 in 2002, and $12,000 in 2003), with certain exceptions for employees with 15 or more years of service with certain types of employers;

9. Any failure involving contributions or allocations of excess amounts as defined above; or

10. Any failure to satisfy applicable requirements under Code Section 403(b)that

   a. results in the loss of 403(b) status for the plan or loss of 403(b) status for the custodial accounts, and

   b. is not a demographic failure, an eligibility failure, or a failure related to the purchase of annuity contracts, or contributions to custodial accounts, on behalf of individuals who are not employees of the employer.

Correction Procedures and Principles

Q 18:28 Which defects are available for correction?

Under the VCT program as revised and renamed by Revenue Procedure 2002-47, the defects that may be corrected are grouped into classifications that are used to determine the applicable sanction. See SQ 18:22 for a list of eligible defects.

Q 18:29 What defects must be corrected, and who determines how they are to be corrected?

The VCT program calls for correction by the employer of all identified defects for all years for which the defects exist, including all closed years. Although the IRS will consider suggestions by the submitting employer with respect to corrections, it will still make the final decision with respect to the final corrections. That decision will be reflected in the final correction statement issued by the IRS.

One problem that employers have identified with respect to corrections is that they do not have records for all years in which defects occurred, particularly where the employer has maintained a 403(b) arrangement for many years. That lack of records makes it impossible for such employers to correct defects exactly for all years even if they were inclined to do so. The missing data creates a significant difficulty for employers desiring to correct their 403(b) programs. Historical data is necessary to properly calculate the MEA limitation not only for the VCT program but also for years through 2001. Revenue Procedures 2001-17 and 2002-47 [2001-7 IRB 589; 2002-29 IRB 130] recognizes that all records may not be available and permits the use of reasonable estimates when it is not possible to make a precise calculation and the probable difference between the estimate and the precise restoration of benefits is insignificant and the administrative cost of determining precise restoration would significantly exceed the probable difference. [Rev Proc 2002-47, § 6.02(5)(a)] The IRS is aware of the problem and is willing to work with employers that do not have full data for all years.

Q 18:30 What additional step must an employer take to complete the correction process?

To complete the correction process under the VCT program, an employer must either initiate or agree to initiate administrative procedures that will prevent the identified operational defects from reoccurring and ensure that the plan is administered properly in future years. Revenue Procedures 99-13, 2000-16, 2001-17, and 2002-47 [1999-1 CB 409; 2000-6 IRB 518; 2001-7 IRB 589; 2002-29 IRB 130] make it clear that having a 403(b) plan document is not sufficient to prove that an employer has compliance procedures, nor is such a document required. The IRS reserves the right to determine final procedures but will first discuss the appropriateness of the final corrected procedures with the employer. If the IRS determines that current administrative procedures are not adequate, it will condition the final correction statement upon the employer's implementing new procedures in the time prescribed in the correction statement.

Planning Pointer. Employers that maintain 403(b) programs subject to ERISA will want to establish compliance practices and procedures not only to satisfy the VCT program requirements but also so that they may argue that SCP or the prior APRSC should apply in any future years' audits that may identify violations.

Q 18:31 Does the VCT program describe any requirements with respect to employment taxes?

Yes. The IRS requires that the employer has initiated or will initiate the proper payment of appropriate employment taxes as part of its VCT submission. Revenue Procedure 95-24 [1995-1 CB 694], Revenue Procedure 99-13 [1999-1 CB 409], Revenue Procedures 2000-16 [2000-6 IRB 518], 2001-17 [2001-7 IRB 589], and 2002-47 [2002-29 IRB 130] cited examples of amounts contributed in excess of the Section 415 limits or the Section 403(b) exclusion allowance that should be includible in an employee's gross income as wages for purposes of determining the amount of employment taxes to be paid in the year of the violation.

Q 18:32 Will the IRS pursue income inclusion for the affected employees?

Revenue Procedures 99-13, 2000-16, 2001-17, and 2002-47 [1999-1 CB 409; 2000-6 IRB 518; 2001-7 IRB 589; 2002-29 IRB 130] state clearly that if a 403(b) program is corrected under APRSC, VCT, or Audit CAP, the IRS will not pursue income inclusion for the affected employees or liability for income tax withholding. However, the correction of a failure may itself result in income tax consequences to an employee (e.g., correction of an MEA violation by distribution of the excess amount).

Q 18:34 What happens once the IRS and the employer have reached agreement as to the corrections, administrative procedures, and sanctions?

Once an agreement was reached under the original TVC program, the IRS issued a correction statement and an acknowledgment letter. The employer must execute the acknowledgment letter and return it to the IRS in accordance with the instructions.

Upon receipt of the acknowledgment letter, the IRS could decide to verify that the corrections were in fact made and that any changes to administrative procedures detailed in the correction statement have been implemented. Such verification is not considered an examination by the IRS of the plan or the employer's books and records. If the IRS verification reveals that the employer has not timely implemented the changes agreed to in the correction statement, the arrangement may be examined by the appropriate Key District Office. The scope of this examination may be expanded beyond confirming correspondence to a full audit.

Once an agreement has been reached under the TVC program, the IRS will issue a closing agreement. The employer must execute the closing agreement, pay the TVC compliance correction fee, and return both to the IRS in accordance with the instructions.

Once an agreement is reached under the TVC program as it existed under Revenue Procedure 99-13 and Revenue Procedure 2000-16, a draft closing agreement is forwarded to the taxpayer. If the taxpayer agrees to the draft closing agreement, a final closing agreement is executed and the corrections must be implemented. Under the VCT program under Revenue Procedures 2001-17 and 2002-47 [2001-7 IRB 589; 2002-29 IRB 130], there will no longer be a closing agreement issued upon agreement, but instead a compliance statement will be issued. The compliance statement is binding upon the IRS and the plan sponsor. The plan sponsor has 30 days from the date the compliance statement was sent to sign and return the compliance statement with the required fee. The IRS will then return a signed compliance statement to the plan sponsor. If the compliance statement is not returned within 30 days, the IRS may refer the case to examination.

Q 18:37   What items will a compliance statement under the VCT program include?

Upon the favorable completion of a correction submission and receipt of a letter from the IRS, an employer will receive a correction statement from the IRS stating the following:

1. The defects identified by the employer or sponsor in its submission;

2. The required corrections for the identified defects;

3. The sanction amount required to be paid by the employer or sponsor;

4. The nature of any revision to the employer's administrative procedures or employment tax procedures or payments upon which the correction statement is conditioned; and

5. The time within which the corrections must be made, including any administrative procedures.

The IRS will not treat the plan as disqualified on account of the failures described in the compliance statement as long as the requirements of the compliance statement are satisfied.

The compliance statement also will state the time frame in which the corrections and procedures are to be implemented.

Q 18:38   Will the issuance of a compliance statement under the VCT program to an employer affect the income tax exclusion for any affected employee's 403(b) plan?

If the compliance statement is properly implemented and all of the conditions specified therein are satisfied by the employer or plan sponsor, the IRS will not seek revocation of the 403(b) plan's income tax exclusion or try to include amounts in any employee's income with respect to the defect. The IRS will, however, require that the employer satisfy any employment tax obligations on amounts that should have been included in income. In addition, correction amounts paid to the 403(b) plan with respect to an employee are includible in the affected employee's exclusion allowance for that year and will be subject to the Section 415 limits.

Q 18:39   What procedure does an employer follow to formally accept the terms of the correction statement under the TVC program?

An employer will receive an acknowledgment letter along with the correction statement. In order to agree formally to the terms of the correction statement, the employer must sign and return the acknowledgment letter to the IRS within 25 days after the correction statement is issued. In addition, the employer must pay the sanction amount specified in the correction statement. If the IRS does not receive the signed acknowledgment letter within the 25-day limit and the sanction amount is not paid, the case may be referred to the Key District Office for consideration of an examination.

After a correction statement has been issued, an employer may not modify a submission request except by a VCT program submission requesting a new compliance statement. If the requested modification is minor and is postmarked no later than 25 days after the correction statement is issued, the correction fee will be the lesser of the original correction fee or $1,250.

Submission Procedures and Requirements

Q 18:43   What information must a taxpayer submit when requesting a 403(b) correction statement?

When requesting a 403(b) correction statement, the taxpayer or his or her authorized representative must submit a letter to the IRS that includes a detailed description of the defects for which correction is sought, a description of the methods the taxpayer will use to correct the identified defects, and all the information needed to support the proposed correction. That information should include the following:

- The number of employees affected and an explanation of how the number was determined (the total number of employees should also be included to show the extent of the violation in the 403(b) plan).

- The number of annuity contracts held by employees.

- The number of related organizations affected by the listed defects.

- A description of the defects and any explanation of how each defect arose, as well as the years in which the defects occurred. This includes, in addition to all open years, closed years (years for which the statutory period has closed). The defects occurring in each year must be identified.

- The amount of applicable earnings (and method of determination) that will apply to any required contributions for the correction method suggested.

- A description of the 403(b) arrangement's current administrative procedures.

- A detailed description of the methods the employer intends to use or has already used to correct defects identified under the submission request. The description should include calculations for each employee affected by the proposed correction.

- Any calculations or assumptions used to arrive at the amount of corrective contributions. For this purpose, the interest rate earned by the plan during the period in question should be used.

- A calculation of the maximum sanction amount related to all of the disclosed violations for the proposed correction (this was required under the original TVC program but has not been required under any of the recent TVC regulations or the VCT program).

In addition, if former participants are to receive correction amounts, the submission should describe a method for locating and notifying such former participants. Such methods may include the IRS letter-forwarding program or other methods such as using the address-only service from a credit reporting agency.

A correction submission must also contain the following:

- A list of other plans maintained by the employer, including other 403(b) arrangements, plans qualified under Code Section 401(a), and simplified employee pensions (SEPs).

- A statement by the employer that, to the best of his or her knowledge, the plan for which the correction is being submitted is not under TEGE examination.

- The location of the Key District Office or the new TEGE Area Office that has jurisdiction over the 403(b) arrangement.

- A statement that the employer has contacted all other entities involved in the arrangement and has received assurances of cooperation to the extent necessary (those parties presumably include insurance companies providing annuities to participants and custodians).

- A statement by the employer under penalties of perjury that the representations in the VCT submission are true, correct, and complete.

- A statement that the employer is eligible to offer the 403(b) program.

Note. The voluntary correction fee was required under the original TVC program but is not required with the new VCT or the prior TVC program until the closing agreement is signed.

If sufficient information is not supplied, the IRS may return the filing to the taxpayer.

Q 18:44 What documents must a correction submission include?

Each VCT or prior TVC submission by an employer must include a copy of the most recently filed Form 5500, if applicable (a Form 5500 is generally applicable if the plan is subject to Title I of ERISA). If a Form 5500 was not applicable, the employer must instead furnish the following:

1. The name of the 403(b) arrangement;
2. The employer identification number; and
3. The other information generally required of tax-exempt organizations when filing a Form 5500.

The submission must also include a copy of any relevant 403(b) documents (copies of plan documents; written descriptions of the 403(b) plans, including summary plan descriptions; and salary reduction agreements) and a statement that the employer is eligible to maintain a 403(b) plan (e.g., that it is a tax-exempt organization under Code Section 501(c)(3) or a public educational organization that is part of a state or a subdivision of a state).

The VCT program or the preceding TVC program also requires the following: the type of employer (i.e., the type of employer for tax purposes) must be stated; the letter must be designated "VCT Program"; and the VCT request under the new VCT program must be filed with one of the four applicable offices for the VCT Program.

Q 18:45 Who may sign a VCT submission?

The VCT or TVC program correction submission may be signed either by the employer or by the employer's authorized representative. If it is signed by the employer's authorized representative, the submission must include a Form 2848, "Power of Attorney and Declaration of Representative," which must be signed by both the employer and the representative. Form 2848 complies with the requirements of Section 9.02 of Revenue Procedure 95-4 [1995-1 CB 397] or Section 11.08 of Revenue Procedure 2002-47. [2002-29 IRB 130]

Q 18:46 What declaration must be included in a correction submission?

The employer must include in its correction submission a declaration under penalties of perjury, as follows:

Under penalties of perjury, I declare that I have examined this submission, including accompanying documents, and to the best of my knowledge and belief the facts presented in support of the VCT request are true, correct, and complete.

The statement must be signed by the submitting employer, not by the employer's authorized representative.

Q 18:47 How and where should the submission request be mailed?

The letter submitting a correction request should be marked "VCT PROGRAM" in the upper right-hand corner of the letter.

Submissions under the VCT program must be filed with the central office. The address for VCT submissions in which the employer is identified is shown in Section 11.12 of Revenue Procedure 2002-47 [2002-29 IRB 130].

Q 18:48 How does an anonymous submission differ under the VCT program?

A VCT submission may be submitted without identifying the employer using the anonymous submission program. The anonymous submission program requires the fee to be paid at the time the application is submitted, not when the correction is settled. VCT program submissions that are not submitted anonymously do not require the fees to be paid at the initial submission.

An employer must respond to any agreement proposed on an anonymous situation within 21 days from the date of the letter of agreement by identifying the plan and plan sponsor.

The anonymous program has been extended indefinitely. [Rev Proc 2002-47, 2002-29 IRB 130, § 10.13 (3)]

Q 18:49 What will happen if a submission request is made by an ineligible employer or the defect identified in the request is not eligible for correction?

If a submission to the VCT program is made by an ineligible employer or the defect identified is not eligible for correction, both the submission and the compliance fee will be returned without review.

Q 18:52 What procedure is followed once the IRS has accepted a submission request?

After accepting a submission request, the IRS agent assigned to handle the case will contact the employer or the employer's authorized representative to discuss the identified defects, the proposed corrections, the proposed changes to the administrative procedures, and the sanction amounts. If the employer and assigned agent reach agreement on all of those issues, the agent will issue a compliance statement to the employer, detailing the agreement (see Q 18:36).

Under the VCT program, after a submission is accepted, an IRS agent will be assigned to the case and will contact the employer or its authorized representative to discuss the identified defects, proposed corrections and changes to administrative procedures, and the sanction amount. The agent will issue a compliance statement, which the employer must sign and return with the compliance fee.

Other Considerations

Q 18:53 What factors should an employer consider when deciding whether to submit a 403(b) plan to the IRS under the VCT program?

Several factors weigh in favor of making a submission under the VCT program. First, now that the IRS has launched an audit program for 403(b) plans, such plans will be the subject of much closer scrutiny, and the odds are greatly increased that a plan will be audited. The IRS audit focus for 2003 includes 403(b) programs at K-12 schools and public colleges and universities, as well as tax-exempt health care entities (hospitals and health care systems). In addition, IRS personnel have indicated in speeches that because the VCT program is now available, if a defect is picked up on audit, the IRS will be less inclined to be lenient.

Nevertheless, for several reasons, some employers may decide to wait before submitting their VCT request. They may have inadequate records to make the final corrections for all years or may fear that the final compliance fee may result in a prohibitive cost. The limited precedents available on the types of defects being corrected or the amounts of sanctions being imposed may also cause employers to hesitate to enter the VCT program. In addition, because an employer must negotiate a final sanction amount with the IRS, there is no way of knowing beforehand the cost of the correction and the compliance fee in total.

Chapter 19

International Tax Treatment

Peter J. Gulia, Esq.
CitiStreet Retirement Services

Almost any business may have employees outside the United States, but academic, research, health care, and other charitable organizations tend to have employees who currently reside in or may return to foreign nations. This chapter addresses some of the international tax issues involved in the income tax treatment of Section 403(b) arrangements, with emphasis on distributions, and explains the effect of treaties that the United States has made with many foreign nations.

Because only a few employees of charitable organizations become wealthy enough to bear significant transfer taxes, this chapter includes only a limited explanation of federal estate tax provisions relating to aliens and citizens who reside outside the United States.

A charitable organization that needs to compute its deduction for contributions to a 403(b) arrangement should seek expert advice about the Treasury Regulations under Code Section 404 and the Proposed Regulations under Code Section 404A.

The word *foreign* is used here, as it is used in the Internal Revenue Code (Code), to refer to any nation other than the United States. Similarly, the term *alien* refers to an individual who is not a U.S. citizen or national. Unless otherwise specified, *citizen* refers to a U.S. citizen and *resident* to a U.S. resident.

This chapter assumes that any participant, beneficiary, or alternate payee under a pension or retirement plan or arrangement or any payee under an annuity contract is a natural person or an individual. It also assumes that any charitable organization is incorporated or organized in the United States and that all 403(b) arrangements are defined contribution in form. The discussion further assumes that any arrangement that was intended to obtain federal income tax treatment under Code Section 403(b) will continue to qualify for that tax treatment. Although the chapter explains that whether a 403(b) distribution may be treated as a pension depends on the facts and interpretation of the particular treaty (if any), the section on withholding assumes that a 403(b) distribution is not compensation for personal services.

Plan Design Considerations

Q 19:11 Should an employer design its plan to address international tax issues?

If an employer knows that it will have citizens working outside the United States or aliens working in the United States, the employer should prepare its plan to address international tax issues. Because many problems can be handled by skillful plan document drafting, the employer should consult a lawyer who has experience in international pension issues.

Q 19:12 What is a foreign trust?

A *foreign trust* is any trust other than a United States person trust. [IRC § 7701(a)(31)(B); Treas Reg § 301.7701-7(a)(2)]

A *United States person trust* is "any trust if a court within the United States is able to exercise primary supervision over the administration of the trust, and one or more United States persons [has or] have the authority to control all substantial decisions of the trust." [IRC § 7701(a)(30)(E); Treas Reg § 301.7701-7(a)(1)]

Even when the trustee (or custodian) is a United States person, a retirement plan trust (or custodial account) is a foreign trust if the trustee (or custodian) is a directed trustee and a non-U.S. employer or plan administrator decides plan distributions or other "substantial decisions." [Treas Reg § 301.7701-7(d)(1)(ii)] Also, if a non-U.S. person has the power to remove, add, or replace the trustee, that power means the non-U.S. person controls substantial decisions of the trust. [Treas Reg § 301.7701-7(d)(1)(ii)(H)]

A nongrantor trust that was in existence on August 20, 1996, and that was treated as a domestic trust on August 19, 1996, may elect to continue to be treated as a U.S. person, notwithstanding the fact that it is a foreign trust. To make the election, the plan administrator must have filed with the IRS in the late 1990s an attachment to Form 5500 or to the plan's other annual report, information return, or tax return. [Treas Reg § 301.7701-7(f); see also Notice 98-25, 1998-18 IRB 11]

Practice Pointer. A non-U.S. employer that expects to establish (or that maintains) a plan that it intends to treat as having the federal income tax treatment of Section 403(b) should consult its expert tax lawyer for advice concerning whether the plan would meet (or would continue to meet) all requirements for federal income tax treatment under Code Section 403(b).

If a non-grantor trust becomes a foreign trust, that "conversion" is treated as a sale of the trust's assets from a U.S. person to a foreign trust. This deemed sale means that the difference between the fair market value of the trust's property and the property's adjusted basis is income subject to federal income tax. [IRC § 684]

Q 19:13 When does an employee need international tax planning?

An employee may need international tax planning whenever more than one nation's law might apply to his or her 403(b) arrangement.

Q 19:14 Why might 403(b) contributions not be desirable for a nonresident?

If an employee is a resident of a nation that taxes wages, personal service income, or income generally, that nation's tax law might not recognize Section 403(b) contributions as an exclusion from wages or income.

Further, investment earnings in a 403(b) arrangement might not be tax deferred for a participant who is a citizen or resident of or is working in a nation that taxes benefit accruals when credited, notwithstanding that no distribution was paid. Moreover, contributions, investment earnings, and distributions may be subject to income tax or other taxes in two or more nations.

In these situations, an employee might prefer to delay a decision about participation in a 403(b) arrangement until he or she can obtain expert advice (see SQ 19:21).

Governing Law

Q 19:15 Can a 403(b) plan be a foreign plan?

Yes. A U.S. charitable organization may choose to maintain a 403(b) plan or program for those of its employees who are nonresident aliens, and such a plan might be a foreign plan (see SQ 19:16).

Q 19:16 Does ERISA apply to a foreign plan?

ERISA's scope does not include a plan "maintained outside of the [United States] primarily for the benefit of persons substantially all of whom are non-resident aliens." [ERISA § 4(b)(4)] However, a plan that includes a U.S. citizen or resident may be subject to ERISA. [See Lefkowitz v Arcadia Trading Co Ltd Benefit Pension Plan, 996 F 2d 600 (2d Cir 1993)]

In any case, an employer-sponsored plan is likely to be treated as maintained inside the United States if the charitable organization employer is located in the United States.

Foreign Income Tax Treatment

Q 19:22 What income tax rates apply in foreign nations?

Although many nations rely on a wide variety of sales, use, personal property, consumption, stamp or document, and other taxes, many foreign nations have one or more income taxes. While a few nations have no income tax, most nations have an income tax in addition to other taxes.

The world's many different income tax regimes vary widely in the kinds of income subject to income tax. For example, some nations tax wage income but not investment income. Personal income tax rates vary widely and frequently, especially in developing nations.

Retirement planning adds the further uncertainty that the tax effectiveness of a current contribution may be based on uncertain future tax rates. For current information, an individual should consult an expert lawyer or accountant.

U.S. Federal Income Tax Treatment

Categories of Taxpayers

Q 19:26 Who is a United States citizen?

For federal income tax purposes, whether a person is a United States citizen is governed by United States law concerning nationality. [Treas Reg § 1.1-(c)]

A person is a U.S. citizen if any of the following applies:

1. He or she was born in the United States. [8 USC § 1401(a)–(b)]

2. His or her parents are U.S. citizens, and one parent had a residence in the United States or in an outlying U.S. possession before the child's birth. [8 USC § 1401(c)]

3. One parent is a U.S. national and the other is a U.S. citizen who was physically present in the United States for a continuous period of one year before the child's birth. [8 USC § 1401(d)]

4. He or she was born in an outlying U.S. possession, and one of his or her parents is a citizen who was physically present in the United States or in an outlying possession for a continuous period of one year before the child's birth. [8 USC § 1401(e)]

5. He or she is of unknown parentage, was found in the United States while under age five, and it is shown, before he or she attains age 21, that he or she was not born in the United States. [8 USC § 1401(f)]

6. He or she was born outside the United States, and one parent is a citizen who was physically present in the United States or in an outlying U.S. possession for not less than five years, and at least two of those years were after the citizen-parent attained age 14 [8 USC § 1401(g)] Some periods of service in the armed forces and periods of employment with the United States Government or an international organization count toward the physical prescence requirement even if the citizen was outside the United States during such service or employment. [8 USC §§ 1401(g), 1401a]

7. He or she was born before noon (Eastern Time) of a mother who was a citizen and who, before the child's birth, resided in the United States. [8 USC § 1401(h)]

   Note. Special rules apply to persons born in Alaska, Hawaii, Puerto Rico, the Canal Zone or the Republic of Panama, Guam, or the U.S. Virgin Islands. [8 USC §§ 1402–07] Special rules also apply to children born out of wedlock [8 USC § 1409]

8. He or she was naturalized according to United States law. [8 USC §§ 1421–30, 1436–51]

   Note. In some circumstances, a child may become a citizen when one parent is (or both parents are) naturalized. [8 USC § 1431–33]

   Note. Some former U.S. citizens may regain citizenship by meeting certain requirements. [8 USC § 1435] For an explanation of how a citizen surrenders his or her citizenship, see Q 19:158.

Q 19:26.1   Who is a United States national?

A person who is not a U.S. citizen may be a U.S. national depending on where he or she was born or to whom he or she was born. A person is a U.S. national if any of the following applies:

1. He or she was born outside the United States in an outlying U.S. possession. [8 USC § 1408(1)]

2. He or she was born to parents who are U.S. nationals. [8 USC § 1408(2)]

3. He or she was found in an outlying U.S. possession while under age five, and it is shown, before he or she attains age 21, that he or she was not born in the outlying possession. [8 USC § 1408(3)]

4. One parent is a U.S. national, and that parent was physically present in the United States or its outlying possessions for seven of any continuous ten years—at least five of which were after that parent attained age 14—and that parent was not absent from the United States and its outlying possessions for more than one year during the ten-year period. [8 USC § 1408(4)]

Q 19:27   Who is an alien?

A person who is not a citizen or national is an alien. [8 USC § 1101(a)(3); Treas Reg §§ 1.1-1(c), 1.1441-1(z)(3)(i)] A person who has filed a declaration of his or her intention to become a citizen but has not yet been admitted to citizenship by a final order of a naturalization court is also an alien. [Treas Reg § 1.1-(c)]

The Internal Revenue Code classifies aliens as resident aliens (see Q 19:28) or nonresident aliens (see Q 19:29).

Q 19:30   What is an immigrant visa?

Generally, an alien who enters the United States must obtain a visa. [8 USC §§ 1101–1365] An immigrant visa (also called a "green card") may be issued to a person who intends to relocate to the United States permanently. [8 USC § 1101(a)(16)]

Even if an immigrant visa holder permanently leaves the United States, he or she will continue to be taxed as a resident until he or she formally relinquishes his or her green card or until his or her status as lawful permanent resident is legally revoked. [IRC § 7701(b)(6)(B)]

Several kinds of nonimmigrant visas are available to a person who comes to the United States on a temporary basis and intends to return home after a short time. [8 USC § 1101(a)(26)] A person who holds a nonimmigrant visa is prohibited from engaging in activities inconsistent with the purpose of the visa. For example, a person who holds a tourist visa cannot obtain employment in the United States.

Income Tax Treaties

Overview

Q 19:48   What is a competent authority request?

If a resident of one treaty nation believes that the other nation is not applying its tax law in compliance with the treaty, that person can apply to the *competent authority* for relief. [Internal Revenue Manual 8732–8733] If a taxpayer makes such an application, the competent authority can either unilaterally grant relief or negotiate with the other nation's competent authority to resolve the issue. The competent authority procedure is perhaps best used for fact questions.

Practice Pointer. In addition to applying for competent-authority relief, a taxpayer should consider taking precautions so that administrative, procedural, or other legal rules will not bar any potential agreement that might be reached by the competent authorities. Some of those precautions include:

- Complying with the procedures for competent-authority relief;
- Filing a protective claim for credit or refund of a tax;
- Delaying the expiration of a limitations period for a refund or other tax adjustment;
- Avoiding the lapse of a right to appeal any tax determination;
- Contesting a nation's adjustment to a tax; and
- Seeking an adjustment to a nation's tax.

Although the taxpayer may consult with the U.S. competent authority in considering these and other precautions, he or she might prefer independent legal advice.

One frequent use of a competent authority procedure is to determine a person's residence for treaty purposes (see Q 19:47).

For the United States, the competent authority is the IRS Assistant Commissioner (International). [IRS Delegation Order 114, as revised in Internal Revenue Manual 1229] In other nations, the competent authority typically is a similarly high-ranking tax official.

Model Treaty

Q 19:66   How does the 1996 Model Treaty treat participation in a 403(b) arrangement?

If a Section 403(b) arrangement is recognized by the foreign nation as a pension plan for treaty purposes and a participant in a pension plan recognized under the law of one of the treaty nations performs personal services in the foreign nation, the following tax consequences apply:

1. "Contributions paid by or on behalf of the individual to the plan during the period that he performs such services in the [foreign nation] shall be deductible (or excludible) in computing his taxable income in that [nation]."

2. Any benefits accrued under the plan or payments made to the plan by or on behalf of the participant's employer during that period shall not be treated as part of the employee's taxable income.

3. Income earned but not distributed by the plan shall not be taxable in the foreign nation until such time and to the extent that a distribution is made from the plan.

4. If the participant makes a rollover (see SQ 19:69), the rolled-over distribution is not taxed by the other treaty nation.

These rules apply only if the participant made contributions to the 403(b) arrangement before arriving in the foreign nation and the competent authority of that nation has agreed that the 403(b) arrangement generally corresponds to a pension plan recognized for tax purposes by that nation.

These benefits cannot exceed the benefits that would be allowed by the foreign nation to its residents for contributions to, or benefits otherwise accrued under, a pension plan recognized for tax purposes by that nation. [1996 Model Treaty and Technical Explanation art 18(6)]

Q 19:67   What should a participant do if he or she receives a distribution that is not a pension for treaty purposes?

Before a participant receives an eligible distribution that is not a pension for treaty purposes, he or she may consider instructing a direct rollover of the distribution into an individual retirement account or annuity (IRA). Later, a distribution from the IRA might qualify as a pension distribution for treaty purposes. The treaty rules concerning the participant's age upon distribution are applied as of the date of the IRA distribution. [Ltr Rul 9143067 (United Kingdom Treaty)]

International Rollovers

Q 19:69   Can a participant roll over a 403(b) distribution into a foreign plan?

If the United States' treaty with the foreign plan's nation follows the 1996 Model Treaty, it may be possible for a participant to roll over a distribution from his or her 403(b) arrangement into the foreign plan. While not free from doubt, the new treaty language is intended to permit a rollover from one nation's pension plan to another nation's pension plan.

For U.S. federal income tax purposes, the rollover must be made according to the regular rollover rules, including (if applicable) the 60-day time limit. [IRC §§ 402(c), 408(d)(3)(A)(i)] This provision is available only to a person who is present in one of the treaty nations to perform either dependent or independent personal services. The person must be a visitor to the host country. A person may use this provision only if he or she was contributing to the plan in his or her home country before coming to the host country.

Also, the host country's competent authority must determine that the recognized plan to which a contribution was made in the person's home country generally corresponds to the plan in the host country. The tax benefits under this provision are limited to the benefits that the host country accords under its law to the host country plan most similar to the home country plan, even if the home country would have afforded greater benefits under its law. [1996 Model Treaty and Technical Explanation art 18(6)(d)]

Selected Treaties

Q 19:79   What does the France treaty say on pensions?

Generally, "pensions and other similar remuneration, including distributions from pension and other retirement arrangements, derived and beneficially owned by a resident of [either nation] in consideration of past employment, whether paid periodically or in a lump sum, shall be taxable only in the nation of which the participant is a resident." [United States-France Treaty art 18(1)(a)]

Q 19:86   What does the Kazakhstan treaty say on pensions?

Generally, "pensions and similar remuneration derived and beneficially owned by a resident of [either nation] in consideration of past employment may be taxed only in the nation of which the participant is a resident." [United States-Kazakhstan Treaty art 18(1)(a)]

Q 19:87   What does the Mexico treaty say on pensions?

Generally, "pensions and other similar remuneration derived and beneficially owned by a resident of [either nation] in consideration of past employment by that individual or another individual resident of the same Contracting State shall be taxable only in the nation of which the participant is a resident." [United States-Mexico Treaty art 19(1)(a), reprinted in TIAS, 1994-2 CB 424; see also 1994-2 CB 489]

Q 19:89   What does the Norway treaty say on pensions?

Generally, "pensions and other similar remuneration paid to an individual who is a resident of one of the Contracting States in consideration of past employment shall be taxable only in that Contracting State." [United States-

Norway Treaty art 18(1), reprinted in TIAS 7474, 1973-1 CB 669; see also 1973-1 CB 693]

"The term 'pensions and other similar remunerations' [sic] means periodic payments made after retirement or death in consideration for services rendered . . . in connection with past employment." [United States-Norway Treaty art 18(4)(a), TIAS 7474, 1973-1 CB 669; see also 1973-1 CB 693]

Withholding on 403(b) Distributions

Pension Withholding for a Foreign Person

Q 19:110 For which foreign nations may a U.S. payer omit withholding on a distribution to a nonresident alien?

Currently, the United States has relevant treaty provisions with the following foreign nations:

- Australia
- Austria
- Barbados
- Belgium
- China
- Cyprus
- Czech Republic
- Egypt
- Finland
- France
- Germany
- Hungary
- Iceland
- India
- Ireland
- Israel
- Italy
- Japan
- Kazakhstan
- Korea
- Luxembourg
- Mexico
- Morocco
- Netherlands
- New Zealand
- Norway
- Pakistan
- Portugal
- Romania
- Russian Federation
- Slovak Republic
- Spain
- Sweden
- Switzerland
- Trinidad and Tobago
- Tunisia
- Turkey
- United Kingdom

A payor may withhold less than the 30 percent tax otherwise required only if the payee is eligible to claim a reduced withholding late under a tax treaty and the payor has received from the payee a properly completed Form W-8 (see Q 19:127).

U.S. Federal Estate Tax Treatment

Federal Estate Tax Treatment of Nonresident Aliens

Q 19:156   How is a nonresident alien's estate taxed for federal estate tax purposes?

For a decedent who was not a citizen or resident at the time of death, the federal estate tax only applies to property that is situated in the United States. [IRC § 2103] It is unclear whether a participant's rights under a 403(b) contract will be treated as property or rights situated in the United States. [See generally Rev Rul 55-163, 1955-1 CB 675; GCM 33827 (May 20, 1968)]

U.S. Expatriate Tax

Q 19:159   How does an individual surrender U.S. citizenship?

A citizen may give up his or her U.S. citizenship by performing any of the following acts with the intention of relinquishing U.S. nationality:

- Becoming naturalized in another nation
- Formally declaring allegiance to another nation
- Serving in a foreign army
- Serving in foreign government employment
- Executing an Oath of Renunciation of nationality before a U.S. diplomatic or consular officer in a foreign nation
- Formally renouncing, within the United States, his or her citizenship during a time of war, provided the U.S. Attorney General approves the renunciation as not contrary to the interests of national defense
- Committing an act of treason

[8 USC § 1481(a)]

For situations in which an individual executes an Oath of Renunciation, the State department prepares and reviews a certificate of loss of nationality. [8 USC § 1501]

When loss of U.S. nationality is put in issue, the burden of proof is on the person who claims that a loss of citizenship occurred. The proof must be by a preponderance of the evidence. [8 USC § 1481(b)]

Chapter 20

Retirement and Estate Planning for 403(b) Participants

John Curran, Esq.
Douglas Rothermich, Esq.
Evan Giller, Esq.
Teachers Insurance and Annuity Association-
College Retirement Equities Fund

The estate and gift tax consequences of qualified and nonquali-fied annuities should also be considered in designing an estate plan for 403(b) participants. Retirement plan annuities can be used to fund trusts that are being established for planning pur-poses and to fund charitable gifts. However, the planner must take into account the complex rules that apply to distributions from retirement plans, particularly the minumum distribution rules and the rights that inure to spouses under certain plans.

In April 2002, the IRS released final and new temporary proposed regulations governing required minimum distributions, which apply for determining such distributions for calender years begin-ning on or after January 1, 2003.

Funding Trusts with Retirement Plan Annuities

Q 20:13   What distribution requirements apply if a trust is the beneficiary of retirement plan assets?

Retirement annuities, whether from a qualified or a nonqualified plan, may be distributed to a trust as an outright distribution following the contract owner's death. Such a form of distribution may be appropriate if income tax matters are not important (e.g., a distribution of a retirement annuity to a purely charitable trust). When the assets are distributed to a trust for the benefit of individual beneficiaries, however, income taxation of the distributions will have an impact. For qualified plan annuities, additional options exist to "stretch out" the payments—so that most of the assets remain in the tax-deferred account for a longer period, deferring further the income taxation of the annuity assets. Also, because the tax-deferred annuities will be subject to income tax only when distributed, stretching out the distributions can allow for greater tax-deferred buildup inside the retirement plan before distributions are made to the trust.

If the only designated beneficiary of a qualified retirement annuity is an individual, that individual can have the option to receive distributions following the contract owner's death over the beneficiary's life expectancy. Additional stretch-out options exist if the contract owner's designated beneficiary is his or her spouse. [IRC § 401(a)(9)(B)(iv)]

If the contract owner's death occurs before his or her required beginning date, the general rule is that distributions to a trust must be made within five years from the date of the owner's death. [IRC § 401(a)(9)(B)(ii)] Technically, the proposed regulations allow the distributions to occur by December 31 of the year including the fifth anniversary of the contract owner's death. [Prop Treas Reg § 1.401(a)(9)-3, A-2]

Q 20:15   What issues, other than estate or income tax implications, should be considered when designating a trust as the beneficiary of retirement plan assets?

Aside from the estate or income tax effects associated with designating a trust as the beneficiary of retirement plan assets, there may be other issues to consider. A trust allows the individual who created it to determine when and how the assets funding the trust may be used. That benefit can give added control that would not be available with an outright distribution of the retirement annuity to a beneficiary.

On the other hand, using a trust can limit options for long-term distributions from a retirement annuity after the contract holder's death. This is particularly true for distributions to a surviving spouse. Distribution of a retirement annuity to a trust for the benefit of a surviving spouse can be structured to allow for minimum distributions during the contract owner's lifetime based on the uniform table, or over the joint life expectancy of the owner and his or her spouse if the spouse is more than ten years younger than the owner. Further, following the contract owner's death, the trustee of the trust can also continue to take distributions over the owner's spouse's remaining life expectancy. The option that is lost, however, with such a form of trust planning (that would be available if the contract owner distributed the retirement annuity to his or her spouse directly) is the opportunity for the owner's spouse to roll over the retirement annuity to an individual retirement account (IRA) in his or her own name. After rolling over the annuity to an IRA, the surviving spouse could then take minimum distributions (after reaching the required beginning date) using the uniform table or (if the surviving spouse has remarried by that time) the joint life expectancy of the surviving spouse and his or her new spouse, and then at the survivor's death, using the beneficiary's life expectancy.

Q 20:16   When should retirement annuities be considered for funding a unified credit trust?

A *unified credit (bypass) trust* is a trust established at death to be funded with the amount of assets that may be sheltered from estate tax by a decedent's applicable exclusion amount ($1 million for 2003 and $1.5 million for 2004 and 2005). This form of trust is typically used at the first spouse's death by a married couple with a taxable estate for estate tax purposes. The trust assets may be held for the benefit of the surviving spouse, if needed, but held in such a way that any unused assets be excluded from the survivor's estate for estate tax purposes.

When unified credit trust planning is appropriate, it often makes sense to fund the trust at the first spouse's death with non-retirement plan assets equal to the deceased spouse's applicable exclusion amount. Retirement plan assets can then be given to the surviving spouse—and several options exist for deferring the income tax on the retirement plan assets until the surviving spouse actually withdraws the funds from the retirement plan. Such a scenario allows a married couple to follow both an estate tax planning strategy that will fully use the deceased spouse's applicable exclusion amount at the first spouse's death and an income tax planning strategy of deferring the income tax on the retirement plan assets for as long as possible.

When there are not sufficient non-retirement plan assets available at the first spouse's death to fund the unified credit trust, however, using retirement annuities to fund the trust may be necessary and appropriate. In such a situation, using retirement plan assets to "fill up" the trust may result in a loss of some of the benefits of income tax deferral (see SQ 20:15). On the other hand, if all of the retirement plan assets are transferred to the surviving spouse for income tax planning purposes, the unified credit trust will not be fully funded. Under such circumstances, a couple's estate plan should consider how to balance the estate tax planning strategy of fully funding a unified credit trust at the first spouse's death with the income tax planning strategy for income tax deferral on the retirement annuity. The decision to fully fund a unified credit trust (at least in part) with retirement plan assets or to transfer all of the retirement plan assets to the surviving spouse to take full advantage of the income tax deferral may depend on a number of factors (the expected size of the surviving spouse's estate at his or her death, his or her life expectancy, and other factors).

If fully funding the unified credit trust at the first spouse's death makes sense, two alternatives for using retirement plan assets to fund the unified credit trust are as follows:

1. Designate the unified credit trust directly as the primary beneficiary of that fraction of the retirement plan assets needed to "fill up" the unified credit trust (after considering all other non-tax-deferred assets available); or

2. Arrange the retirement plan beneficiary designation in a manner that the same result could be attained through "disclaimer planning" (see below), if desired at the time of the first spouse's death.

Under the first alternative, designating the trustee of the unified credit trust as the primary beneficiary for that fraction of the retirement plan assets necessary to fully fund the trust provides a means to fully use the applicable exclusion amount at the first spouse's death. (See Q 20:14 on the impact of designating a trust as beneficiary for distribution purposes.) The participant's spouse or other beneficiaries can remain the primary beneficiaries of retirement plan assets not needed to fully fund the unified credit trust, allowing for the potential of further income tax deferral beyond the participant's death.

It also may be possible to structure the beneficiary designation using a "disclaimer" to provide greater flexibility to do postmortem estate planning following the first spouse's death. If a decedent's spouse or other beneficiaries "disclaim" property or an interest in property they would have received from the decedent, they will be treated as if they had never received the property or interest in property and had predeceased the decedent. Of course, the disclaimer rules under the Code must be followed to avoid any tax consequences for the beneficiary disclaiming (e.g., being treated as having made a taxable gift to the next beneficiary). [IRC § 2518]

The disclaimer rules are quite technical. All of the following requirements must be met for the disclaimer to be effective for tax purposes:

1. The disclaimer must be in writing and be irrevocable and unqualified;

2. The disclaimer must be made within nine months of when the interest in the disclaimed asset is created;

3. The disclaimer must be made before any benefit of the disclaimed asset is received; and

4. The disclaimed interest must pass without any direction from the disclaiming party.

A technique that contemplates the possible use of a disclaimer for an individual's retirement plan assets could be to name the individual's spouse as the primary beneficiary for all of the individual's retirement plan assets, but further provide that if any portion of the retirement plan assets are disclaimed, the unified credit trust will receive the disclaimed assets as the contingent beneficiary. After the individual's death, his or her surviving spouse can then determine if there are enough nonretirement assets to fund the unified credit trust. If there are not, the surviving spouse can decide whether it is more beneficial to continue the long-term income tax deferral on the retirement plan assets or if a portion should be used to fully fund the unified credit trust. If funding the unified credit trust with retirement plan assets makes sense at that time, then the surviving spouse can disclaim a portion of those assets necessary to fill up the unified credit trust. The retirement plan assets then pass to the contingent beneficiary—the unified credit trust. If the unified credit trust qualifies for look-through treatment (see Q 20:14), and the decedent died before his or her required beginning date, the life expectancy of the oldest beneficiary of the unified credit trust can continue to be used to determine the minimum distributions from the retirement plan account to the unified credit trust. If the decedent's death occurs after his or her required beginning date, the surviving spouse's life expectancy can continue to be used to determine the minimum distributions for the retirement plan account to the unified credit trust.

The form of disclaimer planning just outlined allows an individual to take a wait-and-see approach on how his or her retirement plan assets should be used. If full use of the unified credit will provide the best benefit for an individual's family or other beneficiaries, disclaiming may make sense. That may be the case, for example, if the surviving spouse's subsequent death is expected to occur in the near future and the estate tax savings from using both spouses' unified credits outweighs the income tax benefit of slightly longer income tax deferral on the retirement plan assets. Although such a form of planning provides greater flexibility than designating the unified credit trust directly, there may be some risk that the IRS could object to the technique for certain forms of retirement plan assets. For retirement plan assets subject to the Retirement Equity Act of 1984 (REA) [Pub L No 98-397, 98 Stat 1426], some commentators have historically questioned whether the rights given to the surviving spouse by this statute (which is not applicable to IRAs) could preclude the use of a disclaimer under the requirements in the Code. Specifically, these commentators have questioned whether the surviving spouse's statutory rights under REA cause the nine-month period for a disclaimer to begin to run long before the contract owner's death. General Counsel's Memoranda 39858 [Sept 9, 1991] appears to have allowed the use of disclaimers in this manner. Individuals should consult an estate planning attorney about the applicability of this planning strategy in a particular situation.

Spousal Rollovers

Q 20:21 What types of plans may receive a spousal rollover distribution?

Spousal rollover distributions may be made to individual retirement accounts as defined in Code Section 408(a) and individual retirement annuities (other than endowment contracts) as defined in Code Section 408(b), as well as to a qualified trust or an annuity plan, as defined in Code Sections 401(a) and 403(a), respectively; a Code Section 403(b) annuity; or a Code Section 457(b) governmental plan in which the surviving spouse participates. [IRC § 402(c)(8)(B)]

Q 20:22 What are the minimum distribution requirements for funds that have been rolled over by a surviving spouse?

The benefits that a surviving spouse rolls over into his or her own eligible retirement plan become subject to the minimum distribution requirement imposed on such contracts as though originally owned by the surviving spouse. That is true even if the deceased participant's accumulation was subject to minimum distribution at the participant's death. The rolled-over portion is net of any minimum distribution requirement owed by the participant's contract. The surviving spouse can then elect the calculation beneficiary that would apply to the rolled-over funds. [IRC § 403(b)(10); Treas Reg § 1.408-8, A-7]

Retirement Equity Act of 1984

Q 20:27 May the REA requirement for a QPSA or a QJSA be waived?

Under certain circumstances, yes. The requirements for a QPSA or a QJSA may be waived by the participant if an informed consent to such a waiver is obtained from the participant's spouse. [Treas Reg § 1.401(a)(11)-20, Q&As 28, 29, 31]

The requirements for a spousal waiver and consent are as follows:

1. A waiver for both a QPSA and a QJSA must list the specific nonspouse beneficiary who will receive the benefit.
2. The waiver for a QJSA must specify the optional form of benefit being selected.
3. The consent is limited to the specific nonspouse beneficiary or optional form of benefit being selected, unless the plan allows for a general consent that acknowledges the existence of the right to limit the consent to a specific nonspouse beneficiary and optional form of benefit.
4. The waiver for the QJSA must be made no later than 90 days before the participant's annuity starting date in order to be effective.

Furthermore,

1. A waiver and consent contained in a premarital agreement is ineffective.

2. Consent to the waiver of QPSA or QJSA requirements made by one spouse is not binding on a subsequent spouse, except in the case of plan loans.

Appendix B

The Role of the Tax or Employee Benefits Professional in the 403(b) Arena

Janet M. Anderson, J.D.
Michael Footer, Esq.
Mercer Investment Consulting

Since the early 1990s, two forces have been affecting Section 403(b) programs: IRS audits forcing stricter compliance with the rules and competitive pressures bringing about changes in 403(b) products. These concerns have led employers that sponsor Section 403(b) programs to seek the assistance of outside consultants or other tax professionals. Appendix B answers some common questions about the role of the tax or employee benefits professional in the 403(b) environment and provides employers who are eligible to offer 403(b) programs with helpful information concerning the selection and engagement of consultants and other tax professionals.

Q B:5 Should an employer issue a request for proposal (RFP) when seeking to engage a 403(b) professional?

It is not always necessary to issue an RFP when seeking to engage the services of a consultant or other 403(b) professional. Most governmental organizations have procurement requirements that necessitate the issuance of RFPs. At the very least, employers should request a proposal letter from a prospective 403(b) professional that sets out the scope of the project, the fees and expenses, the project team and its expertise, and a timeline associated with the project.

Index

[References are to question numbers and to supplement question numbers (S).]

B

D

G

Section 403(b)(7) custodial accounts, 7:1

separate account investment, 5:8

N

National Association of Insurance Commissioners (NAIC)
model acts, 6:24

Native American tribes
beneficiary designations, S12:16, S12:17

Negative election procedure
salary reduction contributions, 1:25

Netherlands, tax treaty, 19:88

1933 Act. *See* Securities Act of 1933

1934 Act. *See* Securities Exchange Act of 1934

1940 Act. *See* Investment Company Act of 1940

No-action letter, defined, 8:15

No disparity safe harbor
nondiscrimination requirements, S4:33

Nondiscrimination requirements
ACP test, 17:12
ADP test, 4.5
after-tax contributions, S4:6
aggregated annuity program, 4:35
average benefits percentage, 4:19–4:21
average benefits test, 4:15, 4:19–4:22
"benefit, right, or feature," S4:7
benefits, rights, features, S4:32
church plans, 14:27
compensation, defined, S4:25.1
compliance, S4:3
coverage and benefits, 4:1–4:37
coverage rules, generally, 4:13–4:24
cross-testing, S4:30
  special requirements, S4:30.1
current availability test, S4:32
"design-based" safe harbors, S4:7.1
general test under Section 401(a)(4), 4:28
  aggregation of plans, 4:29
  cross-testing, S4:30, S4:30.1
  factors affecting, 4:31
governmental plans, exemption, S4:3
highly compensated employee, defined, S4:4.1
IRC, 1:9
lesser disparity safe harbor, S4:33
matching contributions, S4:7
maximum disparity safe harbor, S4:33

mergers and acquisitions, violations, S16:2
minimum participation rules, S4:9, 4:10–4:12
no disparity safe harbor, S4:33
nongovernmental arrangements, S4:25
non-matching contributions, S4:8
nonsalary reduction contributions, 4:13
Notice 89-23 and, S4:33, 4:34–4:35, S4:36, 4:37
notice requirement, matching contributions, S4:7
overview of requirements, S4:1, 4:2, S4:3
permitted disparity, 4:21, S4:26
ratio percentage test, S4:14
reasonable classification, 4:16
repeal of, effect on governmental plans, 17:16
restructuring plans, 4:27
rules, generally, 4:25–4:37
salary reduction contributions, S4:5
Section 401(a)(4), S4:25, S4:26, 4:28–4:31
Section 414(s) safe-harbor compensation, S4:25.1
Section 415 "long-form" compensation, S4:25.1
Section 415 "short-form" or "safe harbor" compensation, S4:25.1
Section 3401(a) wages, S4:25.1
Tax-Sheltered Annuity Voluntary Correction Program (TVC), 18:20
testing
  average benefits test, 4:15, 4:19–4:22
  cross-testing, S4:30
  general test, factors affecting, 4:31
  how often plans must be tested, 4:24
  ratio percentage test, S4:14
  tax-sheltered annuity plans, 17:11, 17:12
unsafe harbor percentage, 4:18
W-2 compensation, S4:25.1

Nonelective contributions. *See* Contributions

Nonelective deferrals, Section 457, 15:11–15:13

Nonfiduciary
ERISA plan prohibited transactions, 9:85

Nongovernmental employer
nondiscrimination requirements, 1:10

Nonprofit organizations
1933 Act exemptions, 8:11

W

Y